Contents

Notes

Introduction & Overview

Water Awareness

Notes

Operations – Swiftwater First Responder

Swiftwater Rescue Technician

Authors: Martin Bills, Annetta Cooper, Amy Copland, Barry Edwards, Keith Gillespie, Jon Gorman, Daniel Graham, Mark Hogan, Chris Jonason, Paul Jones, Kim Little, Matt McLay, Paul O'Sullivan, Geraint Rowlands, Jim Segerstrom, Mike Soderstrom, J. Michael Turnbull and Phil Turnbull

Illustrations: Carol Davies

Photos: Gaele Atkinson, Martin Bills, Duncan Eades, Daniel Graham, Paul O'Sullivan or as credited

Layout: Daniel Graham, Amy Copland

In conjunction with: Rescue 3 Austria, Rescue 3 Benelux, Rescue 3 Canada (Raven Rescue), Rescue 3 Greece, Rescue 3 Norway, Rescue 3 Spain, and Rescue 3 Japan

Adapted & compiled from the following Rescue 3 International copyrighted material:
►Swiftwater Rescue Technician® Manual ◄► Low to High Angle Techniques™ Manual ◄► Basic Water First Responder ◄► Management of Moving Water and Flood Operation™ Manual ◄► Swiftwater Rescue Technician® 2 Manual ◄► Technical Rope Rescue: Technician™ Level Manual ◄► Swiftwater First Responder™ Manual ◄► Swiftwater Rescue Technician® Advanced Manual ◄

Safety Notice

This Rescue 3 International manual is a basic text to be used in conjunction with Rescue 3 classes taught by Instructors certified by Rescue 3 International. Utilization of this material without certified instruction may be hazardous to life and limb.

Scope of Manual

This manual is designed as an accompanying reference for those undertaking training with Rescue 3 International. It is not a stand-alone document and does not replace training by a qualified instructor.

These notes may be used as initial pre-course reading, an in-class reference, and a post-training resource.

Training courses are only one part in the development of competent Swiftwater and Flood Rescue Technicians. Without post-training practice and experience, students will be unable to develop the necessary levels of skill and judgement to allow them to operate safely and effectively as rescuers in a swiftwater or flood environment.

In addition to the specific techniques and knowledge provided while training at this level, Swiftwater Rescue Technicians must possess the underpinning knowledge delivered at Awareness level and the basic techniques delivered at the Operations level. However, these are included in Rescue 3's Technician level curriculum and do not need to be taken as prerequisite courses.

Introduction & Overview

Notes

History of Rescue 3 International

Rescue 3 International is the world's leading rescue training institution. Its mission is to provide flood, water, and rope rescue training for individuals and organizations with an emphasis on keeping rescuers from becoming victims.

Over its 30 year history, more than 150,000 students in 35 countries have taken Rescue 3's state-of-the-art courses in water, rope, ice and other technical rescue subjects. Rescue 3's growth has been fuelled by a reputation for quality, hands-on instruction; a dynamic curriculum; and using both traditional and innovative techniques that work.

Founded in 1979

The company was founded in 1979 after a California SAR team nearly lost one of its own in a water rescue. A concerned group of emergency responders identified a need for training in areas not commonly covered in the emergency training programs of the time.

The name, Rescue 3, was chosen when the company first started, because the instruction was concerned with all areas of rescue – ground, air, and water – thus Rescue 3.

In 1981, the moving water rescue training program was redesigned into an early form of the current Swiftwater Rescue Technician® curriculum. Swiftwater classes were taught throughout California and slowly spread across the United States.

Demand for professional rescue training was also growing outside the US and so in 1990 Rescue 3 became Rescue 3 International. By the late nineties, Rescue 3 instructors had taught close to 70,000 emergency service personnel. Today, these numbers have grown to over 150,000 students from all over the globe.

Currently Rescue 3 has taught courses or has agents working in many countries, including Argentina, Austria, Australia, Belgium, Brazil, Canada, Chile, China, Colombia, Costa Rica, Germany, Greece, France, Iceland, Indonesia, Ireland, Italy, Japan, Luxembourg, Malaysia, Mexico, Netherlands, New Zealand, Norway, Peru, Puerto Rico, Slovenia, Spain, Sweden, Switzerland, Taiwan, United Kingdom, and Venezuela.

Real World Experience

Rescue 3's instructors are characterized by practical, real world experience and are professionals working in the disciplines they teach, including paramedics, firefighters, law enforcement officers, and search and rescue team members, as well as river guides and military personnel. They all share a passion for saving lives and teaching others to do the same.

Rescue 3 Instructors are also contributing members of the National Association for Search And Rescue (NASAR), the Society of Professional Rope Access Technicians (SPRAT), and the International Association of Dive Rescue Specialists (IADRS).

Notes

NFPA Standards Adopted

In 1999, Rescue 3 undertook a major revision in the curriculum to meet the requirements of the new NFPA[1] 1670 Standard on Operations and Training for Technical Search and Rescue Incidents in the areas of water and rope. They were the first major rescue training company to embrace National Fire Protection Association (NFPA) standards as the basis for curriculum. Today, NFPA standards have grown to become the de facto global standard for technical rescue operations.

Recognized Internationally

Rescue 3 classes are recognized internationally and are validated by many state and national organizations, including many emergency management agencies, community colleges, and fire marshals' offices. They form the core training for many emergency services, rescue teams and water professionals. Personnel from many of the federal Urban Search and Rescue (USAR) teams have taken Rescue 3 classes to meet their water training requirements.

Agency references are available upon request.

Dynamic and Leading Edge

With its global network of instructors, Rescue 3 is in the unique position of receiving constant input on rescue techniques and equipment that have been tested in the field, around the world, and in every condition imaginable. As a result, Rescue 3's curriculum is dynamic and evolves as the rescue field changes and develops. In this way, Rescue 3 is on the leading edge of curriculum development and knowledge of the latest and the best technical equipment available. It strives to be pro-active in serving the needs of a wide range of agencies and rescue programs around the world.

1 National Fire Protection Association

Notes

Overview of Training Courses

There can be no denying the relevance of swiftwater and flood rescue training. Worldwide, there have been countless incidents involving rescuers with inadequate or no training who get themselves and their colleagues into trouble, in, on, or near water, often with tragic results.

The Rescue 3 program provides appropriate training for all personnel who may be deployed in a swiftwater or flood environment, or for those who have a training role within a rescue organization. Courses are an intensive mix of classroom and practical sessions with five levels of training available - Awareness, Operations, Tèchnician, Management and Instructor.

Awareness Training

Water Awareness

This classroom-based course is aimed at personnel who may be working near water but not directly alongside it, or in the water itself. It provides awareness of hazards, and a basic understanding of water rescue techniques.

Operations Training

Basic Water Rescuer (BWR)

This course combines theory and practical skills and is designed for personnel who may be deployed to a still water (flatwater) environment where they may be required to undertake rescues. Includes hazard identification, self rescue and rescue of others.

Swiftwater First Responder

Designed for personnel who may be deployed near a swiftwater environment, but would not necessarily be undertaking rescue work themselves, this class teaches hazard identification and self rescue.

Operations – Swiftwater First Responder

This course expands upon areas covered in Swiftwater Rescue First Responder and includes hazard identification, self rescue and low risk, shore-based methods for the rescue of others. NFPA compliant.

Technical Rope Rescue - Operations (TRR-OL)

This course provides an introduction to rope rescue and covers the fundamentals of low angle rope rescue. Combining theory and practical sessions, the course uses a structured, step-by-step and hands-on approach that makes it easy to learn new skills or fine-tune existing skills. NFPA compliant.

Notes

Technician Training

Whitewater Rescue Technician (WRT)

Specifically designed for the outdoor professional with existing river experience, the core course knowledge and skills are the same as the SRT course, but the emphasis is on whitewater river situations rather than swiftwater and flood rescue.

Swiftwater Rescue Technician (SRT)

Designed to train personnel who regularly work near, in, and on fast-moving water in the knowledge and skills needed to identify hazards, self rescue, and rescue others in a swiftwater or flood environment. Includes in-water, "go" rescues and rope techniques. NFPA compliant.

Swiftwater Rescue Technician – Advanced (SRTA)

Building on the in-water and rope rescue concepts introduced in SRT, this course prepares personnel to work in areas, with extreme swiftwater and difficult access. As a result, it includes technical rope rescue techniques, and introduces search considerations, team management issues, and night operations. NFPA compliant.

Rescues from Vehicles in Water

This specialist workshop for existing Swiftwater Rescue Technicians explores the techniques and skills required to stabilize, access, and extricate victims from vehicles in swiftwater and floods. The course includes theories on vehicle behavior and practical training using an in-water vehicle. Night operations can be included.

(Swiftwater Rescue) Boat Operator (SRBO)

This hands-on course covers the skills required to operate powered boats in a swiftwater environment. In addition to boat handling and crew skills, the course takes bank-based rescue skills covered in the SRT course and applies them to motorized watercraft.

Technical Rope Rescue - Technician (TRR-T)

This course covers concepts and techniques to enable small teams to undertake technical rope rescues in both low and high angle environments. A "building block" approach is used throughout the course so that candidates can progress from key concepts through to the rigging and operation of full systems for raising, lowering and highline rescues. NFPA compliant.

Flood Operations for Emergency Planners and Workers

Designed for those working in floods, but not undertaking a rescue role, the aim is to provide emergency planners and personnel with the necessary knowledge and techniques to enable them to assess hazards and work safely in flood environments. The course is a mixture of theory and in-water practical sessions.

Notes

Management Training

Management of Water and Flood Incidents (MWFI)

Designed to meet the need for incident commanders at water and flood incidents to have the underpinning knowledge and skills to successfully manage such operations. While managers do not need the same level of technical knowledge and skills as specialist water rescue teams, it is imperative that they have a sufficient level of specific knowledge to be able to manage a major water event, plus the ability to safely operate in the warm zone.

Competency-Based Assessments

These rigorous assessments are designed for existing rescue technicians who desire formal endorsement of their competence as Swiftwater Rescue Technicians. Assessment is available at two levels.

SRT Competency-Based Assessment

Covers all the water and rope skills and techniques taught in the SRT course through a series of individual skills tests and scenario-based exercises.

SRT Professional Qualification Assessment

Covers all the skills and techniques taught in both SRT and SRTA courses through a series of individual skills tests and scenario-based exercises. This assessment is equivalent to the testing required for NFPA 1006 certification by third party agencies including Pro Board and IFSAC in the US.

Successful completion of a competency-based assessment can also be used to re-certify rather than attendance at the original training course again. See re-certification information below.

Notes

Re-Certification of Training Courses

Rescue 3 training courses are valid for three years. Upon successful completion of initial training, candidates receive a certificate, ID card, sticker and itemized, personalized skill sheet signed by themselves and the instructor. A copy of the skill sheet is sent to Rescue 3 where the details are entered into a training database. A copy of the original skill sheet is available within 24 hours should it ever be required to verify training credentials for employment or legal reasons.

In some jurisdictions, both the SRT and SRT Advanced training courses have an optional assessment element. Following the training course it is possible for candidates to attend a separate two day assessment course, allowing them to be certified to the NFPA 1006 Standard as competent swiftwater rescue technicians. Rescue 3 International training courses and competency based assessments must be re-certified every three years, unless an employer requires a more frequent re-certification period.

1. If you are within the three year certification period you can re-certify by either:
    a) Repeating your current level of training at a discounted registration fee (i.e. if you have an SRT certification, you can re-certify by attending another SRT course).
    b) Attending the next level of training, if applicable (i.e. if you are an SRT, you can re-certify by attending an SRT Advanced course.) Both your SRT status and Advanced status will then be valid for three years from the date of SRT Advanced certification.
2. If more than three years have elapsed since you have attended a training course, you are no longer eligible to re-certify that course at a discounted price and need to pay the full course fee. You can re-certify by:
    a) Repeating your current level of training (i.e. if you are an SRT you can re-certify by attending another SRT course).
    b) However, you cannot re-certify your technician status by attending the next level of training - you need to re-certify at the current technician level first (i.e. if you attended an SRT course four years ago, you must re-certify your SRT status by attending an SRT class *before* you an attend an SRT Advanced course).
3. As there is no prerequisite for SRT, WRT or TRR classes you can attend even if a prior status is no longer active i.e. if you attended an Operations Swiftwater First Responder course five years ago you can still attend an SRT class.
4. Courses re-certify any previous training at the same or lower level. but do not re-certify any courses at a higher level (i.e. if you re-certify by attending an SRT Advanced class this would re-certify both your SRT and SRT Advanced status. If however you re-certify by attending an SRT this would re-certify your SRT status but not re-certify your Advanced status - you would no longer be active as an Advanced Technician).
5. Water and rope rescue courses must be re-certified separately (i.e. if you are both an active SRT and Rope Rescue Technician you need to re-certify both courses every three years).
6. You must be a current SRT to attend a Swiftwater Rescue Boat Operators course. Both SRT and Swiftwater Rescue Boat Operator courses must then be re-certified every three years.

Notes

7. Training courses can be re-certified by attending the relevant competency-based assessment.

    a) SRT: You can re-certify by passing an SRT Competency-Based Assessment. This will re-certify your SRT status for three years from the date you pass your Competency-Based Assessment.

    b) SRT Advanced: You can re-certify by passing an SRT and an Advanced Competency-Based Assessment (Professional Qualification Workshop). This will re-validate your SRT and Advanced status for three years from the date you pass your Competency-Based Assessment.

    c) If you fail a Competency-Based Assessment and it is more than three years since your relevant training course, your status is no longer current.

8. Rescue 3 Instructors have separate requirements to remain active and do not need to re-certify at technician levels.

Notes

Re-certifying Qualifications

Within three years of original completion

Course attended	**Can be re-certified by**
Basic Water Rescuer	Basic Water Rescuer; SRT
Swiftwater First Responder	Swiftwater First Responder; SRT
Operations Swiftwater First Responder	Operations Swiftwater First Responder; SRT
SRT	SRT; SRT Competency Assessment; SRT Advanced
SRT Competency Assessment	SRT Competency Assessment
Swiftwater Rescue Boat Operator	Swiftwater Rescue Boat Operator
SRT Advanced	SRT Advanced; Pro Qualification Assessment
Pro Qualification Assessment	Pro Qualification Assessment
Technical Rope Rescue	Technical Rope Rescue

If re-certifying at the same level *within three years* of original completion, you will be eligible for a discounted course price.

Notes

Re-certifying Qualifications

After three years of original completion

Course attended	Can be re-certified by
Basic Water Rescuer	Basic Water Rescuer; SRT
Swiftwater First Responder	Swiftwater First Responder; SRT
Operations Swiftwater First Responder	Operations Swiftwater First Responder; SRT
SRT	SRT
SRT Competency Assessment	SRT Competency Assessment
Swiftwater Rescue Boat Operator *	Swiftwater Rescue Boat Operator
SRT Advanced *	SRT Advanced
Pro Qualification Assessment	Pro Qualification Assessment
Technical Rope Rescue	Technical Rope Rescue

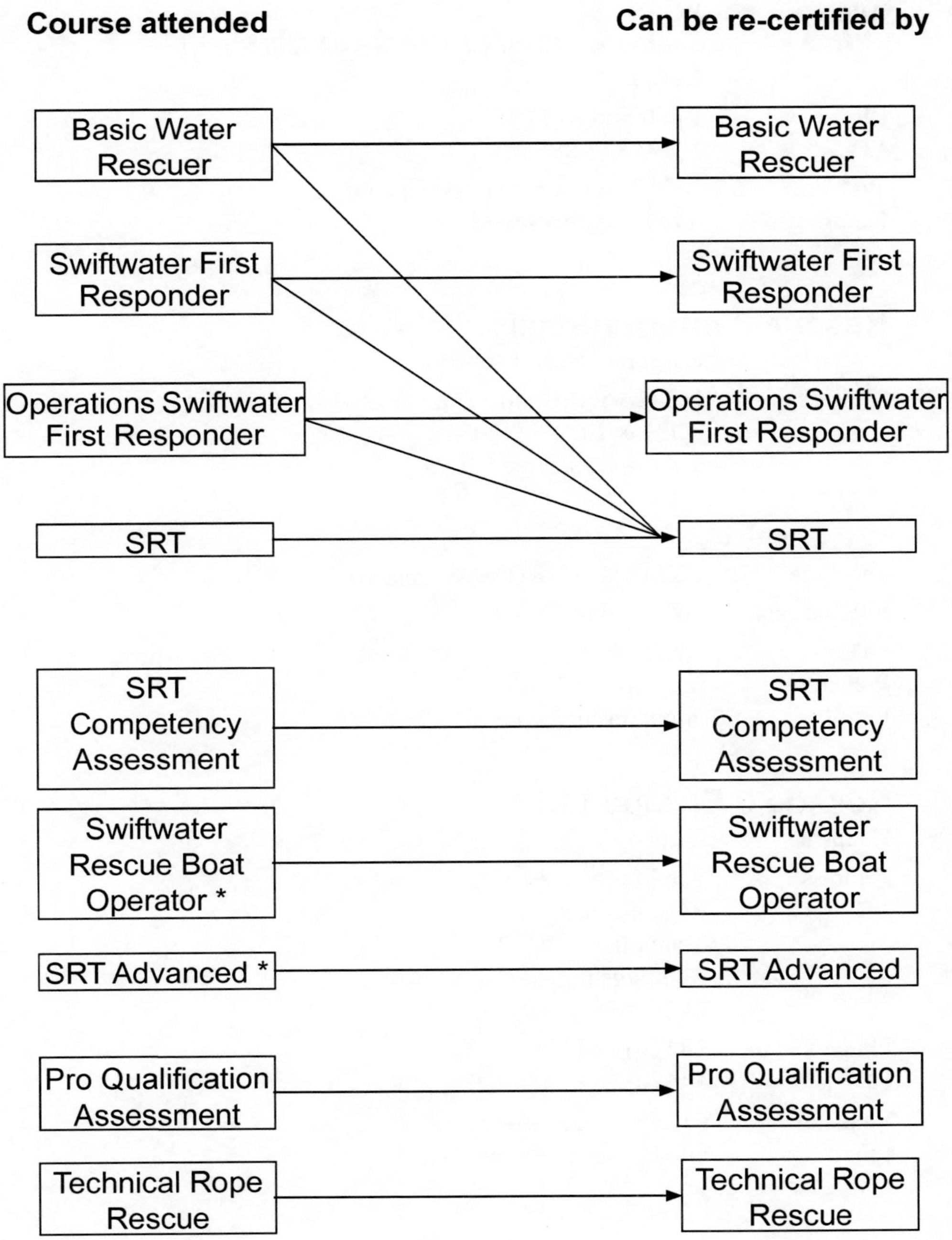

* Must have current SRT

If re-certifying at the same level *after three years* of original completion, you will have to pay the full course price.

Notes

Rescue 3 Contact Details

Rescue 3 Canada (Raven Rescue Ltd.)

Countries **Canada**

Address **PO Box 861**
Smithers, British Columbia V0J 2N0
Canada

Phone **1 800 880-0287**
Fax **1-250-847-8896**
Website **www.ravenrescue.com**
Email **info@ravenrescue.com**

Rescue 3 International

Countries Corporate Headquarters

Address: 11084A Jeff Brian Lane
PO Box 1050
Wilton, California 95693
USA

Toll Free 1 800 457 3728 (US & Canada)
International +001 916 687 6556
Fax 1 916 687 6717
Website www.rescue3.com
Email info@rescue3.com

Rescue 3 Europe Ltd

Countries Europe

Address The Malthouse
Regent Street
Llangollen
Denbighshire
LL20 8HS

Phone +44 (0) 8448 794 773
Fax +44 (0) 8443 580 107
Website www.rescue3europe.com
Email info@rescue3europe.com

Notes

South America

Brazil/Agua Selvagem

Countries	Brazil
Contact	Thomas Schörner
Website	www.aguaselvagem.com.br
Email:	info@aguaselvagem.com.br

Adventure Safety Rescue

Countries	Costa Rica, Guatemala, Belize, Honduras, Nicaragua, Panama
Contact	Philip Perez
Address	P.O. Box# 159-7150 Turrialba Costa Rica
Email	riotribes@yahoo.com
Phone	506-8835-4930

Cascade Safety Institute

Countries	Chile
Contact	Tren Long
Phone	56 45 443627
Toll Free	1-800-292-7238 (United States only)
Email	tren@cascaderaft.com

WaveTrek Rescue

Countries	Ecuador
Contact	Chris Jonason
Phone	360 793 1508
Website	www.wavetrekrescue.com

Esprit Whitewater

Countries	Mexico
Contact	Jim Coffey
Email	jim@whitewater.ca
Website	www.whitewater.ca

Notes

Middle East

Traks PRO

Coutries Kingdom of Saudi Arabia, Sultanate of Oman, Qatar, Kuwait, Bahrain, Yemen, Iran, Iraq, Jordan, Lebanon, Egypt, Syria, Tunisia, Morocco, Turkey, Algeria, Pakistan, Afghanistan

Contact James Falchetto

Email james@traks-me.com

Website www.traks-me.com

Asia

Rescue 3 Japan

Countries Japan

Contact Takahiro Sato

Website www.srs-j.co.jp

Taiwan

Countries Taiwan

Contact Chen Tser Yuan (Frank Chen)

Website www.rescue3taiwan.com.tw

Nomad Adventure Sdn Bhd

Countries Mayalasia and Singapore

Contact Chan Yuen Li

Website www.nomadadventure.com

Himalayan Outdoor Centre

Countries Nepal and Himalayas

Contact Anthony Eddies-Davies

Email enquiries@hoc.com

Phone 977-1-4356644

Website www.himalayanoutdoorcentre.com

Initiative Outdoors

Countries Nepal

Contact Chandra Ale

Email info@initiativeoutdoor.com

Phone 977-1-2111505

Mobile 977-9851014586

Website www.initiativeoutdoor.com

Notes

Oceania

RTG Rescue Training Group

Countries Australia
Contacts Brett Jones, Murray Tucker & Greg Toman
Phone 03 5772 1090
Website www.rescuetraininggroup.com.au

Penrith Whitewater

Countries Australia
Contact Morgen Masuku
Email morgen@penrithwhitewater.com.au

Emergency Management Academy of New Zealand A Division of Tai Poutini Polytechnic

Countries New Zealand
Contact Shane Briggs
Email shane.briggs@emanz.ac.nz
Phone +64 6 3531469
Website www.emanz.ac.nz

Rescue 3 Pacific (a division of Mercalli Disaster Management)

Countries All countries in the Pacific excluding Australia and New Zealand
Contact Steve Glassey
Phone +642102788930
Website www.rescue3pacific.com
Email info@rescue3pacific.com

Notes

Swiftwater Rescue Awareness

Water Rescue Standards

Notes

Rescuers in the US, Canada and Europe are used to operating under the jurisdiction of many standards and regulations. These requirements ensure that organizations are properly trained, equipped and organized to perform their respective services in a safe and efficient manner.

More and more, these standards are including specific information with regard to surface water rescue operations. The following is a brief list of some of the more relevant standards for organizations with a swiftwater rescue responsibility.

Occupational Health and Safety Administration (OSHA) - Regulations that apply nationwide to emergency services, including regulations that specifically address surface and swiftwater rescue.

Federal Emergency Management Agency (FEMA) - Establishes emergency management plans and procedures that influence how state and local agencies respond to major swiftwater and flood incidents. Administers the National Incident Management System (NIMS).

Department of Homeland Security (DHS) - Admininisters FEMA & NIMS but also establishes a standardized typing system for resources used in emergency services. Also developing a National Emergency Services Credentialing System.

American Society for Testing and Materials (ASTM) - Conducts testing and develops standards for equipment used by emergency services.

American National Standards Institute (ANSI) - Assists in the development of standards relevant to rescue equipment.

State Legislation - Often includes legal requirements for emergency services that differ from state to state.

Local requirements - City or county policies, operating procedures and guidelines include emergency services.

NFPA 1670 & 1006 Standards

The National Fire Protection Association (NFPA) is an American organization that develops and publishes standards on equipment operations and performance. These standards are not mandatory; instead an organization can decide if it wishes to be compliant or not. The NFPA does not audit against the standards. Rather, it is the responsibility of the organization to show that it has met the requirements of the published standard.

In 1998, the NFPA published NFPA 1670 – a rescue standard that addresses water rescue as one of its components. In 2000, NFPA 1006 was released which sets minimum standards for emergency response personnel who perform technical rescue operations, including water and flood rescue.

While the NFPA might be seen as American-focused, application of the standards is not limited to the USA. In fact, their comprehensive nature has led NFPA Standards to become de-facto ***global*** standards.

Notes

NFPA 1670 – Standard on operations and training for technical search and rescue incidents (revised 2009)

The intent of this standard is to establish general guidelines for an organization or Agency Having Jurisdiction (AHJ) in assessing hazards, identifying levels of operational capabilities and establishing training documentation and response guidelines. The standard addresses the following rescue disciplines:

- Confined Space Search and Rescue
- Rope Rescue
- Structural Collapse
- Vehicles and Machinery Search and Rescue
- Water Search and Rescue including Swiftwater & Flood
- Wilderness Search and Rescue
- Trench and Excavation Search and Rescue

Note: The NFPA compliant training programs offered by Rescue 3 focus on water and rope rescue.

Levels of Functional Capability

NFPA 1670 identifies three levels of functional capability for technical rescue. It is the responsibility of the AHJ to decide the level or levels at which it wishes to safely and effectively conduct operations at technical rescue incidents. The three levels are:

Awareness – Minimum capability of responders who, in the course of their regular job duties, could be called to respond or could be first on the scene at a technical rescue incident. At this level the responder is generally not considered a rescuer.

Operations – The responder at this level should be capable of hazard recognition, equipment use, shore and boat-based rescues, and participation in a technical rescue under the supervision of technician level personnel.

Technician – A rescuer capable of hazard recognition, equipment use, and co-ordination, performance and supervision of a technical rescue. This may involve search, rescue and/or recovery operations.

NFPA 1670 is aimed at organizations and not individuals. However, by receiving training compliant to the standard, individuals will be an asset to their agency by meeting the overall standard requirements.

A complete copy of the standard can be purchased at www.nfpa.org

NFPA 1006 – Standard for technical rescuer professional qualifications (revised 2008)

Notes

The purpose of this standard is to establish the minimum performance for emergency response personnel who perform technical rescue operations. To be compliant to the standard the individual's performance must be assessed against the standard's criteria. In addition to the individual requirements there are requirements placed on the AHJ such as policy and procedure requirements.

A complete copy of the standard can be purchased from www.nfpa.org.

Rescue 3 International's training courses are compliant with the NFPA 1670 and/or 1006 standards. Training courses are provided at Awareness, Operations and Technician levels, as well as competency-based assessments.

Training Levels

The NFPA 1670 Standard identifies a number of training levels for those who work or respond to incidents near, on, or in water. The level of training required depends on the degree of exposure to a particular hazard—in this case, moving water. Below is a brief description of each training level and corresponding Rescue 3 courses.

Awareness

Qualifies personnel to work in the "cold zone" more than 10' from moving water, in a supporting role for rescue technicians certified to the Operations or Technician level. This course does not qualify personnel to work alongside or in moving water.

- Awareness: Water and Rope Rescue
- Basic Water First Responder

Operations

Qualifies personnel to work in the "warm zone", i.e. a shore-based position within 10' of fast-moving water and in water moving less than one mph. It does not qualify personnel to work in fast-moving water.

- Operations: Swiftwater First Responder

Technician

Qualifies personnel to work in the "hot zone", or in fast-moving water, and to perform "go" rescues.

- Swiftwater Rescue Technician® Unit 1
- Swiftwater Rescue Technician® Advanced
- Whitewater Rescue Technician
- Whitewater Rescue Technician 2
- Management of Water and Flood Incidents

Rescue Philosophy

Notes

Rescue 3 considers there to be four elements in a successful rescue:

- Training
- Practice
- Experience
- Judgment

For a team to be successful in its actions, members must first take courses to gain basic training. In order to become more proficient, team members should practice these skills and techniques further, therefore gaining valuable experience. This may include regular practice at sites that have proven problematic in the past.

As the team becomes more experienced and practiced, members will develop good, sound judgment when dealing with a variety of situations. This judgment is vital when the team is faced with rescue situations in challenging conditions. It is the members' judgment that will be relied upon in order to make the right decisions on how (or how not) to proceed with a rescue.

Having gained experience of what works, what is problematic, the advantages and disadvantages of various systems, and possible solutions – the team members will have the judgment to be able to choose the best solution for any situation without wasting time. This judgment cannot be purchased or fast-tracked, but is the result of much time spent practicing and gaining experience in a variety of conditions and situations.

Rescue Priorities

At all incidents the priorities of all rescuers should be:

1. Self
2. Team
3. Victim

It is vitally important for rescuers to take responsibility for their own actions. This includes personal safety in a hazardous environment such as a rescue site. Unless the rescuer is correctly trained and equipped, the task could be unachievable and produce more victims. Acting on uneducated and misjudged impulses to save a person, such as jumping into the water unequipped or untrained, is highly likely to result in tragedy rather than success. It is paramount that rescuers do not operate beyond their capability.

The above also applies to the team. Individuals have a responsibility to look after their team members and not place them in danger to a level beyond control. There must be backup systems in place so that team members' safety is protected. It is essential that team members all look after their own safety by avoiding undue risks.

Only when rescuers have provided for their own safety, and their team's safety, can they start to perform rescues or operate in a water environment. No work or rescue can exceed the team's capability.

After ensuring the safety of team members and the victim, the risks taken for the retrieval of equipment should be very low – equipment is replaceable, people are not!

And finally, the best rescue is one that does not need to be performed.

Phases of a Rescue

A rescue can be split into several distinct phases.

First, at any rescue site, the initial step must be a scene assessment. This should take into account all the factors that may affect the rescue, including weather, number of victims, their condition and location, capability of the team, water conditions, safety back up, and additional resources.

Once the scene assessment has been performed, a plan can be formulated to safely deal with the situation. The plan should be made up of the following four phases:

1. Locate

2. Access

3. Stabilize

4. Transport

This is known as the L.A.S.T. principle and applies to all rescues.

Initially victims must be located. They may be trapped on a fixed object in the water flow, where they can be quickly located. However, they may be traveling in the water, in which case, a search could last many hours before the rescue can be performed.

Once victims are located, then the team must (where possible) gain access to them by whatever method is appropriate. This could be a simple throwbag rescue to another team member. A victim may be injured and require a boat to gain access.

Once the victim has been accessed, they must be stabilized. This may simply require getting "hands-on" to secure the victim, or entail a full medical immobilization. As a minimum, the victim should immediately be provided with a correctly-fitting buoyancy aid (PFD) and helmet.

Finally, the victim and rescuers will be transported back to safety and onto further care if required.

Notes

A Zoned Approach to Water Rescue

When dealing with water rescue incidents, it is advisable to zone the working area as soon as possible. By only permitting suitably trained and equipped people into each zone, the safety of the team is ensured. Flagging tape or pylons are often used to identify zones.

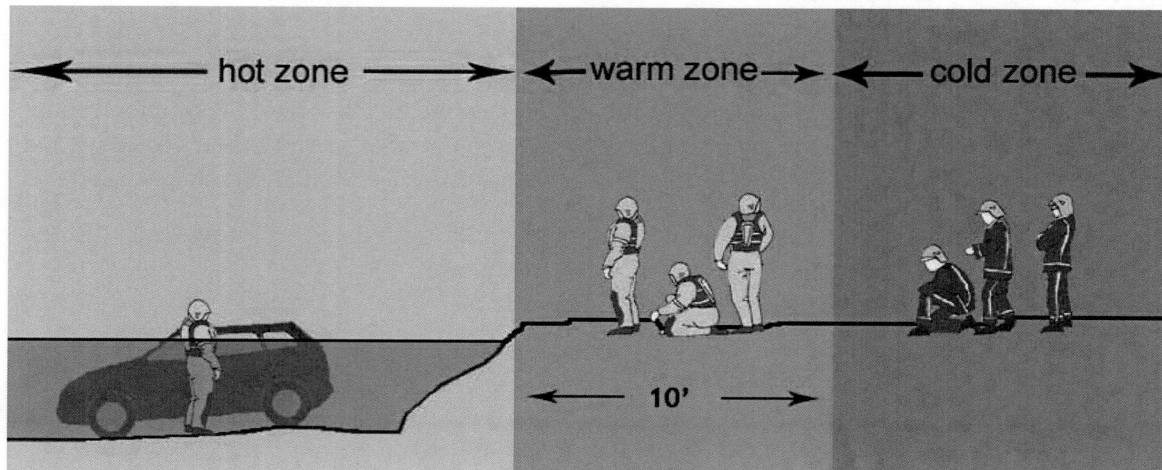

Diagram Aw1: The hot, warm, and cold zones.

The Hot Zone

The hot zone is the area covered by water. This is often the greatest hazard, and must be approached only by people capable of working safely in that environment, essentially those trained to the Technician level. Rescues will be performed by a variety of methods and the personnel operating in this zone must be properly trained and equipped for the situation.

The Warm Zone

This area moves inland, and is generally comprised of the shoreline area within 10' of the water. There is a significant chance that personnel in this area may accidentally slip and fall into the water; therefore they must be properly equipped and trained to deal with this possibility, which generally corresponds to Operational level training. If necessary, this zone can be extended further from the water's edge to compensate for difficult terrain such as slopes or uneven ground.

The Cold Zone

This is the area for personnel trained at the Awareness level. These people may not approach the warm zone and definitely not the hot zone. Personnel in this area must appreciate the dangers of the other zones, but have not undergone the rigorous training required to operate in those zones. Personnel in the cold zone might be medical teams and additional support staff. Regardless of the level of training, however, if an individual does not have appropriate PPE[1], then he must not progress any further than the cold zone.

---

1 Personal Protective Equipment

Notes

These three zones are the working areas required at any incident. Members of the public are kept beyond the cold zone. This ensures that there are no additional victims to deal with, no one to accidentally hinder the rescue effort, or add to the existing challenges.

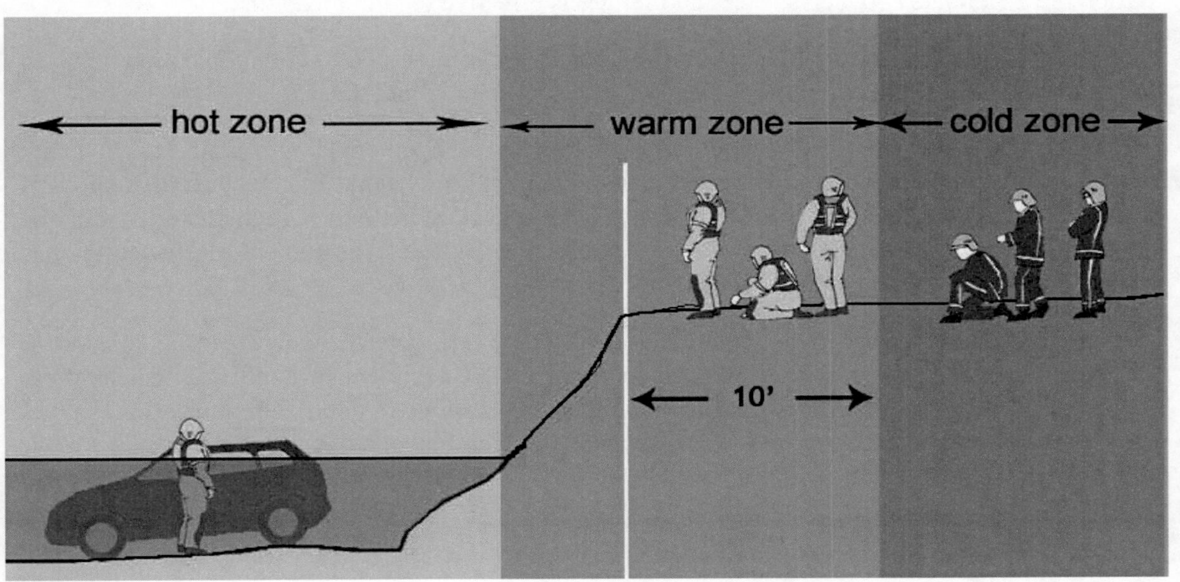

Diagram Aw2: Zones may have to be extended to deal with the topography.

Communications

Notes

Often the difference between success and failure is effective communication.

For an incident to run smoothly, it is essential that there is a method of communication between all members of a team, and between the Incident Commander and the team.

This may be done simply, by voice or signaling to each other. However, there are many more technical methods—for example, a handheld radio system. If a technical method of communication is relied upon, it is imperative that a backup method is immediately available. Rescuers should remember that radios can break, and batteries can run flat. Reliance upon a single method of communication is dangerous.

Whatever method is used, it is essential that all team members recognize and understand it. Where necessary the message should be repeated by the recipient to confirm understanding. Often the river bank is a noisy environment and not conducive to good communication, so it is vital that communications are clear, concise and understood by all.

Hand Signals

The diagrams below show commonly accepted hand signals.

Diagram Aw3: One hand on top of head. **"Okay!"**

Diagram Aw4: One hand extended above head. **"Distress!"**

Notes

Diagram Aw5: Pointing. **"Move in that direction!"**

Diagram Aw6: One hand rotated above the head, then point. **"Eddy out in that direction!"**

Diagram Aw7: Both arms crossed in front of chest. **"Need medical help!"**

Diagram Aw8: Palm shown. **"Stop!"**

Notes

Hand signals – moving a boat

Diagram Aw9: Point positively. **"Move in that direction!"**

Diagram Aw10: Both hands raised **"Stop!"**

Whistle Signals

1 blast	Stop or attention
2 blasts	Attention upstream or move upstream
3 blasts	Attention downstream or move downstream
3 blasts repeated	Emergency or rescue

Radios

Where hand-held radios are used, communications should be disciplined and structured to avoid cluttering the airwaves. This helps to avoid missing important messages.

To prevent damage and to ensure the radios are kept operational, they should be kept in a waterproof case in which they can be easily operated. Water-resistant and waterproof radios are available, although care should be taken not to exceed the rated limits.

Rescue Options

Notes

Many rescuers are familiar with the "mantra" of Talk-Reach-Throw-Row-Go/Tow-Helo for water rescue. Unfortunately, this list of rescue techniques is usually interpreted as a rigid rescue hierarchy, or "order of priority" for attempting a rescue.

Many rescuers believe this list of techniques is set in stone, where the first technique must be considered before the next one is tried. This is far beyond the original intentions of the creators.

Tactical Toolbox

Rather, the variety of rescue techniques should be considered as a "tactical toolbox" of rescue options. Team members with the necessary skills and judgment will quickly choose the appropriate method for the situations they face, and not spend valuable time debating the others.

This manual starts with the simplest rescue techniques and then goes on to cover more complex methods. As techniques become more complex, they require more training, equipment and experience to implement.

These techniques can be divided into two categories depending on the amount of assistance required from the victim.

A conditional rescue relies upon the victim doing something to assist. For example, throwing a rope to the victim would require the victim to have the presence of mind and physical capability to hold onto the rope and grip it tightly until they are safe.

A true rescue requires no assistance from the victim and is used when the victim is incapable of helping himself. The rescuer must do everything, and so must be correctly equipped and trained to perform the rescue. Clearly, the risk to the rescuer is higher, as he or she must go into the hot zone. However, the benefit to unconscious or injured victims is obvious.

Shout & Signal

Communicate with victims by any means available to encourage them to self rescue. Establishing eye contact is very useful. Always maintain a positive attitude and encourage their efforts. Keep communication short and to the point. This rescue can be performed by anybody but as it will likely be performed within three meters of the water's edge, ideally the rescuer would be trained to the Awareness level and wearing appropriate PPE.

Throw

Establish eye contact and communication with the victim to ensure he is expecting an object to be thrown. The object thrown must be buoyant, such as a ring buoy, given that the rescuer will not have any contact with it after throwing. Again, the rescuer is likely to be within three meters of the water's edge and so should be trained to the Awareness level (as a minimum) and be wearing appropriate PPE. After throwing a buoyant object, other techniques will most likely be required to complete the rescue.

Notes

Reach

The length of the reaching aid is the limiting factor. Throwbags, inflated fire hoses, ladders, and wading poles have all been used to good effect. Even though a throwbag is thrown, the rescuer maintains contact with the end of the rope, and so it is classified as a reaching technique.

Wade

Entering shallow, slow-flowing water in order to perform a throwing, reaching, or contact rescue is a relatively low risk option for appropriately trained personnel that can significantly increase the chance of a successful rescue. Particularly in flooded environments, the majority of successful rescues involve wading out to victims and returning with them. Entering slow moving water to wade is the upper limit of the skills of a First Responder.

Craft

Rescuers are now moving into higher risk hot zones, albeit separate from and floating on the water. There are a wide variety of crafts that can be used to perform successful rescues including inflatable pathways, RIBs, PWCs, hovercraft, inflatable boats, rafts, canoes, kayaks, and others. Other techniques are often used in combination with watercraft.

Swim

Using all their skills, Swiftwater Rescue Technicians® will be able to perform in-water, contact rescues where they swim to victims and bring them to safety, regardless of the victim's level of consciousness or injury. Obviously, this is a high risk rescue that should only be performed by the most skilled members of a swiftwater rescue team.

Helicopter or Aerial

These rescues are beyond the realm of the Swiftwater Rescue Technician® course, and illustrate that some rescues will be beyond the skill level of some swiftwater rescue teams. In these instances, other rescuers must be utilized, such as a helicopters or rope rescue teams. Helicopters are often thought of as the best option in any situation, but can be seriously hampered by weather, terrain and darkness. Conversely, a rope rescue team is able to respond in all these conditions. Rescue 3's Swiftwater Rescue Technician® Advanced course teaches the high-angle rope rescue skills and night operations techniques required for these complex rescue situations.

Notes

Rescue or Recovery?

In any rescue, time is a critical factor. Teams are always working against the clock to perform a successful rescue and wondering how long a victim can survive in the given situation.

If a Swiftwater Rescue Team can perform a successful rescue, using the simplest and quickest method, then this is always of benefit to everyone involved. However, when choosing the right option, teams must balance time constraints against the chance of success. There is no point choosing a quick, simple method that will clearly not work. This is why Rescue 3 places such emphasis on practicing and gaining experience and judgment.

In a recovery situation, time is not as critical. Rescuers can wait for water levels to drop, or wait for additional equipment or personnel.

However, the most difficult question often is:

Is this a recovery or a rescue?

or

At what stage do we stop rescue attempts and start treating the situation as a body recovery?

Some situations are clearly a rescue situation (e.g. the victim is head up and still breathing) or an obvious recovery (e.g. a body is found that has been in the water for many days). However, there are many situations where it is unclear whether the response is a rescue or a recovery.

Unless it is a clear recovery situation, all efforts should be made to rescue the victim. Team leaders must make decisions based on available information, but can also face pressure to act from bystanders, family members and the media. Team leaders must ensure that outside pressure does not prompt rescuers and responders to take unnecessary risks and place themselves in undue danger.

Notes

The "15 Absolutes" of Flood and Swiftwater Rescue

Rescue 3 International has identified "15 Absolutes", intended to help students develop an understanding of the basic principles of swiftwater and flood rescue.

General Principles

1 Keep it simple

Many rescues fail because rescue teams try to implement complicated solutions that take too long to set up or are above the ability level of the team members.

2 Always be pro-active

Once organizations and rescue teams recognize swiftwater and floods as potential hazards, they can begin to plan and prepare accordingly. Preparation is not limited to pre-planning the actual response (e.g. training, equipment, personnel, management systems, communications etc.) but can be much broader and include public education and notification systems (e.g. early warning systems for flooding).

As the often quoted line by Benjamin Franklin states, "An ounce of prevention is worth a pound of cure." The number of people who fall victim to water or flood incidents can be greatly reduced through effective public education and risk mitigation, and along with it, the need for rescues.

On scene, pro-activity should be encouraged by ensuring the rescue scene is contained (with upstream spotters and downstream backup) before any rescuers are committed to the water. The person in charge should be pro-active by thinking about alternative plans of action if the initial plan fails. Each member of the team must also observe the surroundings and think ahead to help secure his personal safety and that of others.

Notes

Before the rescue starts

3 The priority at the scene is always self-rescue first, the rescue and security of teammates second and the victim last

The most important person at any rescue is the rescuer. Once the rescuers are in control of their personal safety, then the next level of concern is for their fellow rescuers. Only after that can the victim begin to be considered. To the outsider, this may appear to be a self-centered and unfair approach. After all, the victim is the one in need of rescuing.

However, the victim can only be rescued by those who are in control, do not need rescuing themselves, and have the energy and ability to look after someone else in addition to themselves. If rescuers do not maintain their own safety, they quickly become victims themselves. A team of rescuers that maintains individual and team safety will be a greater rescue asset to the victim than a careless individual rescuer.

4 Always wear a Personal Flotation Device (PFD)

Anyone who is at risk of entering the water (expectedly or unexpectedly) must be wearing an appropriate Personal Flotation Device (either a buoyancy aid or life jacket). Generally, this is defined as anyone who may be in the warm zone (see *page Aw-6*). The type of PFD worn must be appropriate to the operational role of the person. In addition, once contact has been made with a victim, a priority is to also provide him with a PFD. For more information about PFDs see *page Aw-59*

5 Use the right equipment

Swiftwater rescue equipment has progressed a long way in the past 30 years. There is no excuse for putting rescuers and victims at risk through the use of inappropriate, unsafe or improvised equipment. Equipment should be appropriate to the purpose, compliant to any applicable standards, monitored, and tested. Most importantly, rescuers must be familiar with the equipment they are using.

6 Do not use a fire helmet for water rescue operations

This continues from Absolute #5 – "Use the Right Equipment". Fire helmets are generally large with brims that have the potential to cause injuries to the neck if worn in water. There are a wide variety of helmets available specifically designed for use in swiftwater and whitewater environments and one of these should be worn when operating as a rescuer in this environment.

Notes

Before entering the water

7 Always deploy upstream spotters above the location of the rescue operation – ideally on both sides of the river

Swiftwater and flood rescue scenes are often dynamic environments with debris and other river users moving downstream into the rescue site. Upstream spotters can not only warn rescuers of debris and potential hazards, but can also warn other river users of the rescue operation in progress. Clear communication must be in place between the upstream spotters and the incident commander.

8 Always have appropriate downstream backup

There is always the possibility of people being swept downstream at a swiftwater or flood incident. Therefore, it is a priority to have effective downstream backup in place at any rescue. Although throwbags and inflated fire hoses have a role to play here, they are not a definitive backup. A true backup is preferable to a conditional backup (see *page Aw-11*). However, any backup is better than no backup.

9 Always have a backup plan

The incident manager must always be looking at the bigger picture and thinking "What if?" and "What next?". While team members are implementing "Plan A", others need to be putting backup plans into operation. This may mean that additional resources and personnel must be requested -- a process that should be established in advance through pre-planning (for more information see *page Aw-48*).

Notes

Working with rope in the water

10 Never tie a rope around a rescuer

Rescuers have died as the result of being tied to a rope and then trapped underwater, unable to release themselves. If a rescuer is to enter the water attached to a rope, it must be attached to a specialist quick release harness on a rescue PFD.

11 Never tension a rope at right angles to the current if it is to be used for in-water operations

When a rope is tensioned directly across the current and then loaded as a rescuer moves onto it, the water pressure will push the person downstream. The rope then forms a "V" in the downstream current with the rescuer at the downstream point of the "V" unable to move.

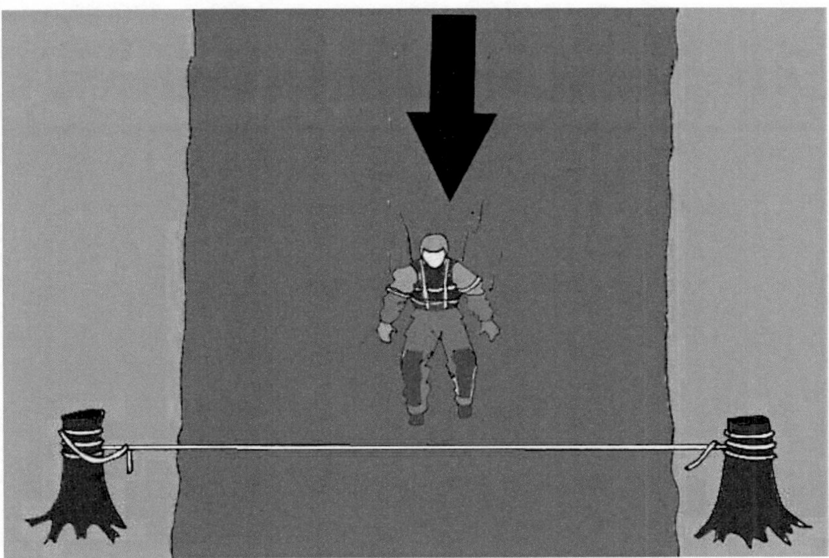

Diagram Aw11: Approaching the rope tensioned at water level.

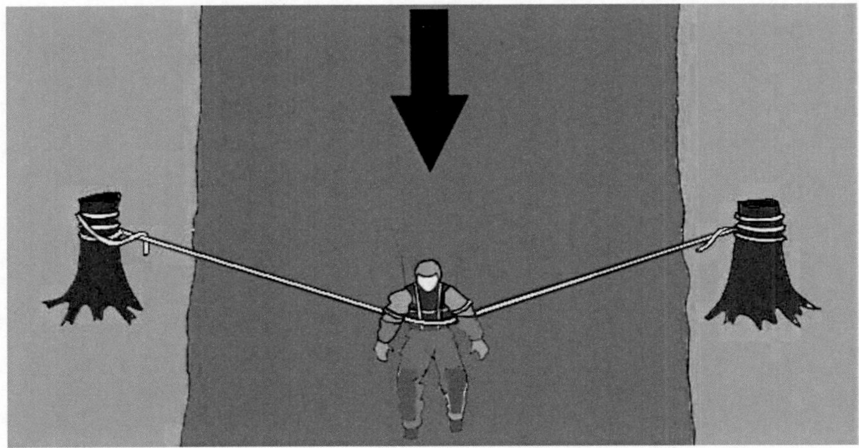

Diagram Aw12: As the swimmer comes onto the rope, a downstream "V" is created, which traps the swimmer and makes it impossible to move the swimmer to either bank.

Notes

12 Never stand inside a loop of rope and always stand on the upstream side of the rope

When operating with rope around water, it is essential to be constantly vigilant to the dangers it creates. Standing in or on loops of rope puts the rescuer at risk of being trapped by the rope. Never stand on rope.

Standing inside loops created by a mechanical advantage system also puts the rescuer at risk of being trapped, or hit by components of the system if it fails.

When using ropes to anchor or recover objects in the water, rescuers must stand on the upstream side of the rope. Then, if the object in the water moves downstream, the rescuer is not knocked over by the rope as it also moves downstream.

Notes

Performing the rescue

13 Never put your feet down if swept away

Attempting to stand up in swiftwater can lead to the potentially fatal situation of foot entrapment. This occurs when a person’s foot is trapped on the river bed by rocks or other objects. The force of the water pushes the body downstream and underwater. The person’s head is also pushed under the water and his entire body can disappear from sight in seconds. Foot entrapments can occur equally often in natural waterways and in flooded areas.

The risk of foot entrapment can be greatly reduced by using correct swiftwater swimming technique until a safe eddy is reached.

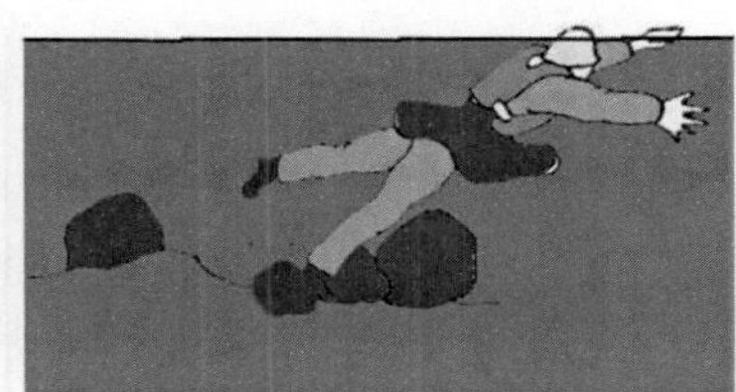

Diagram Aw13: Foot entrapment sequence.

14 Never count on victims to help in their own rescue

Being the victim in a swiftwater or flood incident can be a terrifying experience which greatly affects a victim’s ability to help in his or her own rescue. Even trained rescuers who have been through “victim school” can, through exposure to the rapid cooling effects of water, be unable to assist in their own rescue.

15 Once victims are contacted, never lose them

In the United States, there have been a number of legal cases against rescuers who made initial contact with victims, but then lost contact with them. The rescuers were sued for “abandonment.”

This is one absolute of swiftwater and flood rescue that is not as directly applicable outside of the USA. For example, the risk of being sued for abandonment is not present in Europe. However, rescuers have a legal duty of care for themselves and others, including victims they are rescuing. This requires that once contact is made with victims, every effort should be made to avoid losing contact with them and to ensure they are recovered to safety under direct supervision.

Notes

Moving Water

Consider this: one inch of rain falling over one square mile produces 17.38 million gallons of water, all traveling downhill, toward the lowest point.

Moving water has three key characteristics. Moving water is:

Powerful

Moving water exerts a force on any object it encounters, whether it is a car, rock, bridge or person in the water. This force is dependent upon the speed of the water. As the speed of the current increases, so does the power. See *page Aw-23* for more information.

Relentless

Moving water will exert a continuous force on an object. It never stops. This is unlike an ocean wave which has a cycle of breaking and receding.

Predictable

Water may sometimes look as if it is moving randomly, but to the trained eye it is moving in an orderly and predictable way. Surface features can be "read" and used to predict what is happening under the water.

Channel Characteristics

The nature of rivers and floods are variable, and are determined by four main factors:

- Volume of water flowing
- Channel gradient
- Nature of the channel bed and banks
- Water speed

By understanding how moving water behaves, rescuers can use it, and by doing so, avoid unnecessary or unacceptable levels of danger.

Notes

Volume

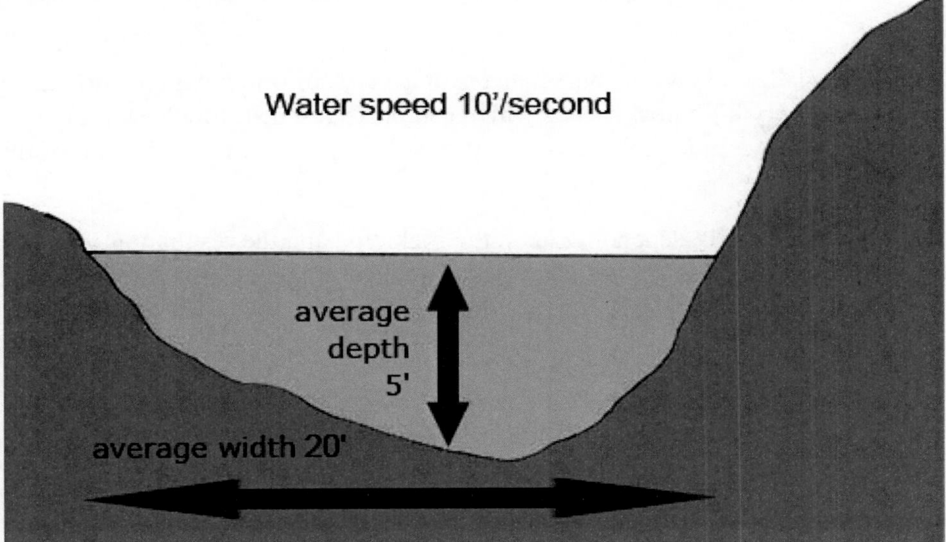

Diagram Aw14: A cross section of a river channel.

By knowing the measurements of a channel at a given spot, it is possible to calculate its flow volume at any point between confluences.

Flow volume is measured in cubic feet per second (cfs^{-1}). Using the above graphic as an example:

Depth	x	Width	x	Speed	=	Volume
5'	x	20'	x	10'/s	=	1000 cfs^{-1}

This calculation is valid only for the area of the river between confluences, ie. between the confluences above and below where the river was measured. Here the channel is carrying 1000 cubic feet per second of water. Above or below confluences, the volume will change.

One cubic foot of water equals approximately 8 gallons, and there are 250 gallons in one ton. Therefore, the river channel above, carrying 1000 cubic feet of water per second, equates to 8,000 gallons of water per second, or 32 tons of water per second.

Channel Gradient

Generally, channel gradient is the main determining factor of water speed. As the channel gets steeper, the water speed increases. The gradient profile is also a critical factor. A gradient of 100' over one mile could be a uniform slope with a high water speed, or a series of slow moving pools divided by sizeable waterfalls.

Notes

Nature of the Channel Bed and Banks

Channel bed and banks will have significant effect on a number of factors such as water speed and hazards.

Smooth-sided, man-made drainage channels can result in very uniform flows and little entrapment risk. They can create very high flow speeds which can make rescue difficult. A straight-running drainage channel will have much higher water speeds than a natural river channel of the same gradient.

Natural river beds vary greatly depending upon the rock type and the resultant morphology (i.e. form or structure), and can present significant risk of foot entrapment.

Water Speed

The speed of the water will be mainly determined by the three factors above (i.e. volume, gradient and morphology).

Constrictions in channels will also increase water speed. The volume of water cannot be altered, so if the channel is constricted, then either the water depth or speed (or both) will increase. Such situations occur both in natural river channels (e.g. where there are mid-stream rocks) and in flood situations (e.g. where there are buildings, cars in streets etc.).

Notes

Force of Water

The relationship between the speed of moving water and the force it exerts is not a linear one. Instead, the force[2] increases by the square of the speed. For example, if the speed of the water doubles, the force that the water exerts on an object is quadrupled.

Current Velocity	Approximate Force on Legs	Approximate Force on Body
3 mph (walking pace)	**75 N**	**150 N**
6 mph (steady jog)	**300 N**	**600 N**
9 mph (running speed)	**675 N**	**1,350 N**
12 mph (fast running)	**1,200 N**	**2,400 N**

Table A1: Rounded figures are based upon research carried out by the Ohio Department of Natural Resources in 1980.
Note: The newton (symbol: N) is the SI derived unit of force.

Water's Effect on People

Water flowing at an easy running pace (7.2 mph) can begin to wash people off their feet in a depth of only nine to 10 inches of water (shin height).

In water approximately three feet deep (i.e. waist depth), water flowing at a slow walking pace (2.2 mph) can make it difficult for people to retain their balance, and as the speed of the water increases only slightly to a fast-walking pace (4 mph), everybody will be washed off their feet.

Of course, these approximations will vary depending upon the height and weight of the individuals, their clothing, the composition of the channel bed, etc.

2 Force is measured in Newtons (N). A mass of 1 kg (2.2 lb) being acted upon by gravity will exert a force of approximately 10 N on the surface it is resting upon. Therefore the force on a person's legs in water moving at 3 mph is equivalent to a mass of 16.5 lbs.

Notes

Transportation of Loads

Rivers and water courses carry loads in a variety of ways. Swiftwater rescue personnel should be alert to hazards and debris flowing beneath the surface.

Top load or surface load

This includes kayaks, rafts and floating debris such as sticks. The top load will also contain swimmers and victims.

Suspended load

Suspended loads travel under the water surface, and are therefore more difficult to identify. These can include debris that is water-logged such as trees or sinking vehicles, etc. Dead bodies are also likely to travel as a suspended load (depending on the state of decomposition).

Bottom load

A bottom load contains heavy objects that will be pushed or rolled along the river bottom and can often be invisible from the surface. In high energy water this could include boulders rolling along the bottom, vehicles etc.

Dissolved load

A dissolved load can be hazardous material or chemicals that have mixed with the water. These solutions may not have been diluted to the point of no longer being harmful.

Notes

Swiftwater Hydrology

River Orientation

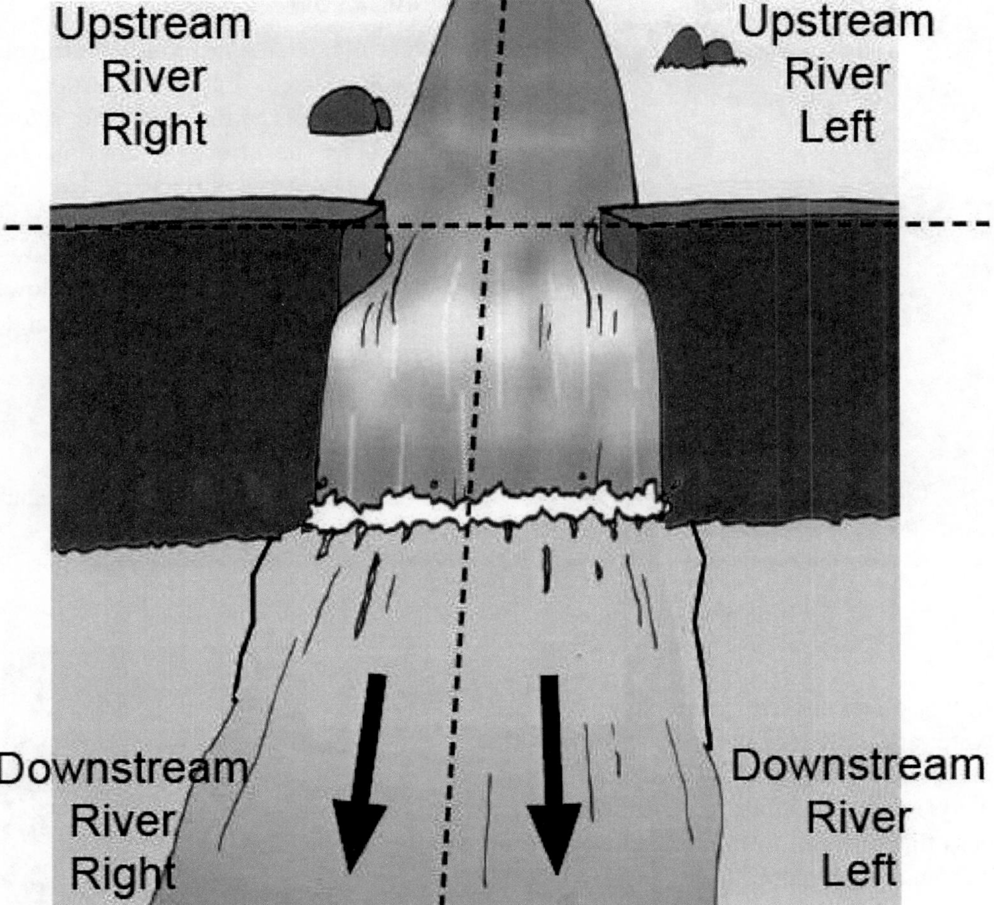

Diagram Aw15: River orientation. Give directions as if facing downstream.

Upstream

The direction from which water is flowing.

Downstream

The direction in which (or to which) water is flowing.

River right

The right side of the channel when looking downstream.

River left

The left side of the channel when looking downstream.

An important thing to remember is that "river right" and "river left" are always determined relative to the flow of the water, not the viewer's perspective. Face downstream for ease of identification.

Notes

Flow Types

There are two types of current flows encountered in moving water channels.

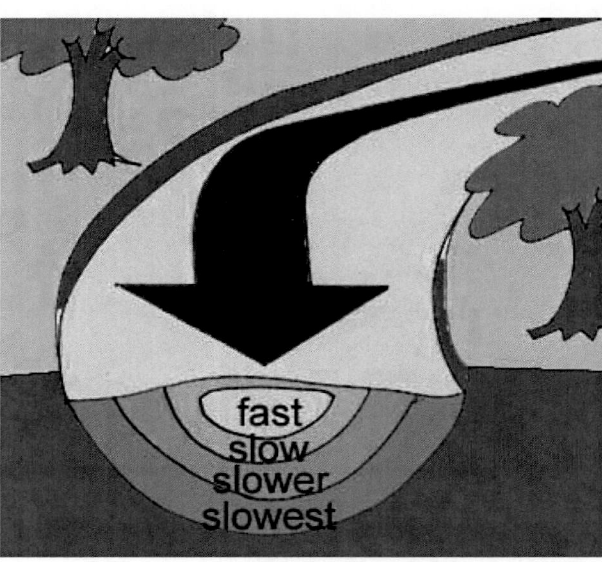

Laminar Flow

The water in a channel does not all travel at the same speed. Layers of water in contact with the channel bed and sides are slowed by the effects of friction. In addition, the water a little closer to the middle is slowed by friction against the slower water beside it. The fastest flow is in the center of the channel just below the surface – furthest from the bottom and bank.

Diagram Aw16: Layers move at different speeds.

Helical Flow

This is a spiralling effect caused by the bank slowing the water at the edge of the river and the faster movement of mid-channel water. It is a relatively unusual feature in natural channels, unless they are full to the top, and traveling at their maximum speed.

Helical flow can push a victim and river debris away from the bank and into the center of the river.

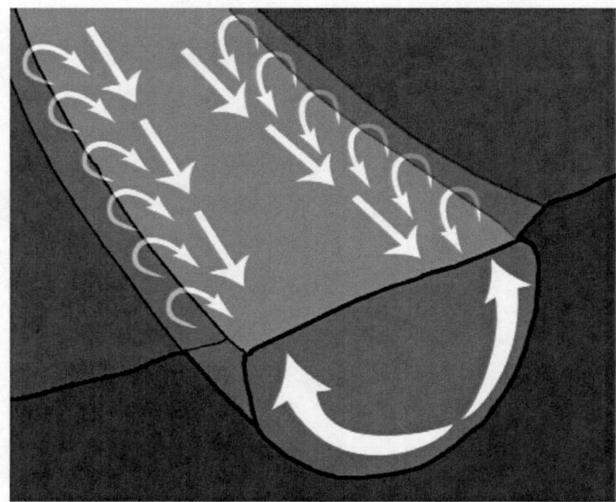

Diagram Aw17: Helical flow pushes objects toward the centre.

Notes

Current Vector

Moving water flows in a straight line until it hits an obstacle. The technical term for the direction the water is flowing is "current vector." Water does not curve around bends in a river or channel; rather it "pin balls" or ricochets from obstacle to obstacle.

As a result, the current creates high pressure areas where it impacts the outside of bends. This can cause erosion, leading to undercut banks. Conversely, there will be low pressure areas (and slower water) on the inside of bends. This can lead to deposition (i.e. build up of sand, gravel or debris) and shallow water on the inside of bends.

An awareness and understanding of current vector is essential in order that personnel to be able to successfully self-rescue and perform rescues. A clear reading of the current vector will enable rescuers to work with the force of the river (where possible) rather than against it.

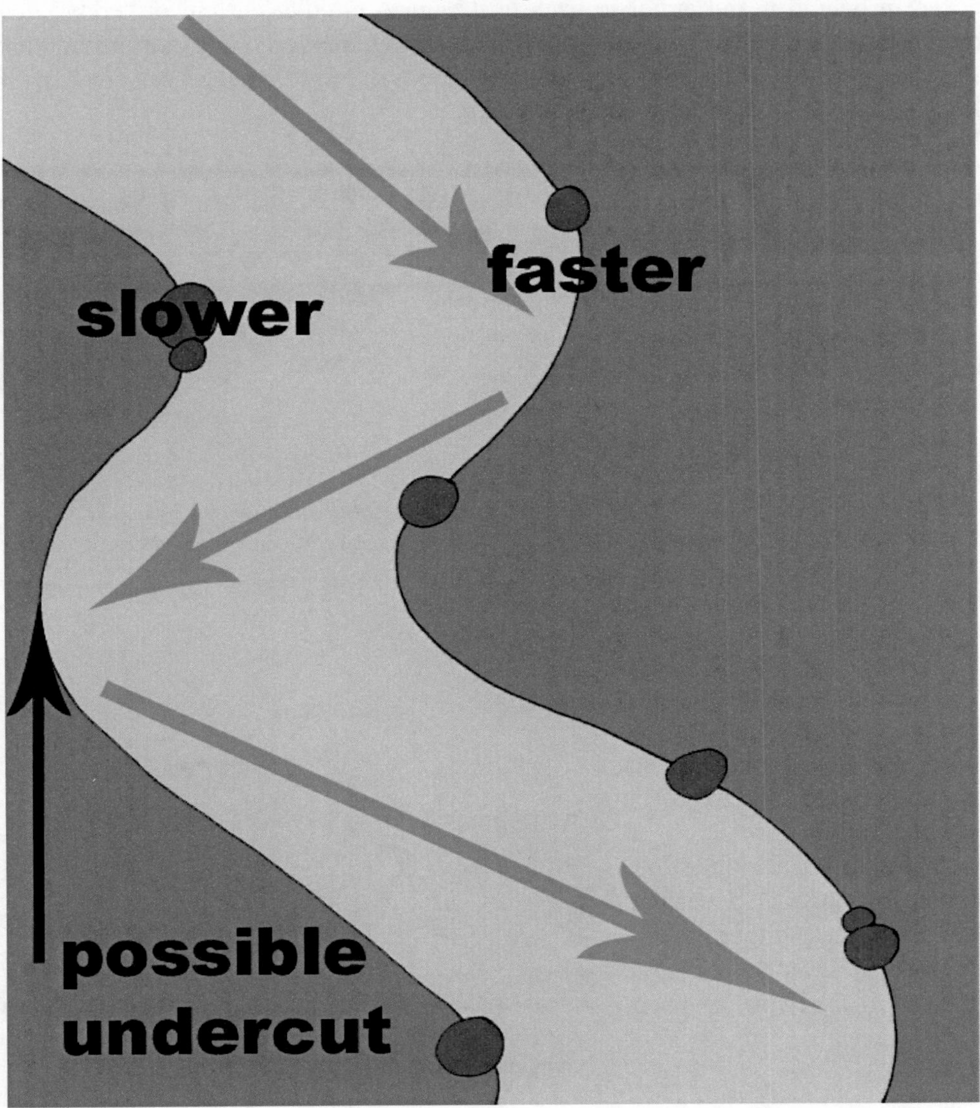

Diagram Aw18: Water "pin balls" off obstacles, creating areas with faster and slower currents.

Notes

Swiftwater Features

Terminology and Definitions

River bed and bank characteristics can create many water features. The type of feature created by any object or obstruction is generally determined by the water level and speed.

Eddy

An eddy is a common river feature created when water hits an obstacle and is deflected away from it. This creates a difference in water pressure downstream of the obstacle that causes water to be sucked in behind it and circulate back upstream. A circular current or "eddy" develops below the obstacle. An eddy is usually an area of calmer, slower water that provide areas of safety for rescuers. However, strong downstream currents or large obstacles can create powerful, violent eddies that can be difficult to enter and exit.

Eddy Line (Eddy Fence)

This is the boundary "line" between the main flow in a river and an eddy. Water currents move in opposite directions on each side of the line. An eddy line (or eddy fence) can range from gentle surface ripples to deep, strong re-circulations.

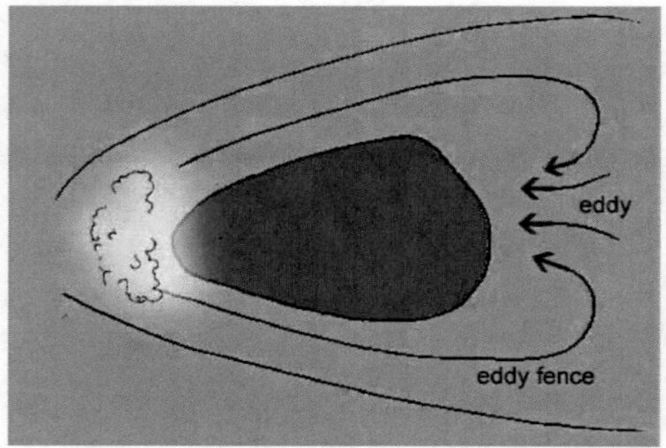

Diagram Aw19: An eddy fence exists between the main current and slower water in an eddy.

Cushion Wave

A cushion wave is created when water hits an object that it cannot pass through. As the water cannot pass through, it bounces off the object before passing to either side of it. The upstream side of the obstacle is an area of high pressure. If an object does not appear to be creating a cushion wave, then the water is either passing through it (like a strainer, see *page Aw-40*), or underneath it (like a siphon, see *page Aw-39*).

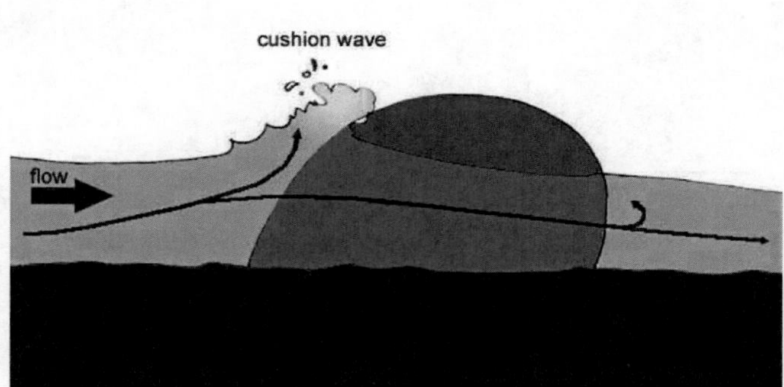

Diagram Aw20: Cushion waves indicate that water is bouncing off something solid.

Notes

Standing Wave (Wave Train)

If an object is deep underwater, a cushion wave is not created. Instead, water passes over and around each side of the object which causes a standing wave to be created on the surface of the water. Standing waves can be large, steep waves with breaking tops (ie. haystack waves) or just gentle surface waves, depending upon the speed of the water, and the size of the underwater object in relation to the depth of the water. A series of standing waves is known as a "wave train."

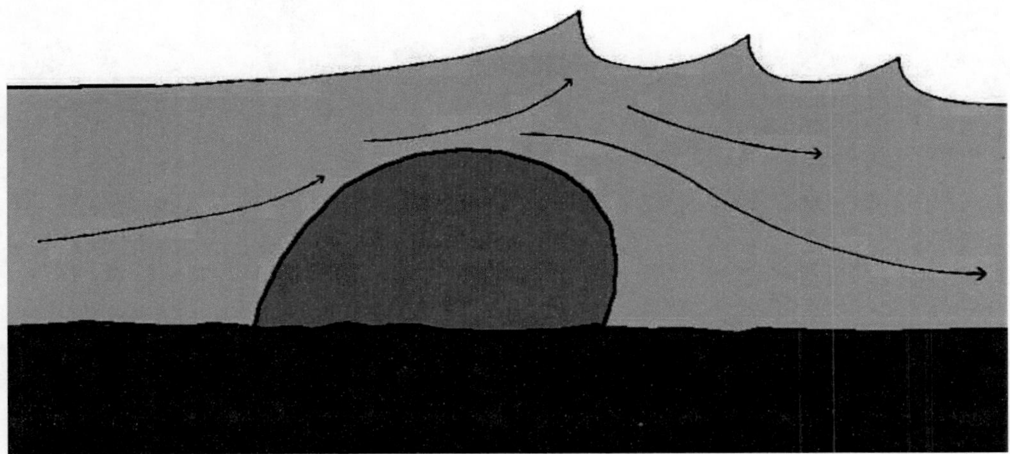

Diagram Aw21: A standing wave is formed by deep water flowing over a submerged object.

Upstream "V"

When water hits obstacles and forms either cushion waves or standing waves, much of the water is deflected to either side of the obstacle. When viewed from above, this creates a "V" shape with the point of the "V" upstream. Any time an upstream "V" is present, there is an obstruction beneath the water, even if it is not visible.

Downstream "V"

If there is more than one object in the flow, then water will be forced between the objects. This flow of water can be identified by a "V" shape pointing downstream, and is known as a downstream "V". This feature is caused by the convergence of water flow between two objects into the channel of least resistance.

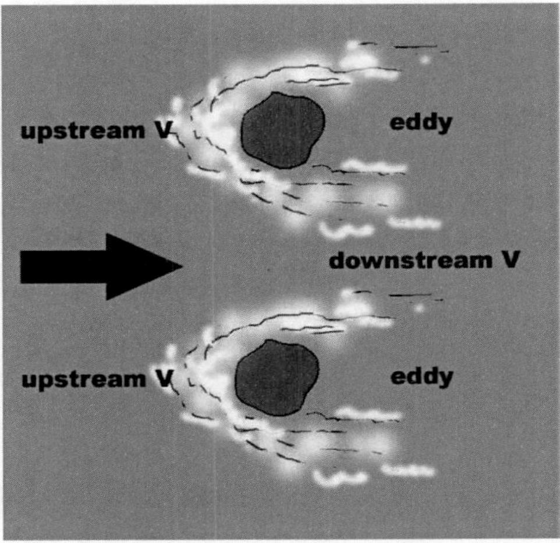

Diagram Aw22: Upstream and downstream "V" are clues as to what is beneath the surface of the water.

Notes

Hydraulic

If the water level rises to the point that water flows over an object, a different water feature is created called a "hydraulic".

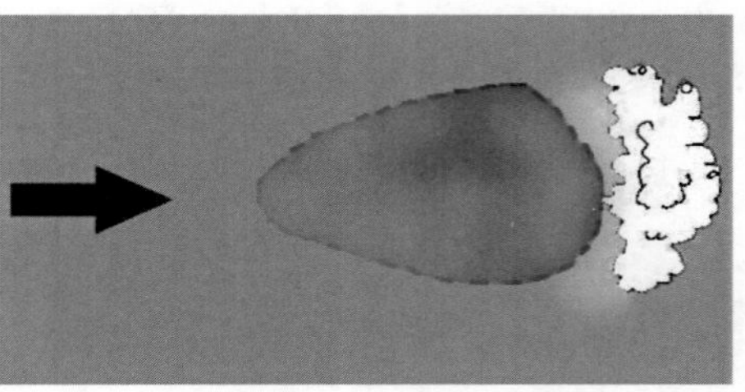

Diagram Aw23: Water flowing over a rock can create a hydraulic.

Hydraulics have many different names including stoppers, holes, pour-overs and many more. As water flows over an obstacle such as a rock, it will flow or fall down the downstream side of the obstacle. In doing so, it will accelerate. This creates a recirculation where the surface water on the downstream side of the obstacle flows back upstream toward the obstacle, while the sub-surface water continues to move downstream.

This recirculation or reverse flow can be dangerous because it can cause an object to become trapped in the hydraulic (hence the name "stopper"). The strength or retentiveness of this recirculation will depend upon a number of features, including volume of water, relative depth of the re-circulating current, and the shape of the river bed.

Where the recirculation is near the surface, and the majority of the water is moving downstream underneath it, the surface recirculation may look dangerous, but it is unlikely to hold swimmers or debris. However, if the recirculation is full depth, then the reverse flow will be much more powerful and more likely to hold swimmers and debris.

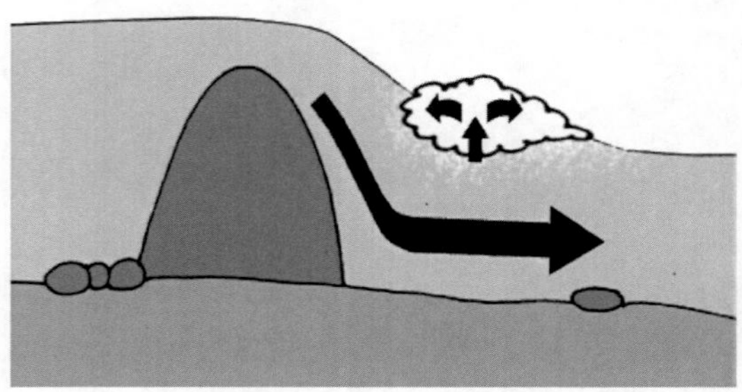

Diagram Aw24: A surface recirculation and a full-depth recirculation.

Shapes of Hydraulics

Notes

Natural hydraulics are often referred to by the shape they make when looked down on from above while facing downstream but this can be confusing. Remember that if the ends of the hydraulic are curved downstream it is “smiling” and if the ends curve upstream it is “frowning”. Hydraulics can also be straight across.

Generally “smiling” hydraulics are considered safer or less retentive than “frowning” or “straight" hydraulics but each hole should be evaluated for other hazards.

Smiling

Water pouring over a smiling hydraulic will create a reverse flow that pushes outward toward the ends. The hydraulic effect or recirculation may be very strong at the center but weakens at the sides, to the point where the water is actually moving downstream. This shape tends to feed items to the sides and so is considered the easiest from which to escape.

Frowning

Water pouring over this hydraulic will tend to feed items to the center and hold them there, making it very difficult to escape. Swimmers can get pulled back into the center of the hydraulic again and again. Sometimes a frowning hydraulic may flush through in the center.

Straight

This is the classic shape of the hydraulic found at the base of a low head dam. (For more information on low head dams, see *page Aw-34)* Straight hydraulics that occur naturally in rivers and floods are often called “ledges”. These can be very retentive hydraulics as there is no variation in the recirculation to flush someone to the side and out.

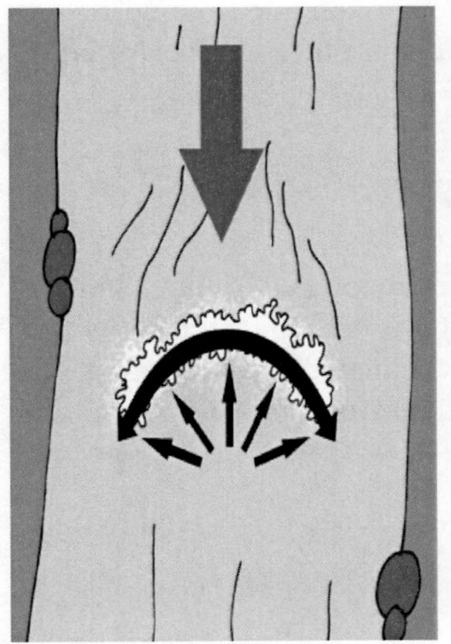

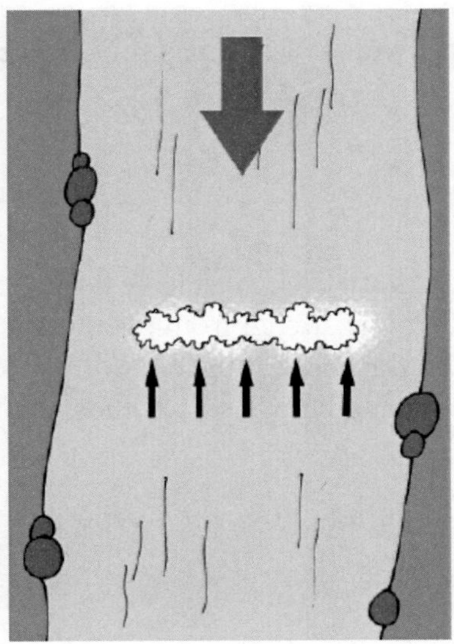

Diagram Aw25: Shape of hydraulics: (left to right): smiling, straight and frowning. The large arrow shows the direction of the main flow, the smaller arrows show the direction that the recirculation will take a swimmer caught in the hole. Note: natural features may not appear exactly as shown. Assess each hydraulic individually.

Notes

More on the Shapes of Hydraulics

Hydraulics or holes with a wave shape at the base are intimidating, but typically less hazardous. Generally, very little water is recycling back upstream. Even huge wave holes will usually just tumble you a time or two before flushing you out.

Ledge holes are not so nice. These go by different names like pour-overs, keepers, sticky holes, etc. The water drops down, goes underneath, and some recycles back upstream. This water moving upstream can be difficult to swim out of. Learn how to identify the ugly ones so you can avoid them.

Big Backwash Is Bad

The length of the re-circulation (or backwash) after a hole (i.e. the distance that water is moving upstream) tells you a lot about its danger and power. If the recirculation is approaching four feet, there is a greater chance that a swimmer will get recycled. If the current moves upstream an even greater distance, it is getting really nasty and dangerous.

Irregular Is Better

A hole or ledge hole that is irregular is nicer, since there are more likely jets of current breaking through the backwash. If swimmers line up with one of those irregular spots, they generally punch through the backwash and out.

Width Is Worse

The worst examples are low head dams, which often have dangerous hydraulics because they are wide, have several feet of backwash, and are very regular in construction and therefore have no current blowing through. If you look carefully, you can spot the horizon line from upstream. A ledge hole that is only a few feet wide is less dangerous, since it won't take as much effort to swim out the side.

Smiling Or Frowning?

Whoever thought of this famous memory trick must have been in a helicopter at the time. Smiling or frowning refers to the view looking upstream from overhead but it is hard to remember which is which when you are on the water. Basically, if the ends of a hole are angled downstream, it will tend to feed you out the end. A frowning hole has both ends angled upstream, and is more likely to hold you.

A hole that is angled relative to the current flow will be more friendly, since it will tend to flush you out the side into the current rushing by.

Unusual Power

Another exception is holes with unusual power moving back upstream. These are rare, but the worst examples have a rock underneath, which aids the backwash. Some low head dams are designed with this feature, making them extra dangerous.

Notes

Closed Ends

Unfortunately, just looking at the shape of the hydraulic is not sufficient. A hydraulic with a smiling shape may feed items to the side, but if that side is closed off by some sort of obstacle (e.g, a concrete wall) a victim is not likely to be flushed out.

Open Ends

An open-ended hydraulic can be easier to escape or rescue victims from. However, an open-ended hydraulic can also be dangerously retentive if other factors contribute to a strong recirculation (see above). Assess each hydraulic carefully.

Water Levels

Hydraulics can also vary hugely depending on water level -- a relatively benign hydraulic at one level can become deadly if the water rises or falls, or vice-versa.

Swimming Out

Swimmers who get stuck in a hole should try several techniques to get out. The first instinct is to swim for the surface, but if that doesn't work try something else!

Swim aggressively for the sides where water rushes by. Remember that water is moving upstream in a hole so use ferrying techniques to move laterally. Alternatively, diving down as deep as possible might get you into water flowing under the recirculation or enable you to push off the bottom. Also, simply changing your shape may cause the hole to spit you out. Keep calm and don't give up.

Notes

Low Head Dams

The fundamental hydrology of a low head dam (also called a "weir") is identical to that of a hydraulic. However, because low head dams are man-made, they can have very strong, uniform recirculations that are highly retentive. Even small, seemingly benign low head dams can hold debris, swimmers and boats. If the sides of the low head dam are "closed" then it can be particularly dangerous. General rules with regard to "smiling" and "frowning" shapes do not work when applied to low head dams – some of the most retentive can be "smile" shaped but with closed-off sides that do not allow for escape.

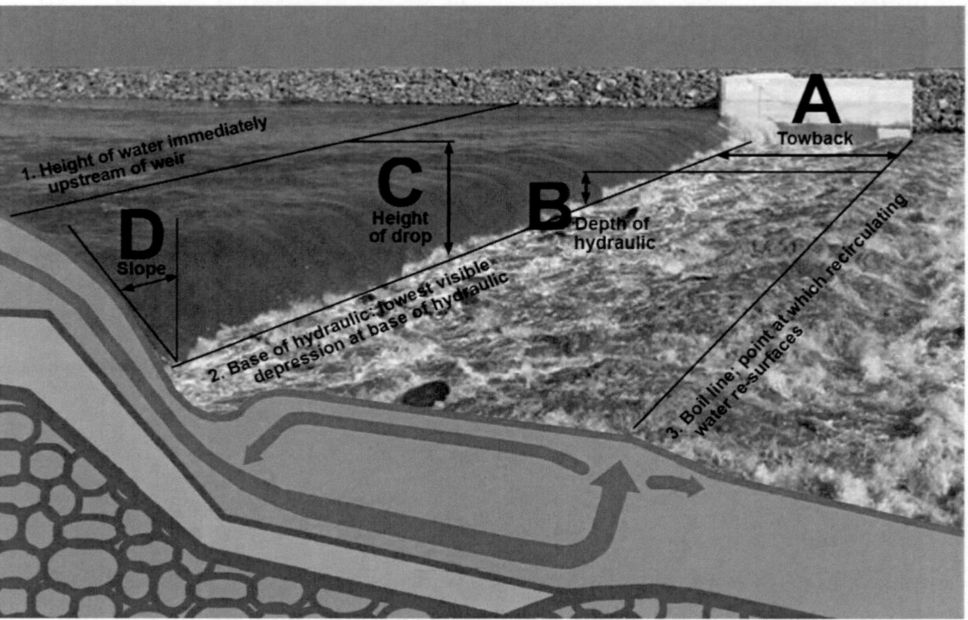

Diagram Aw26: Low head dam cross-section.

Diagram Aw27: Low head dam in Fremont County, Idaho.

Notes

Low head dams will often create full depth hydraulics which can be very hazardous. Other features are routinely incorporated into their construction, such as stilling basins, that can increase the strength of the hydraulic and the distance of the recirculation or "towback" at the base of the dam.

Rescue 3 (UK), in conjunction with the United Kingdom's national *Environment Agency*, has developed a Weir Risk Assessment Matrix. Further details about weir assessment and safety of operations around weirs are taught in two other Rescue 3 courses: *Swiftwater Rescue Technician® Advanced* and *Management of Water and Flood Incidents*.

The assessment matrix is freely available to download from the Rescue 3 (UK) website at

www.rescue3.co.uk/weir.htm

International River Grading Scale

Notes

The International River Grading Scale is a standardized scale to measure the technical difficulty of a particular section of river, and the skill level required to successfully navigate it. Rescuers should remember that this is a recreational scale and does not necessarily reflect how easy (or difficult) it will be to perform a rescue.

Grade I	Fast moving water with ripples and small waves. Few obstructions, all obvious and easily avoided with training. Risk to swimmers is slight; self-rescue is easy.
Grade II	Straightforward rapids with wide, clear channels which are evident without scouting. Occasional maneuvering may be required, but rocks and medium-sized waves are easily avoided by trained paddlers. Swimmers are seldom injured and group assistance, while helpful, is seldom needed.
Grade III	Rapids with moderate, irregular waves which may be difficult to avoid and which can swamp an open canoe. Complex maneuvers in fast current and good boat control in tight passages or around ledges are often required; large waves or strainers may be present but are easily avoided. Strong eddies and powerful currents can be found, particularly on large-volume rivers. Scouting is advisable for inexperienced parties. Injuries while swimming are rare; self-rescue is usually easy but group assistance may be required to avoid long swims.
Grade IV	Intense, powerful but predictable rapids requiring precise boat handling in turbulent water. Depending on the character of the river, it may feature large, unavoidable waves and holes or constricted passages demanding fast maneuvers under pressure. Rapids may require "must" moves above dangerous hazards. Scouting may be necessary the first time down. Risk of injury to swimmers is moderate to high, and water conditions may make self-rescue difficult. Group assistance for rescue is often essential but requires practiced skills.
Grade V	Extremely long, obstructed, or very violent rapids which expose a paddler to added risk. Drops may contain large, unavoidable waves and holes or steep, congested chutes with complex, demanding routes. Rapids may continue for long distances between pools, demanding a high level of fitness. What eddies exist may be small, turbulent, or difficult to reach. At the high end of the scale, several of these factors may be combined. Scouting is recommended but may be difficult. Swims are dangerous, and rescue is often difficult even for experts.
Grade VI	These runs have almost never been attempted and often exemplify the extremes of difficulty, unpredictability and danger. The consequences of errors are very severe and rescue may be impossible. For teams of experts only, at favorable water levels, after close personal inspection and taking all precautions.

Swiftwater and Flood Hazards

The ability to recognize and assess hazards for risk is a vital skill. Each hazard must be identified and addressed before performing a rescue. There are an enormous variety of hazards in swiftwater and flood environments, a small selection of which is outlined below:

Notes

Utility Hazards

Electricity

Clearly, electricity and water do not mix. Power lines may short out or arc. During flooding the height between the power lines and surface is reduced. This is of particular importance during boat operations.

Sub-stations can be flooded, leaving large areas without electricity. In the US, many utility companies have worked closely with State agencies to identify infrastructure that is at risk of flooding. Detailed response plans that provide protection for vital infrastructure are in development.

Although electrical power may be out in an area, many industrial or commercial facilities will have a backup or emergency system. This information should be in an agency's pre-plan.

Natural gas

Gas mains can be ruptured if the earth around the pipe is eroded by flood water. If houses are damaged, then domestic piping can be ruptured and result in leaking gas. Clearly, this poses a significant fire and explosion hazard, particularly if rescuers are operating powerboats in the area.

LPG and oil tanks

The contents of LPG and oil tanks are lighter than water, so that even when the tanks are full they are buoyant. However, if tanks become submerged, they can break free of their framework and float off, venting gas or spilling oil.

Diagram T36: Boy Scout Method

Notes

Chemical and Biological Hazards

All waterways are polluted to some degree. Flood waters can contain significant amounts of hazardous material (hazmat). This may be industrial waste, sewage effluent, fuel, agricultural chemicals, dead animals, and much more washed into the water. These pollutants can cause serious health problems to people working near or in the water.

Personal hygiene is important while working near the water and personnel should be decontaminated following possible exposure. For more information on decontamination see *page Aw-71*.

Possible hazmat sources

Urban

- Fuel and oil from flooded vehicles
- Sewers
- Storm drains
- Fuel storage tanks
- Household waste
- Industrial chemicals

Rural

- Pesticides
- Fertilizers
- Slurry pits
- Septic tanks
- Dead animals

Notes

Physical Hazards

In addition to generic hazards of swiftwater, there are a number of other common physical hazards.

Undercuts

An undercut rock often appears on the outside of a bend, where the current vector has worn it away. The rock tends to lack a visible cushion wave, as the water is traveling under the rock rather than bouncing off it. Consequently, there is a significant risk of entrapment.

Siphon or Sieve

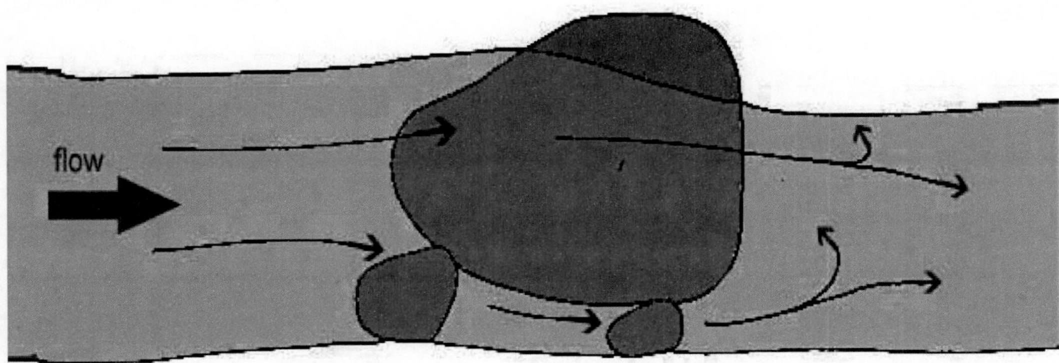

Diagram Aw28: Water flowing under a partially supported object creates a sieve.

A siphon is formed when an object in the flow has a gap underneath it (for example, a boulder perched on a number of smaller rocks). This allows the water to flow underneath the object, as through a siphon. It is a very dangerous feature as it will cause objects (including swimmers) to be sucked down under the object, where they could become trapped.

If water is flowing under an object, there is generally only a small cushion wave (see *page Aw-28*) or even no cushion wave at all on its upstream side. This is a classic sign of the presence of a siphon under the water.

A common example of a siphon is a car standing on a hard surface but surrounded or submerged by moving water The water will travel around the car, but will also siphon between the wheels and under the car. This is a major hazard to anyone operating on the upstream side of the car.

Inspection ("Manhole") Covers

In a flooded environment, inspection covers and drain covers can become displaced by upwelling water as a flood rises. When flood water starts to recede, these open holes then become incredibly powerful and dangerous siphons. The force exerted by these siphons is relentless and very powerful – due to the physics of vortices. A simple wading pole is essential for any personnel wading where these hazards are possible, so that they may probe for and locate uncovered manholes and drains.

Notes

Bridges

Bridge abutments are normally designed to minimize forces from the water, and therefore may not have a cushion wave. This can make it easier for a boat or unwary swimmer to become trapped on an abutment.

Debris

Any kind of natural or manufactured debris can find its way into the water. This can pose a hazard when traveling downstream into a rescue site. Debris can become an entrapment hazard. It can also collect on bridge abutments to form a strainer hazard (see below).

Strainers

A strainer is anything that allows water to pass through it, but not solid objects such as debris, boats or swimmers. Common strainers include trees that have fallen into the water, fences, and railings. The force of the current will hold objects against the strainer indefinitely. The danger that strainers pose to rescuers cannot be understated. It is essential that any strainers on a rescue site are well protected in order to minimize risks to rescue personnel.

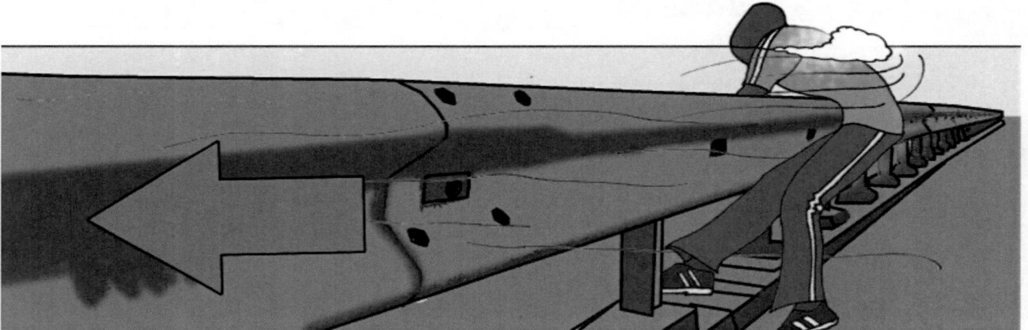

Diagram Aw29: Commonplace structures such as railings can become hazards in a flooded environment.

Cold Water

Water removes heat from the human body much faster than air. Cold water will quickly sap even the strongest swimmer's strength. The dramatic and potentially dangerous effect of cold water on the body cannot be overemphasized. For further information see *page Aw-76*.

Notes

Floods

Although working in floods is essentially the same as working in water, flooding brings some specific issues.

River levels vary greatly depending upon factors such rainfall, snowmelt, release from dams, etc. Most of the time, river level will be within the river channel and therefore its flow and features are relatively predictable. However, as river levels rise they will eventually reach a point where they are "bankfull" and any subsequent rise will see the riverbanks overtopped and the water flowing through the adjacent low areas of land – the floodplain.

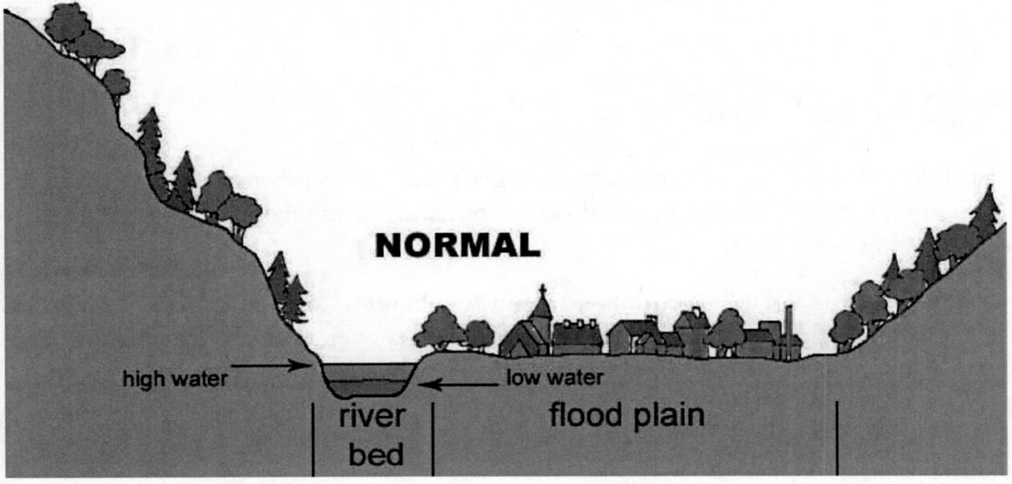

Diagram Aw30: High and low water levels are normally contained within a banked channel.

Generally, the increased volume of water means that most previously-existing river hazards, such as low head dams, become more powerful and dangerous, although some may actually become "washed out" or less dangerous. At high water, there is a new range of hazards as water flows through and around obstacles that were not designed to be in the water. Major hazards are created by parked cars, fences, hedges, gates, road signs, and park benches. In addition, there may no longer be enough clearance for boats to pass under bridges.

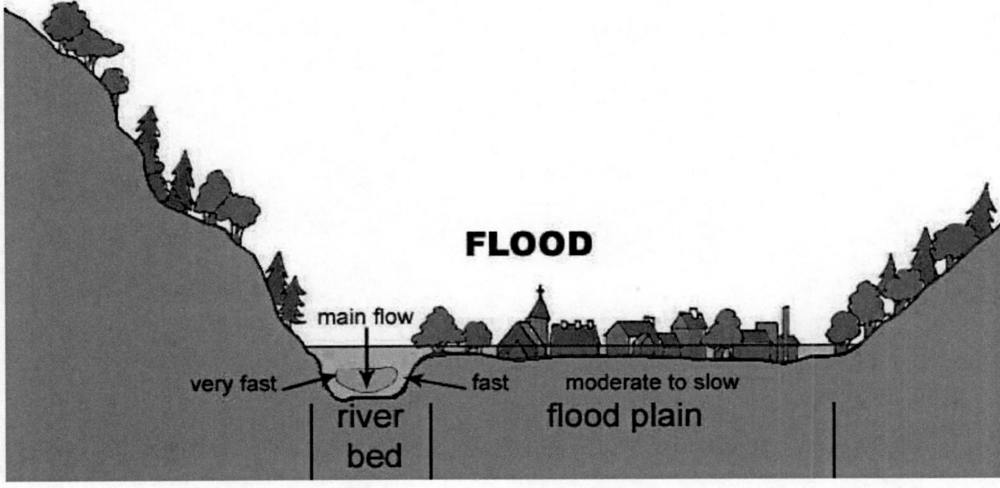

Diagram Aw31: During a flood event the water overtops the river banks and spreads onto the flood plain.

Notes

Flood water will carry large amounts of debris that can build up against houses and bridges, causing structural damage and presenting a significant risk to anyone in the water.

As water flows through the flood plain, there is an increased chance of contamination by hazardous materials such as sewage, agricultural waste, and pesticides.

It is worth noting that once the water overflows the river banks and spreads across the flood plain, this may result in an apparent reduction in the speed of the water. However, the water flowing in the area of the original river channel will still be flowing at its previous rate.

These factors combine to make working in floods a hazardous and arduous task.

The "100 Year Flood"

Floods are often referred to as the "one in a hundred year flood". This does not mean that they will occur once every hundred years, but rather, there is a one-in-a-hundred or one percent chance of such a flood occurring every year.

A "one in two hundred year flood" represents a one-in-two-hundred or 0.5 percent chance of the flood waters reaching a certain height in any given year. It is even possible for two "one in a hundred year" floods to occur on the same river, in the same year, or even in the same month. Looking at historic flood data and river flow measurements allows for computer models to be developed which can be used to produce flood return statistics and detailed flood mapping to aid in the pre-planning process.

Most recently, in May 2010, 100 year floods hit parts of Tennessee, Kentucky and Mississippi as the result of torrential rainfall. The Cumberland River in Nashville, TN reached levels not seen since 1937.

The Four Realities of Flooding

Notes

By their very nature floods are:

1. Multi-agency events

2. Multi-jurisdictional events

3. Hazmat and public health events

4. Long-term events

Rescue teams and emergency planners must understand that floods have their own set of characteristics that differentiate them from other moving water incidents, and therefore also have specific response requirements. With effective pre-planning, specific training and the appropriate equipment designed for these incidents, members of the public will be better protected from the effects of flooding.

At any major flood event, there will be many agencies on-scene. It is essential that these agencies communicate effectively, and work together efficiently.

Flood water does not respect any authority's jurisdiction or county boundaries. As a result, rescue teams will often work with teams from other areas. By establishing common training techniques and equipment in advance, this mutual aid process can be greatly simplified.

The public health implications of large-scale flooding are clear given that large numbers of people may be exposed to contaminants. The very young and the very old are most at risk. Health services in the area may be stretched to capacity.

The long-term nature of flooding cannot be overstated. Flood response can easily exhaust emergency personnel and community members emotionally, mentally, and physically. Irrespective of the resources available, there will always be a call for more. The reality is that years after the rescue response has been completed, members of the public may still be living in temporary accommodation, waiting for their homes to be rebuilt or refurbished.

The Four Phases of Flooding

Notes

Flood incidents may be broken down into four phases. Most floods progress through these phases, although each flood is unique and will therefore progress at its own rate.

Phase 1 – Pre-Flood

In this phase, flooding has not yet occurred. However, it is predicted to occur at some point in the future. This is the time to develop a response plan based on an current hazard assessment that includes historical flood data. This is also a good time to train personnel and invest in equipment. Public education during this phase can be invaluable when a flood event occurs.

Phase 2 – Flash Flood

In the event of a flash flood, streams, rivers, storm drains and wastewater management systems are full. Water begins to escape waterways, to cover roads, and to impact property.

This phase is associated with high speed water. People are caught unaware and lives are in imminent danger. Therefore most technical rescues will occur during this phase, and rescuers will be at their greatest personal risk.

Phase 3 – Expansion

This phase sees streams and rivers clearly out of their banks and water moving across a flood plain. Evacuation may become necessary if structures and occupants are endangered; however, access and egress may be seriously compromised. Hazmat issues begin to surface.

Evacuation generally means people are directed to leave by authorities, and then leave under their own power – which is often not the case in a flood incident. Rescue teams are often required to assist people to wade out safely, or to transport them by boat. This high level of involvement by rescue personnel consumes considerable time and resources. As a result, the term “rescue evacuation” is now being used to properly describe this “hybrid” activity.

Phase 4 – Recovery

In this phase, property owners begin to return, and agencies note an increase in accidents and injuries due to newly-exposed hazards. To offset this, structures and roads should be inspected prior to the public’s return. Infrastructure restoration and hazmat issues are now the most pressing. In particular, hazmat issues may keep public health agencies very busy. Search and rescue work will stop, and turn to search and recovery.

The use of rescue resources (especially inflatable boats) must be adjusted due to the decreasing water levels and emergence of new hazards. Emergency personnel should be closely monitored for fatigue and for negative reactions to personal losses they may have suffered.

Flood Mapping

The ability to look into the future to see how many city blocks and roads might be flooded in a few days is becoming clearer with Flood Inundation Mapping. The National Oceanic and Atmospheric Administration's (NOAA) National Weather Service (NWS) and its National Ocean Service (NOS) Coastal Services Center (CSC) work in collaboration with the Federal Emergency Management Agency (FEMA) and other partners to develop inundation maps for both coastal and inland freshwater flooding.

Sets of maps (referred to as libraries) are being developed which show both the extent and depth of water for various flood levels ranging from minor flooding all the way through to record flood levels. These new flood prediction tools help emergency managers and impacted citizens be better prepared to make important decisions regarding evacuations, moving property, and other mitigation efforts.

Combined with traditional NWS forecasts and flood bulletin information, these new flood maps show the areas of likely inundation based on current conditions and future rainfall. Maps are produced using geographic information systems (GIS) and data gathered for FEMA's Flood Insurance Rate Maps.

These libraries are accessible via the Advanced Hydrologic Prediction Service (AHPS) web portal, the NWS' engine that hosts its vital river and flood forecast information. In addition to displaying inundation maps using the NWS' web interface, decision makers can download these inundation maps and related data for use in their GIS applications (see http://water.weather.gov/ahps/)

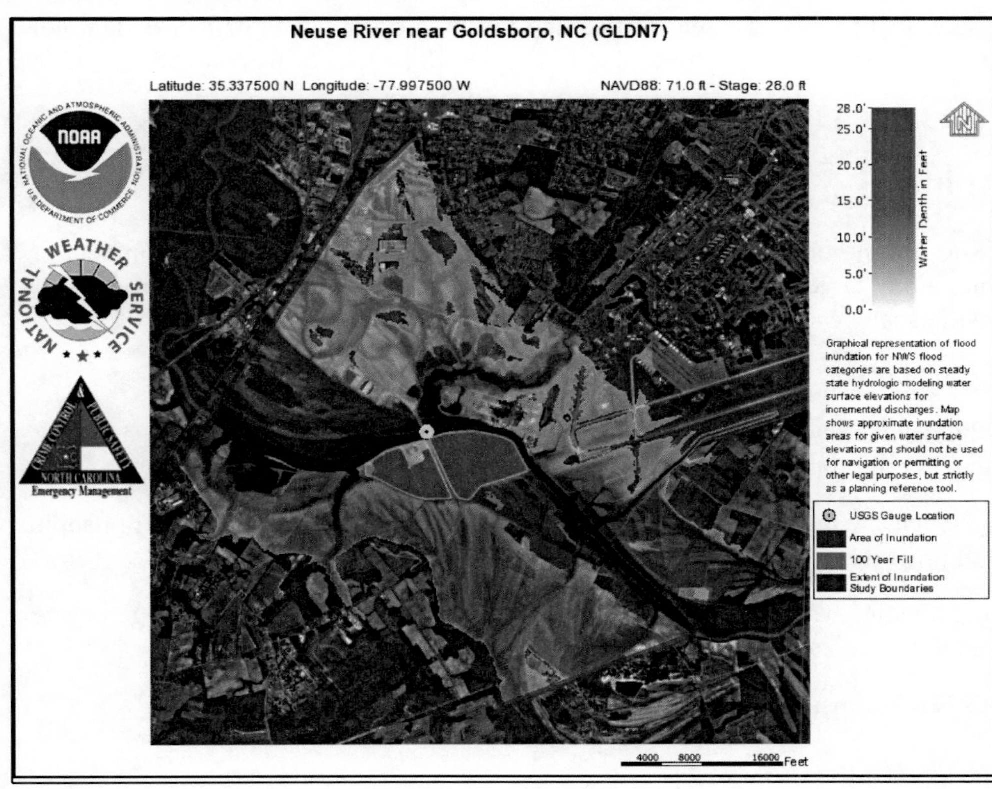

Diagram Aw32 NOAA flood inundation map for the Nuese River, Goldboro, NC.

Notes

Notes

Flood Warnings

NOAA's National Weather Service

In the United States, weather watches and warnings are most often generated through the National Weather Service (NWS) which is a subsidiary of the National Oceanic & Atmospheric Administration (NOAA).

NWS provides local and regional forecasts as well as emergency alerts for severe storms, hurricanes and tornadoes, floods, extreme heat, winter storms, fire, tsunamis, and even solar flares. With 122 Weather Forecast Offices and thirteen River Forecast Centers, the NWS is a useful resource in all jurisdictions within the United States.

Flood watches and warnings are issued for both large-scale, gradual river flooding and rapid flash flooding. Both can be issued on a county-by-county basis or for specific rivers or for points along a river.

NWS warnings allow first responders to implement pre-planned responses including evacuation, placement of flood defenses, initiation of road closures, and pre-deployment of search and rescue resources.

Flood Watch

Issued by NWS to inform the public and cooperating agencies that current and developing conditions are such that there is a threat of flooding but the occurrence is neither certain nor imminent. Timeframe for the onset of river flooding is 12–48 hours; for flash flooding, within six hours.

Flood Warning

Issued by NWS to inform the public and cooperating agencies of flooding that is imminent or already occurring along larger streams in which there is a serious threat to life or property. A flood warning will usually contain river stage (level) forecasts as follows:

Minor Flooding: minimal or no property damage, but possibly some public threat.

Moderate Flooding: some inundation of structures and roads near stream. Some evacuations of people and/or transfer of property to higher elevations.

Major Flooding: extensive inundation of structures and roads. Significant evacuations of people and/or transfer of property to higher elevations.

Record Flooding: flooding which equals or exceeds the highest stage or discharge at a given site during the period of record keeping.

Source: NOAA's NWS website: www.nws.noaa.gov

Notes

Local Flood Warning Systems

Local Flood Warning Systems (LFWS) can be part of a community's preparedness to handle floods. Many areas of the country already have a system in place.

The NWS has information available to help jurisdictions with the complex process involved in determining whether a LFWS could contribute to a community's attempts to mitigate flooding. Other federal and state agencies have instituted programs for helping communities identify and solve local flood problems as well.

LFWS generally "sell themselves" but often it is only after a disastrous flood strikes a community. A "Local Flood Warning System Handbook" is available at http://www.nws.noaa.gov/directives/sym/pd01009042curr.pdf

F.I.N.S.

There are some excellent examples of systems already in place that link flood-related early warning systems directly to the Emergency Services. The Flood Information & Notification System (F.I.N.S.) in operation in Charlotte, North Carolina is a particularly good example.

F.I.N.S. is not intended to be a public warning system. It only notifies emergency responders. The National Weather Service continues to provide flood watches and flood warnings to the news media and public.

F.I.N.S. is a partnership between the City of Charlotte, Mecklenburg County, and the U.S. Geological Survey. This government agency continually monitors rainfall and stream depth levels. Emergency responders are notified when there is a potential or actual problem.

There are three levels for F.I.N.S. notification:

Alert:

When rainfall is intense or streams rise rapidly. The F.I.N.S. system automatically sends the alert via pager, cell phone, and e-mail to emergency responders and Storm Water Services staff.

Investigate:

If the situation gets worse, emergency personnel must personally visit the location of heavy rainfall or flooding. They may barricade streets or take other action as needed.

Emergency:

The highest level. Additional precautions may be necessary such as evacuating residents near the high-water areas.

For further information see http://charmeck.org/stormwater/

Notes

IC

Pre-planning and Incident Management

Dealing with any emergency situation is first a management problem. Management must undertake pre-planning to examine all aspects of a potential problem and devise methods of dealing with it before it happens.

Pre-planning is used to design methods of dealing with anticipated situations and locations, enhance the capabilities of a rescue team, and create a safer scene during incident responses.

Developing a Pre-plan

The first stage to developing a pre-plan is undertaking a hazard assessment. Rescue teams cannot begin to plan responses unless they understand the location and nature of incidents they may be required to respond to.

Records of previous incidents, both recent and historic, are a vital source of information. Rainfall and river level data is also of great benefit.

While planning a water and flood incident response, it is important that managers take into consideration the following four elements:

- Management
- Personnel
- Training
- Equipment

By considering these four elements, in this order, pre-planning will be as efficient as possible. There is little point in investing money in new equipment if it is not fit for the purpose, and the rescuers are not trained to use it.

Rather, preplanning works much more efficiently if management first identifies key personnel to lead a rescue team, and then creates a core team with sufficient numbers. This team then receives appropriate training to deal with specific hazards and incidents previously identified by management. The team is then able to make educated recommendations on the best equipment for the task, and finally, sufficient quantities of the correct equipment is purchased.

Once the basics of the pre-plan have been established, other aspects can begin to be identified such as:

- Communications
- Mutual Aid
- Welfare
- Shelter
- Transportation

Site Planning

Notes

Once pre-planning is complete on a general level, and an overall response determined, it should also be done on a site-specific level for high risk areas and locations within the agency's area of jurisdiction. Such areas may include sections of road prone to flooding; sections of rivers where river users tend to get into difficulties; sites such as fords; or specific structures such as low head dams and sluices.

Information to be gathered on each site may include:

- Location
- Maps and plans
- Access routes
- Communication issues (such as blackspots)
- Specific risks
- Special equipment requirements
- Specialist training requirements
- Team response plan

Once this initial information is assimilated, it should be possible to determine the personnel, equipment, training and management requirements in order to provide an effective response. The development of mutual aid arrangements may be key in providing a response capability.

Site-specific pre-plans also need to include detailed information about transport options, water features and hazards, access, anchor points, and provisions for welfare and decontamination.

National Incident Management System

The National Incident Management System (NIMS) was developed in part to facilitate mutual aid between different jurisdictions and disciplines. NIMS benefits include:

- Unified approach to incident management
- Standard command and management structures
- Emphasis on preparedness, mutual aid and resource management

Compliance and Technical Assistance

ICS is not just a good idea, it's mandated for all first responders by the Department of Homeland Security under the authority of two Presidential Directives. In 2004, DHS established the National Integration Center (NIC) Incident Management Systems Division as the lead federal entity to coordinate NIMS compliance.

A major component of NIMS is the Incident Command System (ICS). The modular format of ICS makes it the ideal system for efficient tactical operations on all swiftwater and flood rescues.

Notes

Incident Command System (ICS)

ICS utilizes specific roles or "positions" that are responsible for preassigned job duties. The system is built progressively as the incident unfolds. This provides rescuers with the flexibility to utilize only the positions required for effective management of a given incident.

While ICS is an efficient way to manage small incidents involving a single agency, it also lends itself to the introduction of nearly any conceivable discipline, responsibility or function as required. This means it is equally appropriate for managing large scale, protracted incidents where numerous agencies are involved.

In addition, the modular format of ICS makes it an ideal management system for dynamic incidents such as water and rope rescues where parameters may change continually.

It is critical that the rescuer be able to implement ICS in order to effectively manage resources at the scene. Comprehensive courses are available, including FEMA's ICS 100: Introduction to the Incident Command System. This course provides the foundation for higher levels of ICS training and may be taken online at www.training.fema.gov/IS/

Components of the Incident Command System (ICS)

While local resources and protocols vary greatly, we have identified the key positions that are most common to typical water and rope rescues. Given that the typical real world rescue is usually carried out with a small team, we have first listed the core team, and then provided additional team members that can be added as the incident grows in scale and scope.

The Core Team

Incident Commander (IC)

The IC is responsible for the overall management of the emergency scene. The IC establishes the incident objectives, determines strategic priorities, and approves the incident action plan among other duties.

Incident Safety Officer (ISO)

The ISO develops and recommends measures for assuring personnel safety and assesses/ anticipates hazardous and unsafe conditions. NFPA 1670 2-5.2.1.1 states "The Safety Officer shall, as a minimum, be trained to the operational level at which the organization is operating."

Single Resource Boss & Team

Single Resource Boss is the generic name for individuals in charge of a single unit or resource, e.g. a swiftwater team or a rope team made up of rescuers trained to various levels (Operations, Technician, Advanced, etc.).

Notes

Additional Positions

Assistant Safety Officer (ASO)

If the incident is large or complex, an ASO may be appointed to assist the SO and oversee specific areas or functions within an incident.

Public Information Officer (PIO)

The PIO develops and releases information about the incident to the news media, to incident personnel, and to other agencies and organizations.

Liaison Officer (LO)

The LO provides a point of contact for assisting and cooperating agencies. The LO will assist the IC in identifying current and potential interagency needs.

Operations Section Officer (Ops)

The Ops Officer manages all of the tactics directly related to the incident objectives. Ops activates and supervises organizational elements according to the incident action plan, requests and releases resources, makes necessary changes to the incident action plan, and communicates changes to the IC.

Logistics Section Officer (Logs)

The Logs Officer provides facilities, services, and materials to support the incident; and helps develop the incident action plan.

Planning/Intelligence Section Officer (Plans)

The Plans Officer collects, evaluates, disseminates, and uses information about the status of the incident and its resources. This information is used to understand the current situation, predict incidents that are likely to occur, and devise alternate plans.

Finance/Administration Section Officer (Finance)

The Finance officer is responsible for the financial, administrative, and cost analysis functions of the incident, including cost recovery, injury reports, and compensation claims.

Branch Director

Branch Directors report to the Operations Section officer and are responsible for implementing their part of the incident action plan. Branches are established as needed by discipline, i.e. Hazmat Branch, Fire Branch, Law Branch.

Notes

Division/Group Supervisor

The Division Group Supervisor reports to the Operations Section officer, or if activated, the Branch Director, and is responsible for implementing the portion of the incident action plan assigned to his division/group. He also assigns resources within the division/group and reports on incident and resource status. Divisions use letter designators, i.e. Division A, B, etc., while groups are established by function and use name designators, i.e. Rescue Group, Search Group, etc.

Strike Team/Task Force Leader

The Strike Team/Task Force Leader reports to the IC or, if the incident is larger, to the Division/ Group Supervisor (see below). He is responsible for performing the tactics assigned to the Strike Team or Task Force. This position also reports on work progress, resource status, and other important information.

Strike Teams are made up of five like resources, e.g. five Swiftwater Rescue Technicians®, five inflatable rescue boats, or five Type 1 fire engines.

Task Forces are combinations of resources that are assembled to perform a specific task. Examples of Task Forces may be one fire engine and three IRBs; a ladder truck and two engines; or an engine, three IRBs and two personal watercraft. Task Forces are more flexible by design and are often better suited to rescue work than Strike Teams.

Using the Incident Command System

Regardless of how small or how large the incident, the ability to manage resources is crucial to the overall effort. ICS offers the most flexible and common sense approach to resource management and should be used on all rescue incidents.

The key to the smooth implementation of ICS is to be familiar with the system as it relates to the jurisdiction. Effective use of ICS can be attained through pre-planning.

Tabletop exercises (with all of the appropriate agencies) are an excellent way to identify deficiencies before an actual incident occurs. The ICS positions can be identified, responsibilities defined, and specific agency concerns addressed well in advance of a call out.

Notes

Size-up of Flood and Swiftwater Rescues

Upon arrival at a water or flood incident, a scene assessment must take place. This is known as "size-up" and is generally much easier for locations where a pre-plan exists.

Size-up has been defined and redefined many times, but it always boils down to two simple factors for the Incident Commander:

- Identify the problem
- Decide what to do about it

Outlined below is a process to assist ICs in making the best decisions possible, while keeping rescuers safe.

Everyone's Responsibility

Size-up, whether it is done well or poorly, affects the overall outcome of any emergency and can make the difference between a successful rescue and a fatality.

However, size-up is not exclusively the job of the Incident Commander. Every member of the team should be aware of his environment and the situation and should pass relevant information on to his superiors. Given that swiftwater and flood incidents are so dynamic, with conditions changing constantly, a concerted effort by all rescuers to continually assess the scene will assist the Incident Commander in making sound decisions.

Situational Awareness

Size-up does not begin when you arrive on-scene; rather, it includes your prior knowledge of the area, your available resources, and much more. This base knowledge is then combined with the rapid assimilation of current information in an effort to obtain as complete a picture of the incident as possible.

The military has long called this "situational awareness" and it is critical to good quality, timely decision making. As critical as initial size-up is, the ongoing evaluation of an emergency scene is just as critical. In other words, don't lose your situational awareness once you have earned it.

Achieving Situational Awareness

The most valuable sources for achieving situational awareness are:

Personal observations

Personal observations tend to yield a great deal of information largely because the information is firsthand. These observations can identify the type or nature of the incident, the magnitude of the incident, the number of victims, the victim's physical/mental condition, and numerous other vital pieces of information.

Notes

Information Gathering

When the IC cannot see the rescue scene, or parts of the rescue scene, he will have to rely on information gathered by other responders. This information is still very useful, but to the degree possible it should be gathered by knowledgeable personnel who have experience in the type of incident unfolding and can describe the information accurately and in detail. Sound incident action plans are based on sound and timely information.

Pre-Planning

Preplan information can make a valuable contribution to size-up. It can include the location of access and egress routes; needed resources; location of hazards including utilities; hazardous materials; confined spaces; and hazards such as low-head dams, strainers, etc.

Interviews

Interviews with victims, witnesses, and bystanders can provide information such as the incident location, number of victims, victim histories, the nature of the rescue, and other useful information. Don't rely on second-hand information if the original source is available.

Notes

Team Briefing

Before rescue team members can be deployed, the team leader must thoroughly brief them to communicate the rescue plan, identify hazards, confirm tactics, and establish team roles. There are many formats for team briefing, one of which is the SMEAC system used by many emergency services and armed forces. SMEAC stands for:

- Situation
- Mission
- Execution
- Administration
- Command and Control

Situation

Includes general information about the situation including what has happened, the number of victims, the location of victims, environmental information, time available and so on.

Mission

More specific information about the task the team is requested to undertake and a clear description of the goal the team is expected to achieve.

Execution

Details of how the task is going to be performed, the equipment to be used, other teams that are involved, the time constraints for operation, etc.

Administration

Information about where equipment can be found, when welfare breaks will take place, where decontamination facilities are, where cordons are located, etc.

Command and Control

Information about who is in charge of the operation within the team structure and above the team structure, details of the lines of communication between team members, and details of communication from the team to the command post.

Resource Management

Notes

As mentioned in an earlier section, the National Incident Management System (NIMS) was developed in part to facilitate mutual aid between different jurisdictions and disciplines in the US.

In order to ensure that emergency responders have the information they need to request and receive the appropriate resources during an incident, NIMS has established a standardized resource management process. It includes methods for typing, inventorying, ordering, and tracking resources in order to facilitate their dispatch, deployment, and recovery before, during, and after an incident.

Resource Typing

In the past, one of the problems faced by incident managers when calling in additional resources was the lack of a benchmark or criteria to which they could refer. At best ICs might be able to obtain information about the number of people in a swiftwater team, and perhaps any specialized equipment they could bring. Often, ICs would discover that one agency would have a very different level of "Technician" training than another, making it difficult to know whether it was truly capable of the task at hand.

However, resource or "team" typing was developed to improve the ability of ICs to make informed decisions. Measurable standards that identify capabilities and performance levels serve as the basis for categories.

It is very important that the same criterion is used across the board for resource typing. The National Integration Center (NIC) Incident Management Systems Integration (IMSI) Division has been leading the national resource typing effort for several years to identify resources that are especially valuable for mutual aid in disasters. Team typing only works if the same criterion is used by everyone. A "Type 1" team in Sacramento, California needs to meet the exact same requirements as a "Type 1" team in Charlotte, North Carolina. Otherwise the vast potential benefits to incident commanders at major disasters won't exist.

As a result, swiftwater/flood teams from coast to coast can now be categorized as Type I, Type II, Type III, or Type IV when rated in the following areas:

- Team capabilities and structure
- Boat operations capability
- Team skills
- Team training
- Team equipment inventory

Consequently when additional resources are required, the incident management team can be task focused. Team members can select a swiftwater team (or rope team or dive team etc.) with the capability, personnel, and equipment best-suited to the specific incident, and be sure that the team will be able to deliver (see chart below).

Team Capability and Structure

Resource typing for swiftwater and flood teams outlines the range of tasks that each type of team must be capable of undertaking; the number of team members required; and the breakdown into managers, team leaders and team members.

Boat Operations Capability

It further sets out whether the team must have boat capability, and what type of boat is required. This is not design specific, but is determined by operational remit. For example, rather than stating a team needs to have a 5.5 m RIB with a 40 hp engine; the typing requires a team have a motor boat fitted with a prop-guard, capable of transporting at least six persons, and the ability to progress upstream in 10 mph water.

Team Skills and Training

Typing details the skills that team members must possess. Some skills are considered "core" and need to be possessed by all team members, such as shallow water operations. Other skills need only be possessed by a certain number of team members. For example, a team may only need one or two members with animal rescue skills. Typing also establishes a schedule for recertification or refreshing of core skills, and specialized training required by certain team members.

Team Equipment Inventory

This component of resource management sets out the equipment that each type of team needs to have. The inventory covered includes:

- PPE for team members
- Communication equipment
- Decontamination equipment
- Navigation equipment
- Technical equipment
- Boat equipment (if applicable to team type)
- Medical equipment

There is obviously the potential for a vast difference in capability between different types of teams. This is reflected in the cost requirements to set up and operate each type of team. Only larger, full-time search and rescue organizations will have the capability to meet the requirements for more advanced teams.

However, even small (including volunteer) organizations can run highly effective lower level teams, which if properly typed will be able to undertake vital work in major flood operations and for all local and regional water risks.

With resource typing in place, Incident managers can deploy teams from any agency, knowing the operational skills of the team. This will not only ease the burden on managers, but also ensure that only trained personnel are operating in the hot and warm zones.

Notes

Personal Equipment

Rescue teams carry a vast range of equipment, depending on their areas and levels of operation. Awareness level personnel are not rescue team members, but do need to have knowledge of the equipment used as they may perform a supporting role in the cold zone (see *page Aw-6*).

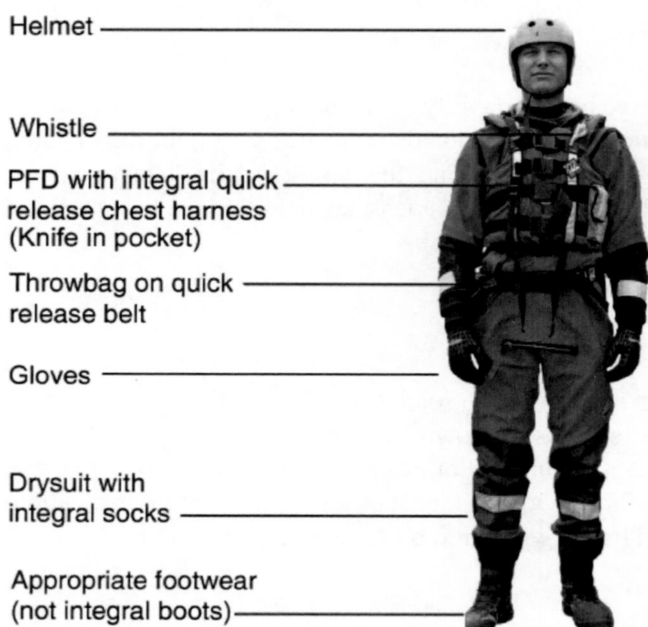

Protective clothing suitable for the task is essential. Just as firefighters would not wear a drysuit to attend a fire, the same approach must be adopted for water rescue.

NFPA 1952 includes standards for wetsuits, drysuits, gloves, footwear, helmets and PFDs. Based on this standard, it is up to the AHJ to determine the correct mix of equipment for its response area.

Before equipment is chosen it is necessary to look at the hazards from which personnel need protection. This directly relates to the zones in which personnel will be operating. In a water rescue, the most obvious hazard is the water itself. However, the hazmat issues of water rescue and in particular flood events must also be taken into consideration.

Drysuits

PPE[1] must protect the wearer from the water itself and from contact with it, for both thermal and hazmat purposes. Certain drysuits fulfill this purpose and will fit a range of people, as long as the seals fit effectively. However, some of the more breathable suits will not protect against certain pathogens and chemicals so always check with the manufacturer. The NFPA specifies drysuits must protect the wearer from water-borne pathogens.

A drysuit offers a barrier but no impact protection or thermal properties. Therefore, a drysuit requires additional thermal clothing to be worn underneath. Thermal and impact protection can be easily regulated by adding or removing layers depending on the conditions.

Many different styles of drysuit are available. The NFPA specifies suits should have an integral sock but many suits will have only ankle seals. Integral boots have the advantage of being complete and easily put on and they can protect the feet from hazmat. However, many boots tend to be difficult to swim in, or have soles that do not offer much grip. Also, integral boots cannot be removed if the boot is caught in an underwater entrapment. The drysuit would have to be compromised by cutting off the boot.

A better option is to use integral socks on the drysuit and use separate specialist water rescue boots, hiking boots or industrial safety boots. This option allows greater flexibility as boots can then be the correct size for the end user. Naturally, latex socks are more fragile than integral boots and care must be taken not to puncture them.

Wetsuits

Notes

Wetsuits work by trapping a layer of water between an individual's skin and the suit material, which is then warmed by body heat. However, they offer no protection from hazmat as the skin is in constant contact with water.

Neoprene wetsuits offer good insulation and impact protection as well as some inherent buoyancy for rescue swimmers. However, to provide the best thermal qualities, wetsuits need to fit snugly. This makes them quite specific to individuals. In addition, the NFPA specifies that the suits have long sleeves and cover the legs to the ankle.

Personal Flotation Devices (PFDs)

The most critical piece of equipment for anyone within 10 feet of the edge of the water is a good personal flotation device (PFD). ("Lifejackets" are not for rescuers.) The U.S. Coast Guard (USCG) website states, "Nine out of ten drownings occur in inland waters, most within a few feet of safety. Most of the victims owned PFDs, but they died without them. A wearable PFD can save your life ... if you wear it."

PFDs For Rescuers

In the United States, all PFDs are approved by the U.S. Coast Guard. Originally "life jackets" were designed primarily to float people on their backs in a position that made it easy to breathe. Life jackets were not designed to swim in or as rescue devices. However, over the last 20 years, PFDs were developed with specific models for rescuers that provide necessary buoyance but also the mobility required for swimming. New PFDs are more visible with reflective tape, have a quick release harness, and have add-ons like pockets and attachment points for rescue items like knives and glow sticks.

The USCG recommends the following PFDs for emergency responders:

- Type III - for boat-based activity in calm, inland waters
- Type V - for special uses and work purposes
- Type III/V - multipurpose jackets that fit criteria of Type III & V

However, many PFDs in the above categories will not necessarily meet the minimum requirement for 22 lbs. of flotation set by the NFPA for surface water rescue. Check the label before you buy.

Fit is Key

While proper buoyancy is critical, fit is also very important when selecting a PFD. Try to find one that provides the proper flotation while still fitting properly. Comfort is important too, because if it is uncomfortable, it won't get worn. For more on buoyancy and fit, go to the USCG website.

Inflatable PFDs

Inflatable PFDs have gained popularity over the past several years due to their comfortable fit. While these jackets certainly can be more comfortable, their need for a method of activation can be the device's Achilles heal. Some vests are equipped with a manual activator which requires

Notes

conscious thought and effort to deploy. In the case of a head or spinal injury or a slow reaction time, this may not be possible. Conversely, some vests are equipped with an automatic activator which is initiated by water pressure. While removing the need for the wearer to deploy the vest, automatic inflation vests absolutely will inflate under pressure, including when the wearer is trapped in the fuselage or passenger area of a sinking helicopter or motor vehicle. This unwanted activation will trap the wearer inside the sinking equipment. They are therefore not recommended by the NFPA for rescuers.

Helmets

The NFPA sets standards for helmets for surface water operations in the 1952 Standard. These helmets are designed to protect the head from impacts and must float. They must also be designed in such a manner that water will flow easily through them and not create a choking or injury hazard by “bucketing” or retaining water.

They must have a strong strap system and any metal parts must be corrosion resistant. The foam lining must not absorb so much water that it becomes heavy and uncomfortable to wear.

This standard does not address helmets to be worn in motorized or non-motorized boats.

Working at height helmets (EN 397) and mountaineering helmets (EN 12492) are designed to protect against objects falling from above. Most have a cradle that has a space between it and the top of the helmet. This space absorbs the energy from an impact. These helmets are not appropriate for use in swiftwater as the space can act as a bucket, catching the current, filling with water, and possibly leading to neck injuries. In extreme cases, the helmet could be ripped off, leaving the wearer unprotected.

Just because a helmet has holes does not mean it is meant for use in the water. Holes are usually intended for ventilation.

Footwear

Good footwear for the water rescue environment has always been a compromise. Recreational water shoes often have thin soles, making them unsuitable to work on rough river banks. Today there are a number of very good supportive boots available on the market and some even have climbing grade rubber soles. Water boots tend to take severe abuse from contaminated water, rough terrain, and long periods of being soaked followed by rapid drying.

Boots do not need to be waterproof (a drysuit with socks accomplishes this and so the wearer is protected from hazmat) but they must be non-slip on rough terrain, be flexible enough to swim in, and offer protection to the sole and toe area. Neoprene boots offer good insulation and will sustain constant drenching without rotting, unlike hiking boots. However, hiking boots may offer more grip and support on uneven terrain. Some industrial work boots are available. They are similar to hiking boots, but with additional steel or composite shank and toe-cap protection. The

downside of using industrial boots is that they are heavy and do not drain well. This can be a distinct disadvantage in the water.

Notes

Gloves

Hands need protection in the water environment from both cold and abrasion and possibly hazmat. Neoprene gloves with reinforced palms offer warmth and some degree of protection from sharp objects. The NPFA specifies a cut-proof palm. However, if gloves are too thick, handling ropes becomes difficult and they do not offer any protection from hazmat. True dry gloves will provide hazmat protection but they become very cumbersome to swim in and for handling ropes etc.

Whistle

A whistle that will continue to function after immersion in water is a vital tool for anyone operating at a water incident. Whistles can be used either to attract attention when in trouble, or as a communication system with specific calls. Swiftwater environments often have high levels of background noise created by the moving water, and in many cases whistle blasts can be heard when vocal communication is not possible. They are also particularly useful during night operations.

Knives

Anyone working near the water environment with ropes must carry a knife. Ropes in water can become tangled and entrapped very easily. The knife carried needs to be very sharp, easily available and yet secure. However, there are pros and cons to any knife. A sheath knife can be knocked loose, and especially if it has a sharp point, could easily cause injury. Conversely, a folding knife is tied to a lanyard that is attached to a PFD, but if it is dropped while open, it could thrash around in the water, causing injury. Folding knives can also be difficult to open while wearing gloves.

Throwbags

Notes

A throwbag is a standard water rescue tool and should be carried at all times when within 10' of moving water. It is comprised of a specialized water rescue rope contained in a bag for easy throwing.

Diagram Aw38: Comparison of throwbag types & sizes

Throwbags are available in various lengths depending upon their intended use, the most common being 50' to 75' long. The rope used is predominantly polypropylene; however, some specialist throwbags use ropes combining more than one material, such as nylon and spectra. All have a low melting point and therefore are unsuitable for high-angle rope rescue applications.

Must Float

NFPA Standards state the rope used in throwbags must float, as must the bag. Keeping the rope and bag on the surface of the water makes it easier for the victim to grab the rope and minimizes the chances of the rope tangling in debris. For more information on NFPA Standards for throwbags, see page Ops-24.

Notes

Throwbags must be highly visible. The bags must be easy to pack and contain the rope easily and securely. Additional features such as lightstick holders, reflective tape and belt attachment points are all useful options, but increase the price.

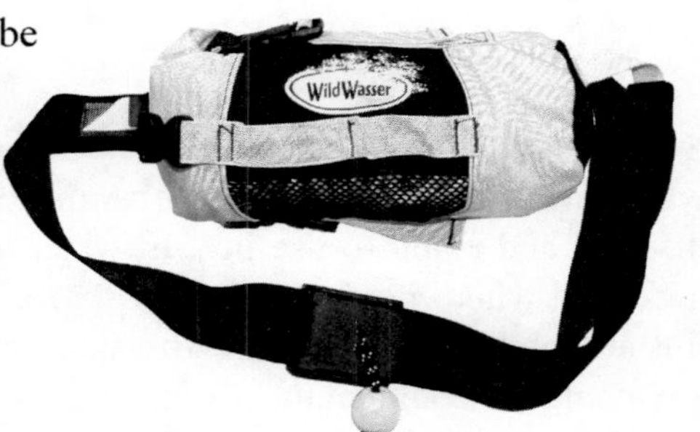

Diagram Aw39: Throwbag with waist belt

Rope Diameter

Rope diameters vary and the thicker the rope, the easier it is to handle. Obviously, the thicker the rope is, the heavier it will be, and the larger the bag will be. Thicker rope also means that people with smaller hands may have difficulty throwing coils.

Commercially manufactured throwbags are available in a variety of lengths between 30' and 125'. Smaller bags are easy to stow, carry, and throw but have limited range. Larger bags can be difficult to throw but are invaluable on wider channels. Remember, you can always make a long rope easier to throw by removing a few feet of rope from the bag before throwing, but its much harder to make a short rope longer.

Lights

When personnel are working at night they need adequate lighting. This may be provided by portable generators and flood lighting, or from vehicles.

Diagram Aw40: Handheld spot light for search operations.

Personnel in the field need personal lighting. Head lamps are ideal as they give a hands-free capability and shine light wherever the individual looks. Head lamps are good for lighting the immediate personal space. LED bulb technology now delivers a pure white light and an extended battery life. When selecting a headlamp, keep what style of helmet you use in mind. The headlamp will often ride on the rim of the helmet and therefore mustbe held in place by clips, friction, or some other combination of active and passive retention measures. Back up lights and batteries should be carried.

For search operations, head lamps are generally not powerful enough and do not cast light a sufficient distance. For this task, powerful handheld spotlights are required.

For Swiftwater Rescue Technicians® who will operate in the water the flashlights, head lamps and spot lights must be waterproof.

Emergency lights for personnel, such as cyalume glow sticks, are advisable. Although they do not provide working light they are very effective for marking equipment, or even for personnel if their personal lights fail.

Notes

Swim Fins

Swim fins can greatly increase a rescuer's speed when swimming in water. However they can be difficult and tiring to use in swiftwater and are awkward when moving about on shore. Normal diving fins are too large for use in swiftwater, but specialist river fins are available from a number of manufacturers.

Eye Protection

Eye protection is not normally worn in a swiftwater rescue environment. This is because specific hazards to eyes are relatively low, and operational issues, such as fogging, are more of a hindrance. If an additional risk to rescuers' eyes is present (such as using hydraulic cutting tools on a vehicle in the water) then suitable eye protection should be worn. Eye protection is also recommended for powerboat operations because of bugs, debry, and spray.

Buoyant Aids

Although relatively rare in swiftwater rescue, for many years lifeguards have used buoyant aids to reduce the risk posed by the victim. Many different designs are available. They all work on the same basic principle of providing a large amount of buoyancy in an easy-to-grip shape and a length of rope that allows rescuers to distance themselves from the victim.

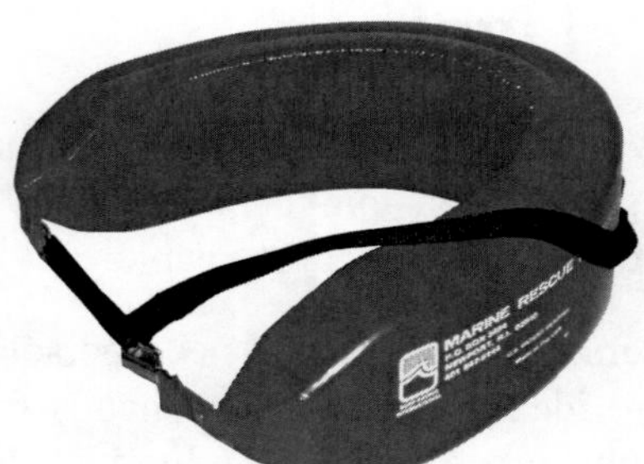

Notes

Team Equipment

Rescue teams carry a vast range of equipment, depending on their area of speciality and levels of operation. Awareness level personnel are not rescue team members, but need to have knowledge of the equipment used as they may perform a supporting role in the cold zone (see *page Aw-6*).

Inflated Fire Hose

As many swiftwater rescuers are fire fighters, fire hose is often easily available at moving water incidents and has many uses. Capping and inflating a fire hose with compressed air gives a number of water rescue options.

The hose can be used as a reach rescue tool in flat or slow moving water. It is also useful in low head dams, where the hose is pushed out into the reversal or towback to reach the victim. It can be used in a pendulum rescue, lowered from a bridge, or as a downstream backup when set up as a diagonal. For more information see *page Aw-59*.

To be utilized as above, ensure that the following are readily available:

- Lengths of standard fire hose
- Cylinder(s) of compressed air
- Caps for the hose ends
- Inflation/deflation control system

For most applications, the hose is inflated between one and three Bar.

Diagram Aw43: Fire hose can be used to perform a variety of reach rescues.

Notes

Boats

Boats come in many shapes and sizes and have a multitude of uses. No boat exists that fulfills all the needs of the swiftwater and flood rescuer and so compromises are necessary. No matter what craft is used, it is critical for rescuers to understand its capabilities and limitations.

Flood events can be divided into four phases (*see page Aw-44*) that require different activities and potentially different types of boats for evacuation, rescue, search and rescue, search and recovery. The high speed water conditions associated with a Phase 2 flash flood event may require a fast powerful craft to deal with water velocity. Phase 3 (Expansion) and Phase 4 (Recovery) of a flood event may require a more robust, puncture-proof craft.

Each craft has advantages and disadvantages, so think carefully about the end use of the boat and don't be swayed by the exciting image portrayed in the catalog. The sheer number and variety of boats currently on the market is huge and can be confusing so have a good sense of your specific needs:

- What will the boat be used for?
- How will it be transported?
- On what type of water will it be used?
- Where can it be launched?
- How many crew are needed to operate it safely?

Rescue 3 currently offers 3 motorized boat operations courses (*Flood Rescue Boat Operator, Swiftwater Rescue Boat Operator,* and *NIMS Rescue Boat Operator*).

Inflatable Rescue Boat

These tend to be smaller boats with a raft-like construction. They can be rolled up for transportation and launched very easily. They have a rigid transom on which to attach an engine, and can have a semi-rigid floor, i.e. a number of aluminium strips covered with Hypalon. They sometimes have an inflatable keel which improves directional control and helps in rougher water. IRBs tend to be forgiving and maneuverable in whitewater and can also be handled reasonably efficiently without the motor. Some also have compartmentalized tubes which allow rescuers to isolate compromised sections.

This type of boat is proving to be very popular with a lot of emergency services and rescue teams due to its versatility and friendly handling characteristics, along with its ease of carrying and launching. However, its ability to carry loads or people is not as great as other boats, and the boats can become very unstable if overloaded. As it is lightweight, it can easily be waded in shallow water.

Rigid Hull Craft

Rigid-hulled boats come in a huge variety of shapes and sizes. They can have flat bottoms or deep V's. They can be made of a wide variety of durable materials such as aluminium, wood or plastic. Some boats have a double skin or built-in buoyancy compartments that keep the boat afloat if it swamps. Those that have a flat bottom tend to have good initial stability, although they will feel more unstable in rough water. The deeper the "V" a boat has the less initial stability it will have, but it will handle rougher weather and waves better.

Notes

Rigid-hulled boats also tend to have more "freeboard", that is, higher sides. This can make it more difficult to load victims into the boat. Almost all will need a trailer and slipway to launch. This type of boat is easily available and can be very versatile as long as the limitations of its particular design are understood.

Rigid Inflatable Boat (RIB)

These have a combination of a rigid hull and keel with inflatable tubes much like that of a raft. The larger size of a RIB (compared to the IRB) allows it to use much more powerful engines. The rigid hull gives the boat speed and directional stability, while still having the forgiving nature and stability of the inflated side tubes. Larger ribs can have a central console with a wheel and throttle control, which gives a better view of the water and victim, however, there is less directness of steering response in boats steered with a tiller.

As with other rigid-hulled craft, an RIB usually needs to be launched from a trailer.

Personal Water Craft (PWC)

PWCs suffer from the bad image of being "the hooligan's tool of choice". This statement has to be revised due to the increased use of the PWC in water-based rescues recently. The PWC has long been used in surf rescue where its power, speed, and maneuverability have earned it a reputation as a formidable rescue craft. Due to the jet drive, there is no prop to foul or injure victims in the water. However, if the jet intake gets clogged, the PWC loses power instantly.

This craft is still in its infancy for river or moving water rescue, though its potential is considerable. PWCs require trailer launching.

Whitewater Raft

These range in size from 10' to 18' and are usually made of a rubberized material called Hypalon. They can also be made from PVC which is lighter but not as tough or abrasion resistant. Whitewater rafts are easily carried and launched almost anywhere. Due to their lightness, they are easily waded through shallow water.

Whitewater rafts for rescue applications are almost always paddle powered and obviously rely on a high skill level from the crew. Most rafts now come with inflatable floors with simple self-draining holes which allow the raft to run difficult water without the crew needing to bail water. The tubes of the raft are also compartmentalized to prevent a puncture from deflating the whole boat.

Rafts provide a very stable platform for numerous rescue scenarios and so can be a huge asset to the rescue team. They can be used successfully in low head dam rescue, on a high line, and for quick access to submerged vehicles, either free paddled or on a tensioned diagonal rope system.

Notes

Types of Propulsion

When choosing the boat, the method of propulsion must be decided at the same time. The choice between motorized and non-motorized (i.e. paddle powered) depends on the call out area or type of incidents expected. The *Swiftwater Rescue Technician*® course includes some basic paddle boat handling. For training in motorized boats, Rescue 3 offers a Swiftwater Rescue Boat Operators course.

Whatever type of craft is chosen, it is essential to be aware of its limitations when it is paddle powered as opposed to motor powered. For instance, a large RIB is extremely difficult to paddle, due to the deep V hull that makes directional changes difficult and the fact that the crew sits high above the water, especially near the bow. However, a small IRB or whitewater raft is easily paddled and maneuvered, and even waded.

In addition, all paddle powered boats can only move downstream. While it is possible to move upstream in eddies, non-motorized boats are at the mercy of the direction of flow. For a crew to be able to paddle a boat efficiently in swiftwater it must have trained and practiced together on a regular basis. However, the deployment speed of a paddle boat can be a huge advantage in a rescue scenario.

Other Craft

Inflatable rescue craft

- Extremely maneuverable
- High skill level required
- Limited carrying capacity
- Purpose-built for easy victim retrieval
- Can be used for unstable surfaces such as ice

Notes

Kayak

- Extremely maneuverable
- High skill level required
- Very limited carrying capacity
- Durable
- Good for hasty searches
- Very specialized craft with limited application

Canoe

- Maneuverable
- High skill level required
- Limited carrying capacity
- Specialized craft with limited application

Rescue Boards and Sleds

- Variety of designs available for mud & ice work, swiftwater and to be used in conjunction with a PWC
- Useful to support a swimming rescue
- Quick to set up
- In-water option - victim exposed to the water

Personal Safety and Survival

Notes

Falling In

Falling into the water is a foreseeable hazard when personnel are working near to water; therefore all team members should be aware of the danger and prepared for this. All personnel who work within the warm zone (within 10' of moving water) must be dressed in suitable PPE which will provide protection if they fall in. Personnel should be aware of the area they are working in and understand basic hydrology should they fall in.

Diagram Aw53: Defensive swimming in proper PPE.

Upon immersion, a PFD or life jacket is designed to float wearers on their backs with their faces clear of the water. Personnel should adopt the defensive swimming position on their backs with their feet and backside as high as possible. This position will enable them to see where they are going, protect them from underwater obstructions and foot entrapment, and enable them to negotiate hazards and catch a throwbag.

Personal Welfare

Welfare is an important issue when personnel are committed to rescue scenes. Working in harsh environments quickly takes its toll on stamina. Personnel will require regular breaks, rotation of teams, feeding, re-hydration, warming, cooling, etc. It is essential that team leaders and managers recognize this and make provisions for the welfare of the team members, victims and any others involved in an incident.

At major flood events many teams will be required to allow for adequate rotation and resting of teams. Accommodation will be required so personnel can rest, sleep and recuperate away from

Notes

the scene. Team members should be aware of their own limitations and ensure their team leader is aware when they need rest, food, water or sleep.

Decontamination

Working in or around water may result in contamination of workers. This is even more likely in floodwater conditions.

Water can be contaminated by a variety of sources—from chemical substances and biological agents in and around water, to polluted water containing toxin-producing algae or micro-organisms. Household waste such as sewage is an obvious contaminant, as well as chemicals from a variety of sources (such as households or local industries) causing skin and eye infections. Agricultural and rural areas carry their own contaminants.

Good hygiene is an effective control measure. Keep open wounds covered. Decontaminate hands, face, and equipment thoroughly before eating, drinking or smoking. After completing operations, decontaminate and then shower thoroughly. Equipment should be decontaminated following use, or prior to meal breaks. Often the cross contamination chain can be broken in this manner. The most important decontamination stage with textiles (drysuits, buoyancy aids etc.) is drying – ensure that they are thoroughly dried after use.

A course of inoculations against Hepatitis A and up-to-date Tetanus shots are advisable for people working in polluted environments. Further medical precautions and advice should be sought from occupational health and medical departments.

Decontamination can be conducted by a dedicated team member or small team equipped with alcohol-based hand gel and face wipes specifically formulated to eliminate waterborne bacteria, cleaning chemicals and specialized equipment. At large flood incidents, a similar level of care could be achieved by mass decontamination stations provided by the emergency services.

Decontamination should be an integral part of the risk assessment process and pre-planned for at the required level. Inter-agency collaboration is paramount for large scale flooding decontamination.

Working at Night

Working in darkness greatly increases the risk to rescuers. Rescuers should be more aware of their own and other team members' safety at night.

It is good practice for personnel to wear lights such as cyalume sticks to ensure they are visible to others, and a head lamp is useful as it keeps the hands free to operate and provides personal task lighting. The scene should be lit with flood lights as much as possible. Personnel within 10' of water should never work alone and always be suitably equipped.

A powerful spotlight will be valuable, to assist with location of hazards and searches for victims. Spotlights may be aided by the use of night vision equipment and thermal imaging. It should be noted that thermal image cameras do not "see" through water. However, they are useful for locating heat sources on the bank or above the water.

Notes

Drowning & Related Conditions

Defining Drowning

There are many different definitions of drowning and even experts often disagree. This makes comparison and analysis of data from different researchers very difficult. Consequently, in 2005 the World Congress on Drowning developed a new definition for drowning which will greatly assist in drowning research and help establish a more accurate picture of the global incidence of drowning.

The now-widely accepted definition is:

"Drowning is the process of experiencing respiratory impairment from submersion/immersion in liquid."

The Congress also established three outcomes of drowning:

- Death
- Morbidity (illness or ill effect)
- Life with no morbidity (no ill effect)

There was also a decision to discontinue use of the terms wet, dry, active, passive, silent, and secondary drowning. Thus a simple, comprehensive and internationally-accepted definition of drowning has been developed.

Global and National Statistics

According to these definitions, drowning is the third most common cause of accidental death globally (after road traffic accidents and falls). The World Health Organization and the International Lifesaving Federation estimate that of the 1.2 million people who die from drowning every year—more than two people each minute—more than 50 percent are children. There are perhaps eight to 10 times that many who experience a near-drowning event but who reach safety alone or are rescued by others. It should be noted that deaths during floods, traffic accidents, and suicides are not included in this figure. Due to the lack of accurate reporting methods (even in developed countries), we can be sure that this is a significantly low estimate.

In the United States, the Centers for Disease Control and Prevention reported that in 2007 there were 3,443 fatal unintentional drownings in the United States, averaging ten deaths per day. Approximately one quarter of these deaths occurred in children 14 years or younger. Deaths were highest in the toddler age group and among adolescent and young adult males. An additional 496 people died in boating-related accidents from drowning and other causes. Significant factors in the majority of deaths are the lack of safety equipment (such as life jackets) and the influence of alcohol.

Floods, which include flash floods, river floods, and urban/small stream floods, cause approximately 76 deaths annually in the US, according to National Weather Service statistics. However, more than half of these deaths are due to people being swept away by current after leaving a stalled vehicle.

Notes

"Near Drowning" or "Secondary Drowning"

As noted above, these terms are no longer in official use because they cause confusion about the causes of drowning. However, they are often used to describe situations where the victim either survives, at least temporarily, following aspiration of fluid into the lungs, or when death occurs at a later time following an initial aspiration of water.

In cases where someone may have aspirated water, he or she must receive medical attention immediately, even if alert and fully rational, and regardless of whether or not there is evidence of water in the lungs (such as chest pain, coughing, breathing difficulties, white or pink foam around the mouth or nostrils).

The irritating effects of water on the lungs can lead to complications up to 72 hours later that can lead to death. It should be noted that it does not require complete submersion to drown and it is possible to aspirate sufficient water during intermittent submersion of the face.

The Drowning Process

Upon submersion, conscious people will normally attempt to hold their breath. Contrary to popular belief, the determining factor in the ability to breath-hold is not a lack of oxygen nor a build up of carbon dioxide, but rather the build up of nervous impulses that starts when inspiration stops, until the desire to breathe becomes overwhelming. This impulse can be reduced by swallowing or other movements that move the respiratory muscles without actual inhalation. It is possible that a natural instinct to keep breath-holding by swallowing is the reason why large volumes of water are found in the stomachs of some drowning victims.

Immersion in cold water can sometimes lead to a little-understood reaction that suppresses the desire to breathe. See Mammalian Diving Reflex page Aw-74 for more information.

Inevitably, after a varying amount of time, the victim will start to inhale water and eventually fall unconscious – although it should be recognized that at this point the victim will still have cardiac output. As the victim becomes increasingly hypoxic (starved for oxygen), the heart will stop working.

FOR FURTHER INFORMATION:

Essentials of Sea Survival by Frank Golden and Michael Tipton (2002). Published by Human Kinetics

Handbook on Drowning: Prevention Rescue and Treatment by Joost Bierens (Editor) (2005). Published by Springer

Notes

Hydrostatic Shock

Hydrostatic shock occurs when a victim is immersed in water for a long period of time. The water exerts pressure on the body, in particular on the legs as they float deeper in the water. This in turn reduces blood flow to the legs, causing blood to pool, and artificially maintains high blood pressure in the body overall. When a victim is rescued and pulled from the water in a vertical position, the pressure on the body is instantly lost, which causes blood pressure to drop rapidly, a loss of consciousness, and potentially cardiac arrest.

However, the victim must come out of the water. The water is the more dangerous of the risks present. To minimize any rapid drop in blood pressure, victims should be rolled from the water in a horizontal position and then transported prone up a river bank or over the side of a boat.

In particular, issues with hydrostatic shock have occurred when victims have been winched into a helicopter using only a single strop. As a victim is held vertically while being transported, they can lose consciousness which drops their head forward and blocks their airway. Correct procedure is now to double-strop all victims pulled from the water (one strop under the armpits, and one strop behind the knees) and transport in a prone position.

Mammalian Diving Reflex

The mammalian diving reflex is the ability of warm-blooded animals to optimize their respiration (conserve oxygen) when diving under the water. This reflex is exhibited strongly in aquatic mammals (seals, otters, dolphins, etc.), and to a lesser extent in other mammals, including humans. Diving birds, such as penguins, have a similar diving reflex.

Triggered by Cold Water

The diving reflex is triggered specifically when cold water contacts the face – water that is warmer than 70°F does not cause the reflex, and neither does submersion of other body parts. Also, the reflex is always more dramatic in young people, which can allow them to survive longer immersions.

A full understanding of humans and the mammalian diving reflex is still not known. However, it involves several key factors, such as vascular constriction (limiting of blood supply), bradycardia (slowed heart beat), and blood shunting or shifting within the body.

Blood vessels constrict in parts of the body (such as the hands, feet, arms, and legs) that can tolerate a decrease in oxygen and still function. The body slows and eventually stops blood supply to these areas. Organs like the brain and heart, which demand a constant supply of oxygen, are the last to be cut off from blood supply. Because of decreased circulation in many parts of the body, the heart does not have to work as hard, which reduces the amount of oxygen used throughout the body.

Notes

With less need to pump blood, the heart slows and, in an average person, the pulse rate decreases by 10 to 30 percent.

For humans, there are many factors that influence the onset of the mammalian diving reflex including the temperature of the water, lung volume, physical conditioning, the body's position in the water during immersion, ability to breath-hold, psychological state, and depth of immersion. Each of these can play a significant role in how the heart responds.

Contributes to Survival

There are well documented cases of people (particularly young people) who have survived for extended periods immersed in very cold water, often under ice. The exact mechanism that allows this to happen is not fully understood, but it is often attributed to the mammalian dive reflex. Rescuers must remember that this is a very rare condition and it only occurs in very cold water.

Notes

Common Medical Conditions in the Water Environment

Hypothermia

When responding to a swiftwater or flood emergency, rescuers must always be on the lookout for signs of hypothermia caused by immersion in cold water. Hypothermia is of particular concern to swiftwater and flood rescue personnel because water conducts heat away from the human body 25 times faster than air through the process of conduction. In addition, swimming at any speed further accelerates heat loss from the body through the process of convection.

Hypothermia is best defined as when the body is no longer able to maintain a normal core temperature of 98.6°F due to environmental factors. Classically, hypothermia is defined as a core temperature below 95°F, with varying degrees of severity as the body chills further. At a core temperature of around 82.4°F heartbeat irregularities may occur - called cardiac arrhythmias - which can prevent the heart from pumping blood properly. The heart will stop beating completely at around 64.8°F, causing death, although there have been survivors of hypothermia with much lower recorded core body temperatures. Remember the classic adage "No one is dead until they are warm and dead."

Rescuers should also be aware that even when not causing hypothermia, the effects of cold on the human body can drastically reduce flexibility, strength and stamina. Strength decreases by an average of three percent for every 1°F drop in muscle temperature. Below the body temperature of 80°C, muscle fatigue occurs earlier, and strength is reduced. Muscles in the forearm can cool to this temperature within 20 minutes of immersion in water at 54°F. Consequently, it is possible for rescuers to become incapable of performing their required tasks without becoming hypothermic. In addition, hypothermia will complicate the management of any other injuries, and may worsen certain conditions

Signs and symptoms

In the early stages, symptoms of hypothermia are shivering and feeling cold. This leads to a lack of fine motor control, loss of judgment, and uncontrollable shivering. If the victims are able to talk and move themselves, then this is a good indication that they are only mildly hypothermic and will recover with appropriate thermal protection;

Signs of definite hypothermia include loss of coordination, slurred speech, and pale skin. At this point, the victims will usually be capable of re-warming, providing they are protected from the cold.

As hypothermia becomes more severe, the victim will stop shivering, have a definite altered mental status, and lose interest in survival. If the victims are unable to move, or are unconscious, then this is a good indication that they are severely hypothermic and need to be carefully and rapidly evacuated to a definitive care facility. If left untreated the victim will become unconscious and eventually die.

Notes

Treatment

Remove or protect the victim from a cold, wet or windy environment. Remove any wet clothing, and insulate with thermal layers. If wet clothing cannot be removed, then provide a vapor barrier (such as a plastic "survival bag") over wet clothing. Research has demonstrated that a vapor barrier will trap a layer of air that serves well as thermal insulation for wet victims.

Foil "space blankets" do not act as vapor barriers. They are designed to reflect radiated body heat and a hypothermic victim is radiating very little heat. They provide no protection against conductive heat-loss (for example sitting on a rock) or convective heat-loss (the route from which most heat is lost from a hypothermic victim). However, they are very compact in size and lightweight in comparison to other products available.

Textile or down insulation is highly insulating when dry, but it is bulky, heavy, difficult to compress and drops significantly in performance when wet. Nor is it windproof or waterproof.

The "Blizzard Survival" range of products offers a very effective means of treating hypothermia in a swiftwater rescue environment. They provide an effective vapor barrier, protection from the wind, and trap air in the "ReflexCell" technology to provide protection against conductive heat-loss. The Norwegian Air Ambulance uses bubble-wrap to tightly wrap up the victim, to similar effect.

If the victim is mildly hypothermic, and is alert and capable of swallowing, high-energy drinks may be administered. Victims should avoid exercise until they feel re-warmed (a minimum of one hour of treatment).

In severe hypothermia, victims are at risk of suffering spontaneous ventricular fibrillation. They should be handled extremely gently, and kept horizontal. Ensure that the victim's head is well covered with warm hats. Do not administer anything by mouth. Do not rub extremities.

External heat sources may be used, although there is a lack of experimental evidence to confirm their effectiveness at stabilizing the core body temperature. Heat packs should be placed on the groin, armpits, and neck. Avoid placing them directly in contact with the skin as this can lead to burns.

Always Attempt to Re-Warm

As the body cools, oxygen requirements drop significantly, and victims can appear very lifeless. Always attempt to rewarm someone suspected of hypothermia -- remember that a hypothermic victim is not dead until they are warm and dead.

Hyperthermia (Heat-Related Injuries)

At the other end of the spectrum is hyperthermia which occurs when the body can no longer dissipate enough heat to balance the heat being absorbed from the surrounding environment. This leads to several problems listed below.

The best cure is prevention: remain hydrated and take steps to cool down when necessary, before any negative impact from heat occurs.

Notes

Heat Cramps

Heat cramps are the result of a chemical disruption caused by profuse sweating, or in short, an electrolyte imbalance due to loss of salt. It is most often seen in people in good physical condition while exercising or working hard in hot conditions.

Signs and symptoms:

- Sudden onset of cramps in the legs, and/or the abdomen
- Possible low blood pressure
- Nausea
- Rapid pulse
- Pale, moist skin
- Normal core body temperature

Treatment

Remove victims from the hot environment and cool them down. Provide fluid replacement by mouth if they can tolerate it, but use fluids with sodium (like sports drinks) if possible. Plain water may worsen their condition.

Heat Exhaustion

Heat exhaustion is caused by dehydration and loss of body fluids. When water and electrolytes are not replaced, circulation slows down, affecting the vital organs.

This may be as a result of operating for extended periods during hot weather.

Signs and symptoms

- Headache and weakness / fatigue
- Rapid shallow breathing
- Pale skin, and sweating (possibly profuse)
- Muscle cramps, unsteadiness, dizziness and nausea

Treatment

Remove victims to a cooler environment as quickly as possible. Remove as much clothing as practicable (particularly drysuits). Lay them down and allow them to rest. Rehydrate the victims with cold (lightly salted if possible) water or an electrolyte solution. If possible, apply cold compresses and fan them. If victims vomits, they should go to hospital.

Heat Stroke

Heat stroke is a true medical emergency!!!

Unfortunately, the line between heat exhaustion and heat stroke is often blurred. The principle difference is the presence of cardiovascular shock in heat stroke. However, if in any doubt, err on the side of caution.

Notes

Heat stroke is characterized by a high core body temperature of over 104°F. At this temperature, the body is effectively being cooked and severe damage to the kidneys, liver, and nervous system can result.

Signs and symptoms

- High temperature (> 104°F.)
- Hot, reddish, dry skin
- Rapid and strong pulse initially, becoming weaker
- Deep breathing initially, becoming shallow and weak
- Mental confusion
- Headache
- Nausea or vomiting
- Convulsions
- Sudden collapse

Treatment

Remove victims to a cooler environment as quickly as possible. Remove as much clothing as practicable (particularly drysuits). Lay them down and allow them to rest. If they are conscious, rehydrate with cold (lightly salted if possible) water or an electrolyte solution. Apply ice packs to the neck, armpits and groin. Aggressively fan them with cool air. Wet them with cool/tepid water. If possible, monitor their temperature, and as it declines, reduce cooling efforts – avoid causing hypothermia.

Traumatic Injuries

The most common injuries in swiftwater or flood incidents are to the extremities including hands, feet, arms and legs. Injuries can include cuts, bruises, fractures and dislocations. Most traumatic injuries are extremely painful, but not life threatening. Fractures of the bones in the extremities generally present as painful, deformed, and swollen limbs. The main concern is whether victims have a pulse and sensation distally (at the end of the limb). If they do not, you may have to reposition the limb to facilitate taking a pulse.

Open fractures have a high risk of infection when exposed to water and other contaminants. Reducing a dislocation is a valuable technique that can be learned in advanced first aid courses. Splinting is another valuable skill that can be learned in a first aid course. As a rule, splinting involves the immobilization of the joint above and below the fracture. Always check for a pulse and sensation before and after any intervention.

Major Fractures

The most serious fracture involves the largest bone in the human body -- the femur (thigh bone). It is surrounded by major blood vessels running down the inner thigh that, if punctured by bone fragments from a break in the femur, can cause enough bleeding to be a serious life threat. While all bleeding should be stopped, it is critical that you perform a thorough victim assessment to be certain you don't miss any life threats before addressing bleeding. If a victim has a fracture of the femur, or any bone in the torso, one must have a high index of suspicion that there were such significant forces involved that other injuries may be present.

Notes

Internal Injuries

In addition, always look for less obvious internal injuries. Internal injuries can be difficult to detect and may quickly become a life threatening condition.

Bleeding

The human body has approximately 1.5 gallons of blood circulating at all times. This blood carries oxygen to all tissues, and then carries out waste products from the body.

Bleeding can be life threatening. It can also be distracting from other life threats. There are some basic questions to ask about bleeding: is it flowing, spurting, or oozing?

Oozing

Oozing blood is easily stemmed with simple bandages and is not a serious concern

Flowing

Flowing blood indicates a venous source and is fairly easily controlled. Even so, a victim can lose a large enough amount of blood from venous bleeding to develop shock and eventually die.

Spurting

Spurting blood indicates an arterial bleed and this is a life threat that must be controlled quickly or the person will "bleed out" and die. The preferred method to control bleeding is by direct pressure, generally using some type of bandaging material. After applying the bandage, apply direct pressure over the wound. Do not remove the bandage. If it bleeds through, apply more bandages on top of the first one and reapply pressure.

It is protocol in many areas to use pressure points above the level of the wound. However, studies have found that this is neither consistent nor totally effective, not to mention time- and resource-consuming. Tourniquets are coming back as a viable method of stopping serious bleeding. The most effective and least damaging (to nerves and muscle tissue) is a commercially available tourniquet with a wider band, no sharp edges, easy to use windlass (tighten), and a way to secure it when finished. If applying a tourniquet, one should be trained in its use, apply it slowly, release it when the bleeding stops, check the wound regularly, and be sure to document the time it was applied.

Other methods to stop serious, spurting bleeding include commercially available hemostatic agents, or clotting agents.

Shock

Notes

Shock is defined as inadequate tissue perfusion, or not enough blood circulating in the body's tissues and vital organs (heart, brain, lungs, liver, kidneys). It can occur as a result of any of the injuries listed above.

There are several types/causes of shock, but in general the signs and symptoms include low blood pressure (hypotension), overbreathing (hyperventilation), a weak rapid pulse, cold clammy grayish-bluish (cyanotic) skin, decreased urine flow (oliguria), and mental changes (a sense of great anxiety and foreboding, confusion and, sometimes, combativeness).

The human body is generally very good at compensating for the early stages of shock. The heart rate, blood pressure, and respiratory rate will increase in an effort to deliver oxygen to all the vital organs. However, when enough blood volume is lost, no amount of compensation will maintain oxygenation and the system will fail. This failure is evidenced by falling vital signs, and eventually coma and death.

Shock is a major medical emergency. It is common after serious injury. Emergency care for shock involves keeping the patient warm and giving fluids by mouth or, preferably, intravenously.

Waterborne Illnesses

Notes

In addition to the many injuries that can occur in conjunction with moving water, there are several waterborne illnesses that personnel should be aware of as well. These illnesses may appear many days after exposure and are often difficult to diagnose, and so it is important to recognize their signs and symptoms.

Leptospirosis and Weil's Disease

Leptospirosis is a bacterial infection caused by organisms called Leptospires that can cause death in some rare cases, but go virtually unnoticed in others. These bacteria can survive for days or even weeks in moist conditions, but only a few hours in salt water. Different strains of the Leptospira bacteria can infect a wide range of animals. The strain carried by rats, mice, and voles is the one that most frequently infects humans. The organisms are excreted in the animal's urine, which can contaminate water including muddy riverbanks. The likelihood of becoming infected is greater from stagnant or slow-moving water, particularly in high water and flood conditions.

Leptospirosis occurs worldwide but in the US is most common in temperate or tropical climates, particularly in Hawaii. It is an occupational hazard for many people who work near and in lakes and rivers including the military and first responders and is a common occurrence after flooding in densely populated centers especially in developing countries.

Method of Infection

The Leptospires most commonly enter the body through breaks in the skin, such as minor abrasions and small cuts. An alternative route of infection is through the mucous membranes of the nose, mouth or eyes.

Preventative measures for personnel:

- Cover cuts and broken skin with waterproof plasters
- Wear suitable PPE
- Do not touch rats with unprotected hands
- Wash with soap (or alcohol gel) and dry hands thoroughly prior to eating, drinking, smoking
- Shower after becoming immersed in open water
- Decontaminate on-site after removing PPE
- Avoid cross-contamination from PPE

Signs and Symptoms

The usual incubation period is four to 14 days, but can be up to 30 days. Usually a flu-like illness occurs, with fever, shivering, severe headache, vomiting and pain in the back and calves. The second phase of the disease leads to meningitis (swelling of the brain lining), liver and kidney failure, and subsequent jaundice. Death may occur in approximately 10 percent of jaundiced patients. Again, most people who contact this bacterial infection recover fully, and some have no symptoms at all.

Notes

Treatment

A doctor's diagnosis is by clinical suspicion - a blood test can rarely confirm the illness in time to effect treatment, although it may subsequently confirm it. Antibiotics during the first few days will help in limiting the infection and are often prescribed prior to confirmation of blood tests.

Weil's disease is often used as the "layman's term" for a Leptospiral infection. In fact, the true definition of Weil's disease (the most serious form of the infection) is when the patient has become jaundiced due to liver damage.

It should be noted that deaths from Leptospirosis are rare. According to the Center for Disease Control the reported incidence of leptospirosis is 100–200 cases per year in the United States with at least half of these in Hawaii. Leptospirosis is likely under-diagnosed in the United States, with reported incidence depending largely upon clinical index of suspicion.

For further information

www.cdc.gov
www.leptospirosis.org

Hepatitis A

Hepatitis A is a virus present in feces and is therefore present in water contaminated by sewage, such as in flood conditions. All personnel in and around inland waterways and flood operations personnel are potentially at risk. The virus is contracted via the fecal-oral route.

Hepatitis has a variable incubation period of 15-50 days. Onset is usually abrupt, producing fever and abdominal discomfort followed by jaundice. Many infections are relatively mild, but in some cases progress to prolonged and severely disabling disease.

A vaccination against Hepatitis A is available, and personnel at risk should seek advice from their doctors or occupational health advisors.

Blue Green Algae

Cyanobacteria, also known as blue green algae, is frequently found in fresh water and can be contacted through swimming or wading. During extended periods of warm, calm weather this algae multiplies and forms a bloom on the surface of the water. The blooms may look like jelly or paint and are normally blue-green in color, though can also be red, brown or black. The blooms can appear and disappear with changing weather.

The majority of blooms produce allergens or toxins which can vary considerably in potency. Although ingestion of small quantities of concentrated bloom can be fatal, human deaths are extremely rare. However, there have been numerous cases of animal deaths, which can add to contamination problems in an already flooded area.

Notes

Signs and symptoms of algae reactions can include:

- Dermatitis
- Eye irritation
- Gastroenteritis
- Joint and muscle pain
- Pneumonia
- Liver damage
- Neurological conditions

Gastrointestinal Illness

Ingestion of bacteria that cause gastrointestinal infection is a significant risk for swiftwater and flood rescue personnel. Sewage contains large numbers of organisms and even seemingly clean waterways can contain harmful bacteria.

Salmonella infection is probably the principal bacterial risk, but Campylobacter, pathogenic Escherichia Coli, Listeria and Cryptosporidium may also be present. Gastrointestinal illness is characterized by frequent and watery bowel movements, but is fairly short-lived. Treatment includes rest and plenty of fluids to prevent dehydration.

For further information

www.cdc.gov

Notes

General First Aid in the Moving Water Environment

The following is a general review of issues related to medical considerations in the water environment. It is not intended to be a complete synopsis of patient care. Anyone working around moving water is encouraged to take a comprehensive first aid course from a certified professional. In the US, first responders are subject to the Good Samaritan law that protects them from liability as long as their treatment does not extend beyond training or certification. Finally, nothing contained in this section should discourage personnel from following local medical protocols.

Rescuer Safety

Removing a victim from the water is a high priority, but rescuers should first consider their personal safety. Assess for hazards and ensure the safety of team members ***before*** the rescue begins. Once the rescue is started, do not focus on it to the detriment of the team. Be sure to take appropriate body substance isolation precautions (generally driven by local protocols).

Initial Assessment

Determine a level of consciousness. This process starts while approaching the victim. Ask victims if they are OK. If they answer clearly, then they are alert. If the answer is unintelligible, or there is no answer, they may have an altered level of consciousness. Look the victim over as you approach, and assess any immediate life threats. The two most immediate threats involve breathing and bleeding, both of which can be recognized immediately.

At the same time, quickly scan for the mechanism of injury (MOI). Finding out what caused the incident will help rescuers understand the possible injuries and their severity.

ABC Assessment

The standard systematic ABC (airway, breathing and circulation) assessment can be done in a very short time. As you perform this assessment, always stop to counter any life threats that you discover.

A – Airway

Is the airway open and unblocked? If not, perform a standard “head tilt - chin lift”. Could there be possible cervical spine injuries? If there is any doubt, one should assume there are injuries to the neck/spine and proceed accordingly, performing the standard “jaw thrust” maneuver. Apply manual C-spine stabilization simultaneously when opening the airway. Remember that a victim who is not breathing will surely die, so while all efforts should be taken to stabilize the neck and back, opening the airway takes precedence.

Notes

B – Breathing

Is the victim breathing? If not, and the airway is opened, do spontaneous respirations resume? Are they adequate? Does the chest rise and fall evenly? Ideally, respiration rate should be between 12 and 20 breaths per minute.

If victims are conscious, can they speak in full sentences and/or cough? If they cannot, then treat for an obstructed airway. Are there any audible breath sounds? Snoring respirations indicate an obstructed airway (generally found in an unresponsive victim). Reposition the airway to allow more airflow. Stridor (high-pitched sounds on inspiration) also indicate a partially blocked upper airway. This is generally caused by inflammation or mucous – which should lead you to suspect an antihistamine response (asthma, allergic reaction). Wheezing (high-pitched sounds on expiration – and sometimes inspiration) also indicate an antihistamine response. Gurgling indicates that the victim has some form of fluid in the air passages – water, blood, vomit or mucous.

C – Circulation

Check for any hemorrhage (bleeding) as you approach the victim. Severe bleeding is a life threat and must be addressed at this stage (bleeding and shock will be addressed later). If none is discovered, move on. Can you feel a pulse? Check the radial pulse. If no pulse is found, check the carotid pulse in the neck. If no pulse, consider attempting CPR. Take into account location, how many people are on scene, and how far it is to advanced medical care.

Note the rate when checking the pulse. This is done by counting the beats for 15 seconds and multiplying by four. This will give the beats per minute. 70 - 90 is normal. Illness and/or injury may increase the pulse rate. A rate over 150 is an indicator that something is seriously wrong, while a pulse under 50 is not usually enough to keep a person conscious. Is the pulse regular or irregular? Is it strong or weak? If possible, take the blood pressure. Record all findings – this will be the baseline for this victim.

Neurological Assessment

Following the ABC assessment, the next step is a neurological exam to determine the victim's level of consciousness. A commonly-used method is to categorize the victim into one of four levels based on the mnemonic "AVPU":

"A" - Describes an **alert** victim capable of conversing.

"V" - Victim responds to **verbal** stimuli, but can't converse.

"P" - Describes someone who only responds to **painful** stimulus

"U" - Describes a victim that is totally **unresponsive**

Injury and Exposure

Notes

The next concern is for injury. Perform a thorough physical examination to assess for additional injuries. Look for deformities, bruising, lacerations, tenderness or swelling, rash, and any other clues that may give insight as to the extent of injury.

Beginning at the head, progress to the neck, chest, abdomen, extremities and back. Compare injured limbs to uninjured limbs.

While it is necessary to visually look at and palpate during an assessment, be sure to take the victim's body temperature into account. In water and/or during a traumatic event, the victim will lose body heat rapidly and this must be taken into account. Look for signs of hypo or hyperthermia depending on the weather. Failing to maintain adequate body temperature in a victim will ultimately worsen the victim's condition with most injuries or illnesses (see Hypo- and Hyperthermia, page Aw-20).

Interview

If the victim is conscious, perform an interview that includes questions about the event, the victim's own history, and any interventions that have been performed prior to your arrival.

The **SAMPLE** mnemonic will assist in remembering what to ask.

> **S – Signs and symptoms:** Symptoms are completely subjective. It is what victims tell you they feel.
>
> **A – Allergies:** Is the victim allergic to medications? Bee stings? Are there any known food allergies?
>
> **M – Medications**: Is the victim being prescribed any medications? If so, what are they for? Any herbal remedies? Any illegal drugs?
>
> **P – Past medical history:** Diabetes, heart problems, breathing problems, seizures, etc.?
>
> **L – Last oral intake:** When was the last time the victim ate or drank anything?
>
> **E – Events leading up to the illness or injury:** What was happening prior to the event that brought you on scene?

Many of these questions will lead to other questions that can help paint a more complete picture of what took place.

Once the initial assessment is complete, go back periodically and check to make sure nothing has changed. This is known as the "ongoing assessment". Make certain that bandages are still controlling any bleeding, that the victim is still alert and warm, etc. This ongoing evaluation will continue until the patient care is transferred.

Notes

Patient Packaging & Evacuation

Patient packaging is the term used to describe the process of preparing the victim for evacuation or transfer to paramedics. Once the assessment and initial treatment is complete, and the victim is ready to be moved, the packaging of the victim is an important component of the rescue.

Victims are generally packaged in a litter or Stokes basket when available. Some injuries will require the use of a spine board inside the litter. A vapor barrier is also important in order to maintain warmth and provide protection from the elements. Be sure to reassess the victim after the packaging process.

The next step, evacuation, is a critical component of any rescue. Early in the incident, quickly plan for how the victim is to be removed from the environment and to definitive medical care.

Swiftwater Rescue Operations

Supporting the Swiftwater Rescue Technician®

Notes

As well as being prepared to work around the water and undertake shore-based and shallow water wading rescues, one of the main roles of first responders trained to the Operations level is to support teams of Swiftwater Rescue Technicians® at an incident. To enable this, a responder will have the ability to self rescue, work in shallow water, handle a paddle boat safely, and perform basic rope work.

A first responder will be expected to help and support in technical rescues, but will not be expected to perform them. This may include providing downstream safety cover or assistance with victim handling. Flooding operations may include evacuation of people from properties using shallow water working skills. At a scene of major flooding, Technicians may be in short supply and utilized for technical rescues. Therefore it is first responders who will be used to undertake the majority of evacuations and safety preparations.

Perhaps most of all, the first responder can support the Technician by being trained and equipped to work safely in the water environment. This is a great help, as the Technicians will not have to perform the simpler, lower risk rescues themselves. The Incident Commander and specialist teams can be confident that all personnel working in the water environment are equipped, trained and competent to work safely.

Working in Floods

Notes

Although a flood is a moving water incident with many similarities to a typical swiftwater rescue, there are also differences when dealing with flooding.

Early command and control needs to be established and maintained. Incident command is vital to communicate, plan, allocate, control, brief and debrief the many multi-agency teams that may be involved.

Changeable Water Levels

Consideration must be given to weather conditions that will influence water levels, particularly current rainfall, predicted rainfall, tidal influences, and land drainage. The continually changing conditions will affect the type of approach rescuers take to a situation.

Flood water can be very changeable with regards to depth, flow, speed, and volume. Generally these rates can be predicted by relevant agencies who can give an approximation of expected water levels.

Hazardous Materials

Flood water can be flowing and moving in places it was never intended to be. Once rivers overspill their defined channels and interact with the wider environment, there is a whole new set of physical, biological and chemical hazards to deal with. Rescuers need to be constantly looking out for new hazards.

Flood water is almost certainly contaminated. It is possible that the water has come up through the sewer system and has been contaminated with effluent including chemicals or petrochemicals. Consideration should be given to such issues as testing and sampling the water, and decontamination of personnel, equipment, and PPE. All floods should be treated as hazardous material incidents, and suitable de-contamination processes should be adopted. Monitoring the health of personnel exposed to flood water is strongly advised. For further information on decontamination see *page page Aw-71*.

Where personnel are committed to the water as a wading response, they should be appropriately dressed in a drysuit, buoyancy aid and helmet. If waders are to be used instead of drysuits, consideration should be given to the possibility of the wearer stepping down into a deeper area of water and becoming immersed, from which it can be very difficult to recover. In the event of immersion in waders, the skin will be contaminated with flood water which may result in infection and illness. For more information on equipment see *page Aw-58*.

All personnel operating in flooded areas should be issued with a suitable wading pole to allow them to check for underwater hazards. For more specific information see *page page Ops-8*.

Diagram Ops1: Shallow water wading with a pole.

Boat-Based Rescue

Notes

Many bank-based rescue techniques can have limited applications in floods due to the wide coverage of the water. The effective use of both motor and paddle boats are a critical flood response asset. Motor and paddle boats require specialist training both to allow crew to operate the boat in a swiftwater and flood environment and to apply bank-based techniques such as throwbag and swimming rescues from these boats. Such training is available through the Rescue 3 International *Swiftwater Rescue Boat Operator* and *Swiftwater Rescue Technician®* courses.

If boats are being used then the choice of boat types will be an issue (for more information on boat types see *page Aw-66*). When the water is deep and fast-flowing, powered inflatable boats work well. When the water becomes shallow, it may be necessary to use hard bottom boats. Rescuers may also be able to wade in the water with boats to perform rescues. However if the flow is too fast or the depth variable, then more advanced rescue techniques will be required, such as an aerial rope rescue or a helicopter.

Evacuation and Search

Many people may need rescuing from a flooded area. Not all of these rescues will be technical rescues and incident managers need to decide who is to be rescued first and which rescue teams are best capable to deal with individual incidents – resource or team typing is of a great help here (*see page Aw-56).*

Where rescuers are moving large numbers of people, consideration should be given to how they will be transported. Personal flotation devices (PFDs) in a full range of sizes, from small child to XXXL adult, will be needed for members of the public. These should be clearly marked and a different color from those used by responders.

During an evacuation, people will need advice about what personal possessions they can realistically bring with them. Family pets can be problematic to deal with – many people refuse to leave without their pets. People who have been rescued will need help and advice about emergency shelter and accommodation.

Search is a major consideration in flood events. Not all victims will be obvious. House-to-house searches are required to ensure no one is left trapped. This can be extremely time consuming and require many personnel to search effectively. Once an area is searched, it should be marked accordingly and the incident management team informed in order to avoid replication of work. This is usually done with spray paint on the outside of the property. If at all possible try to place markings on an area which can be easily replaced or covered up later, such as doors or roofs.

Notes

Swimming in Swiftwater

It is important for all personnel working in the warm zone (page Aw-6) to be able to self-rescue using both defensive and aggressive swimming methods.

Defensive Swimming

When in swiftwater and unsure of the situation, the defensive swimming position is the default low-risk option. This is sometimes incorrectly called the "safe swimming" position. Swimming in swiftwater is never without risk. The position is correctly termed "defensive" because it is designed to reduce the chance of injury and potential foot entrapment.

In the defensive swimming position, swimmers are on their backs with their feet pointed downstream. Their hips are as close to the surface as possible. This position helps to minimize the chance of impact injury in moving water, as swimmers can "fend off" objects using their feet.

The arms can be used in a large backstroke action which slows the swimmer down, and allows the swimmer to set a "ferry angle" across the current.

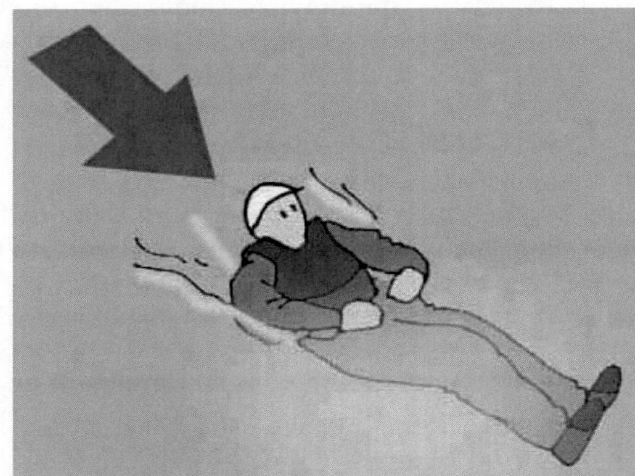

Diagram Ops2: Defensive swimming position

Aggressive Swimming

Aggressive swimming techniques can be used to cross river currents and make rapid progress to a safe eddy in areas that the swimmer has assessed as being low risk.

To swim aggressively, swimmers roll onto their front in the water. Their head remains oriented upstream. The swimmer can now use a more front crawl stroke combined with a powerful kick to maneuver in the water at a faster rate.

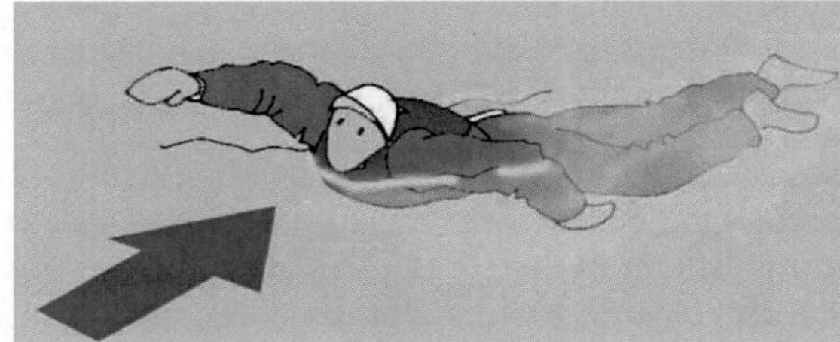

Diagram Ops3: Aggressive swimming position

Ferry Angles

When swimming across a current (both defensively and aggressively) the angle between the current vector (see *page Aw-27*) and the swimmer's body orientation is very important. This is known as the "ferry angle". Good swiftwater swimmers will constantly adjust their angle to allow the water to carry them to their destination with the minimum of effort. They let the water do the majority of the work.

As a general rule, an angle of approximately 45° to the current vector is good. By swimming at this angle the water flows more easily along the body and does not greatly impede the swimmer.

Movement downstream will be minimized while swimmers move laterally in the direction that their head and body is pointed.

A ferry angle wider than 45° increases the force of the water against the swimmers' bodies. The current causes them to "lose ground" and pushes them downstream with little lateral gain. Also, they will no longer be able to fend off objects with their feet, and risk taking impacts in their abdomen and chest.

Notes

Diagram Ops4: Ferrying in a defensive swimming position.

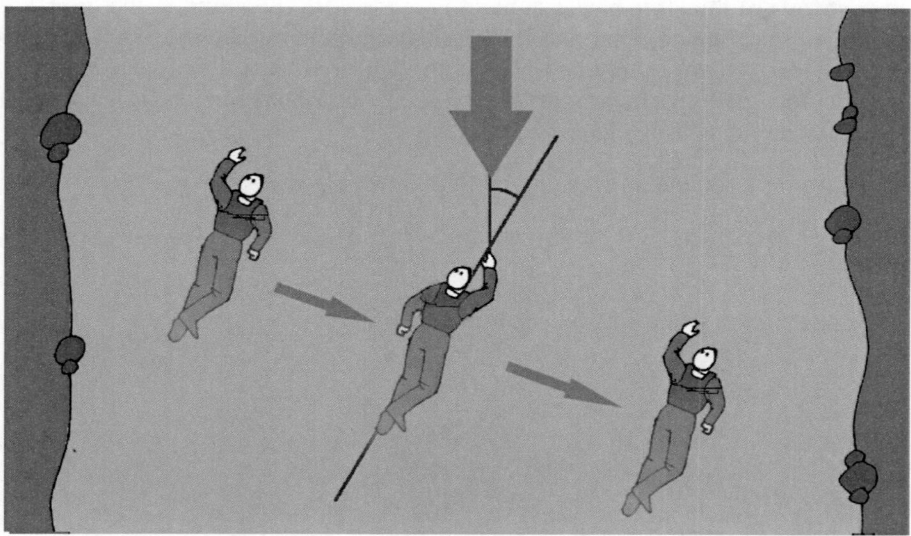

Diagram Ops5: Ferrying in an aggressive swimming position.

Notes

Swimming a Wave Train

When swimming through a wave train (see *page Aw-29*) it can be difficult to breathe and see. If possible, take breaths when in the trough between waves. If breathing is attempted at the top of breaking waves the spray or foam can interfere with breathing.

Diagram Ops6: Breathing at the bottom of a wave in a wave train.

Dealing with Strainers

Strainers (see *page Aw-40*) are very dangerous hazards and should be avoided at all costs. If a swimmer is carried downstream toward one that cannot be avoided, it is essential to try to get on top of the strainer. It is almost impossible to assess if there will be a clear route under the strainer.

To maximize the chance of getting on top of the strainer, the swimmer should aggressively swim directly head-first toward the strainer. As contact is made with the strainer, the arms are used to pull the body up and over the strainer and the momentum generated used to lift the legs up and over the strainer. Clearly, swimming head-first at an identified hazard is a very high risk option. However, this method gives the swimmer the best chance of keeping his airway clear of the water, even if he is unable to fully clear the strainer.

Entrapments on strainers can occur even in very slow moving water.

Diagram Ops7: Practicing the strainer drill.

Eddy-line Roll

Good swiftwater swimmers will use the water to assist their every move. Features such as eddies (see *page Aw-28*) are useful as resting places, or as a place to exit the water.

When swimming into an eddy, the swimmer will have to overcome the force of the eddy line. One techniques for doing this is to swim at 90° to the eddy line and simply punch through.

A more advanced technique is an eddy line roll. Swimmers approach the eddy line from the main current and roll over the eddy line. They need to place an arm deep into the water in the eddy, acting as a brake and thus locking them into place. This method, when done correctly and at the correct time, can be highly effective and energy saving. Good swimmers will feel the water of the eddy line start to twist them, and rather than fighting it, will work with the water and roll with it into the eddy.

Notes

Notes

Shallow Water Techniques

Shallow water working techniques are a vital skill for the first responder.

There are various ways of moving in a shallow channel, either as an individual or as a team. By using these techniques, particularly the team methods, the safety of team members is increased.

Before attempting a shallow water technique, first responders should consider the following factors. All these factors interact, and no one factor will determine the success or failure of the crossing.

Depth

Water depth, if it can be determined, is a limiting factor. Clearly, shallow water techniques will only work in shallow water. Where possible, the water depth should be determined in relation to the shortest member of the team.

Speed

Water velocity is usually the most obvious danger. Even ankle-deep water can move fast enough to knock rescuers off their feet. For more information on water speed and the forces of water, page Aw-23.

Channel Bed

The surface under the water can pose many hazards to wading rescuers. An extremely smooth, slippery surface will severely limit the depth and speed of water that a rescuer can cope with. An uneven boulder-strewn channel bottom will provide many opportunities for rescuers to injure or entrap themselves.

Personnel

The technique to be used will be dependent on the number of trained personnel available.

Before starting to wade, personnel should consider all of the risks and hazards highlighted in the Water Awareness section of this manual. Generally as a group, hazards can be successfully negotiated due to the strength of the configuration and mutual support.

Single person crossings work well for an unavoidable situation, but it is far safer to cross with the support of others. Where possible, a pole of some sort should be used to feel the channel bed ahead of the rescuer.

Diagram Ops8: Single person crossing.

Group Wading Techniques

Notes

The group techniques "line abreast" and "line astern" both use the water to their advantage. The upstream person takes the force of the water while the others are in an eddy and can support the front person.

Diagram Ops9: Line abreast.

The line abreast technique works better in low energy environments where rescuers can expect a reasonably flat surface. Urban environments lend themselves to this technique. However, when carrying the pole, it can be difficult to check the ground ahead, leaving rescuers vulnerable to underwater hazards like open drains.

Line astern works well in faster-moving water as the rescuers can brace against the current by leaning forward on a wading pole and the pole can be used to probe for hazards in rough terrain.

Diagram Ops10: Line astern.

Notes

The wedge is a solid option for a team and can be used to carry injured persons in the center where they are sheltered and supported. The use of a litter basket keeps one hand free to balance against a teammate.

Diagram Ops11: Wedge crossing.

Diagram Ops12: Wedge crossing with litter.

Victims must ***never*** be tied into the litter basket during water operations and if possible, should be wearing a PFD. If the victim requires immobilization (in the case of a suspected spinal injury), then a different option is required for safe evacuation.

Tethered Crossings

Notes

When using shallow water crossing techniques, a tethering system may be used to help secure the rescuers. All rescuers who are committed to the water will have a rope tether attached to the cows-tail on the quick release chest harness on their PFD. This rope then runs back to a belayer who holds the end of the rope in a position of safety on the bank. Should the wading rescuers lose their footing, they are attached to a rope which will serve as a pendulum and swing them back to safety at the bank.

If this method is used with two rescuers, then it is possible to place a victim between them and cross the channel. If the rescuers lose their footing they assume a defensive swimming position and return to shore with the help of the belayed rope. The rescuer who is downstream of the victim during the crossing keeps hold of the victim throughout.

Diagram Ops13: Tethering.

The Clean Rope Principle

Notes

This is not a technique, but rather a way of thinking and operating. Very simply, if a rope is used near, on, or in the water, the clean rope principle dictates that there be no knots or loops tied into a rope which may cause an unintentional snag or chock. This is due to the fact that when a rope has been released into current, an accidental snag or chock will bring it to an abrupt halt. If this happens during the recovery of a rope it may be inconvenient (or even cause the rope to be lost), but if a rope snags or chocks when a person is entangled in it, the results can be fatal.

It is impossible to accomplish many of our rescue techniques without violating the clean rope principle, but we should attempt to follow it whenever possible. For example, anytime a line is crossing current, provisions must be in place for the system's quick release. When utilizing a tension diagonal (see "Tensioned Diagonal" on page Tech-41) this is best accomplished by releasing the downstream end, with no knots or loops (a clean rope). It should be noted that hitches are superior to knots whenever a quick, clean release is desired.

There are many that advocate the application of the clean rope principle to the use of throwbags. This is accomplished by removing knots and loops from the rescuer-held end of the throwbag rope. The advantages are obvious. If for any reason the rescuer releases the rope it will be less of a threat, although the bag itself remains a hazard. There are of course tradeoffs to be considered. A short loop in a figure 8 knot on the rescuer-held end of the line provides a superior gripping point for the rescuer and facilitates a quick-connection to another rope length. These features are highly prized by many experienced rescuers.

Concerning throwbags it is universally agreed that any loop on either the rescuer-held end, or on the bottom of the throwbag itself, must be very small. This will prevent anyone from slipping his or her hand through the loop, thereby risking entanglement. The bottom line is that ropes and moving water represent a dangerous mix, and the clean rope principle is one way the trained rescuer can help improve the odds.

Throwbag Rescues

Notes

The throwbag is a basic yet essential rescue tool for all rescuers working around the water. A throwbag rescue is a conditional rescue -- in order to be successful, victims must hold onto the rope that is thrown to them. However, many victims of swiftwater and flood incidents may be physically or psychologically unable to hold on to the throwbag.

Techniques for throwing the bag accurately and effectively must be practiced regularly to ensure skills are retained. The ability to throw a throwbag accurately, the ***first*** time, could be essential to a successful rescue. Consequently rescuers should practice several different methods of throwing throwbags to ensure that they are able to cope with different eventualities.

There are many different methods of throwing a throwbag. Generally people find that the underarm technique gives better accuracy, although less range. It can be useful if there are overhanging branches or lines.

Usually the overarm technique delivers more power and range but less accuracy. The overarm technique does not work well with overhead obstructions, but if throwing from a boat or with low level obstructions it is very effective.

Diagram Ops14: Underarm throwing technique.

Diagram Ops15: The bent-overarm or football technique.

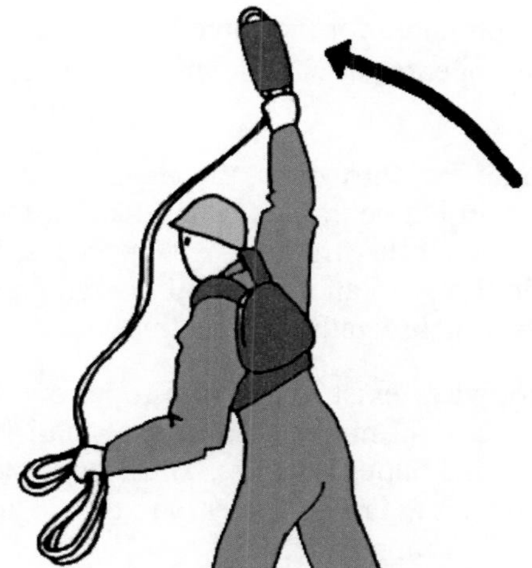

Diagram Ops16: The straight-overarm technique.

Notes

The sidearm technique is useful if there are obstructions both overhead and underfoot, but it can be difficult to aim accurately.

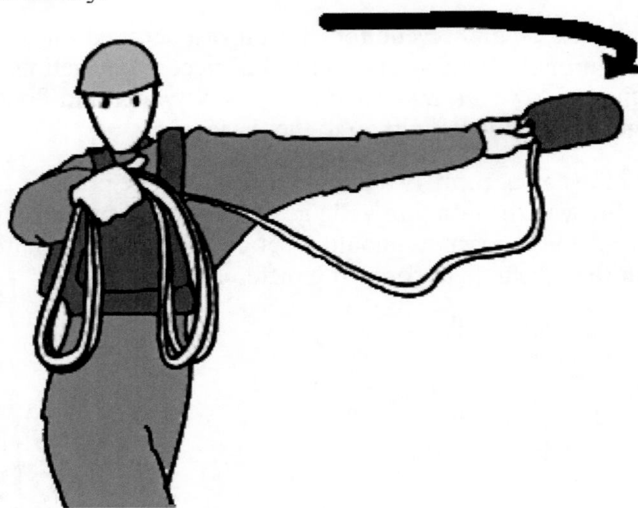

Diagram Ops17: Sidearm throwing technique.

Points to remember when using throwbags:

- Before you throw the bag, assess if there is a safe area downstream for the victim to pendulum (swing) into and to be recovered from.
- By removing some line from the bag before throwing, you allow yourself some spare rope that can be let out later if needed, to reduce the load or lower the victim further downstream.
- Shout or blow a whistle and make eye contact with victims to warn them you are about to throw them the rope.
- Aim at and beyond the victim. It is better for the bag to be on target and 10' past the victim than 3' too short.
- Be prepared for the force once the victim makes contact with the bag. Consider paying out rope, or moving downstream to reduce the shock, or brace your body well.

The rope may be thrown in the bag, which is usually more effective, more accurate and longer range. However if the first throw is unsuccessful (or a second throw to another victim is required) coils may be quickly gathered and thrown.

While many ways exist to coil the rope, one of the more successful methods is to use small lap coils (also called butterfly coils). These are quick to make, tend not to tangle, are easy to throw, and pose minimal entrapment risk.

Diagram Ops18: Making lap coils in preparation for line throw.

Belaying

Belaying simply means "controlling the rope". The rescuer may adopt one of several belaying options. The method adopted will depend upon many things including the terrain underfoot, the anticipated forces, the equipment available, and the number of personnel. Belayers should ensure that they are choosing a technique that is safe and appropriate for the task.

Notes

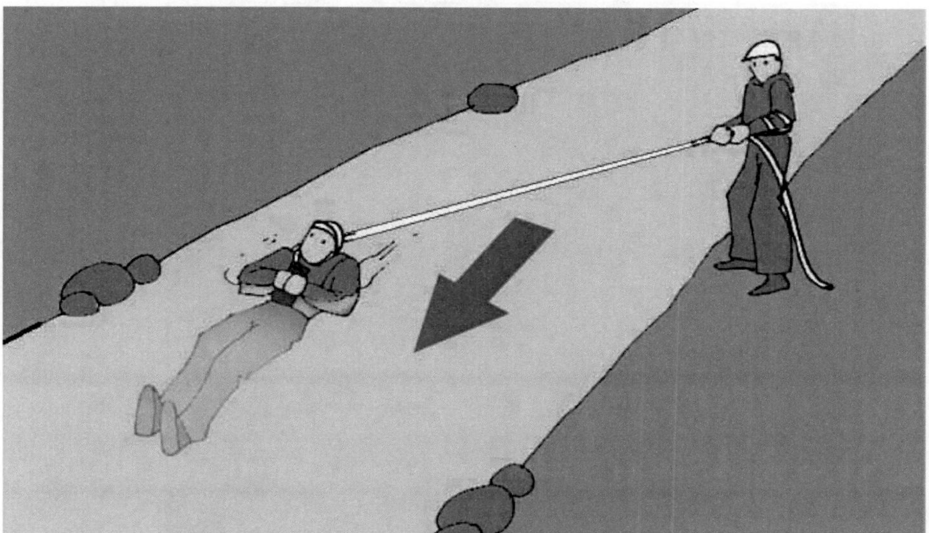

Diagram Ops19: An open bank allows the rescuer walk down the bank to perform a dynamic belay to minimize the forces on the victim.

Dynamic Belay

The dynamic belay involves belayers staying on their feet, bending their knees and bracing against the load on the rope. If required, the belayer is able to walk downstream steadily with the rope to reduce the force felt by victims as they pendulum into a safe eddy.

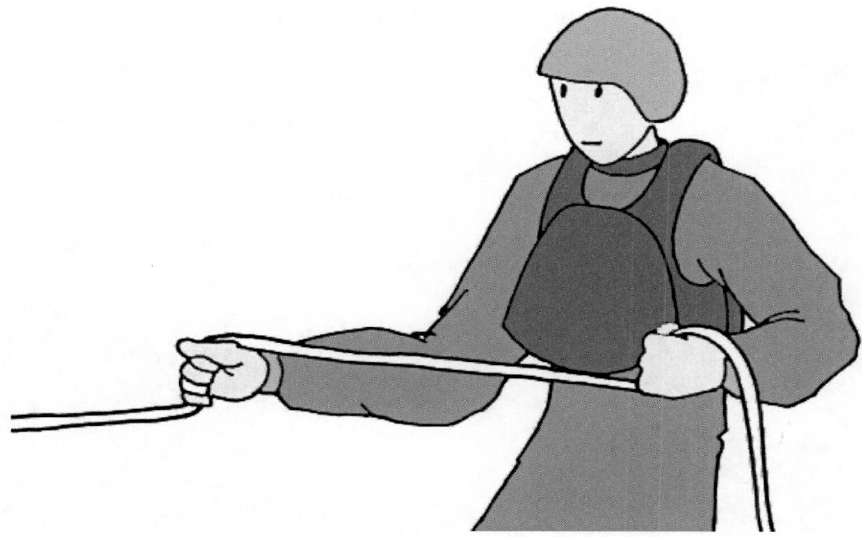

Diagram Ops20: The "Fireman's Grip" on the rope. This overhand grasping technique maximizes the grip strength of the rescuer, while ensuring they can release the rope cleanly at any time.

Notes

Sitting Belay

Alternatively, a static sitting belay may be used. This method is generally safer for the rescuer, although may result in a larger force on the rope for the victim. By having the rope wrapped around the body, with the loaded side upstream, it allows increased control by the rescuer, and will slightly increase the amount of friction on the rope.

Diagram Ops21: Sitting body belay.

Vector Pull

A vector or deviation pull may be used to retrieve the victim in certain circumstances. However, this will greatly increase the force applied to both the belayer and victim.

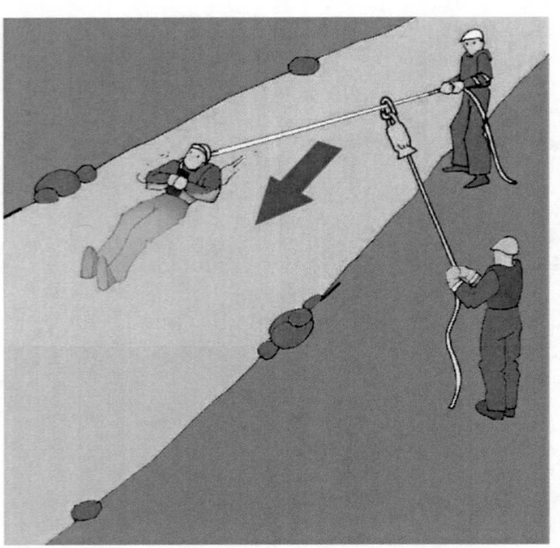

Diagrams Ops22 and Ops23: The setup and application of a vector pull.

Inflated Fire Hose Rescues

Notes

Fire and rescue services carry fire hoses and compressed air in abundance. By inflating a fire hose with the assistance of a control system (see *page Aw-65*), the rescuer can create a very versatile piece of water rescue equipment.

The hose can be used for the following techniques:

- Reaching aid
- Downstream diagonal
- Drop from a bridge
- Reach tool in a low head dam

It must be remembered, however, that the diagonal method is only usable on channels approximately 100' - 125' wide. Beyond this the diagonal is too long and becomes unusable. The speed of the water can also render this technique more or less effective.

Diagram Ops24: Inflated fire hose as a reach rescue.

Diagram Ops25: Inflated fire hose as downstream diagonal.

Notes

Diagram Ops26: Inflated fire hose dropped from bridge to upstream swimmer.

Diagram Ops27: Inflated fire hose into low head dam.

Looping Methods

All of the above inflated fire hose techniques are limited by reliance upon the victim. They are all conditional rescues (see page Aw-11). Victims must be able to hold on to the hose while they are pulled to safety. This is particularly difficult in moving water and compounded by the effect of immersion and cold (see *page Aw-76*).

The following two methods have been developed for moving water incidents. Both use a short length (10'-15') of inflated fire hose. The hose is attached to a floating rope in such a way that the hose will wrap around the victim and hold him in the loop of the hose. The reliance upon the participation of the victim is reduced, but not removed entirely.

Victims still need to lift their arms, so that the hose wraps around their chest. These methods are unlikely to work with unconscious victims.

Long Beach Method

Notes

Developed by the Long Beach Fire Department in California, this method has been successfully used for a number of rescues in high speed water drainage channels.

The key concept is that the end of the hose nearest to the bank has a pulley attached, and a floating rope is fed through this pulley. One end of the floating rope is then secured to the end of the hose furthest from the bank and the other end either tied off in such a way that it can be released under load, or given to a belayer. Clearly, a long length of floating rope is required.

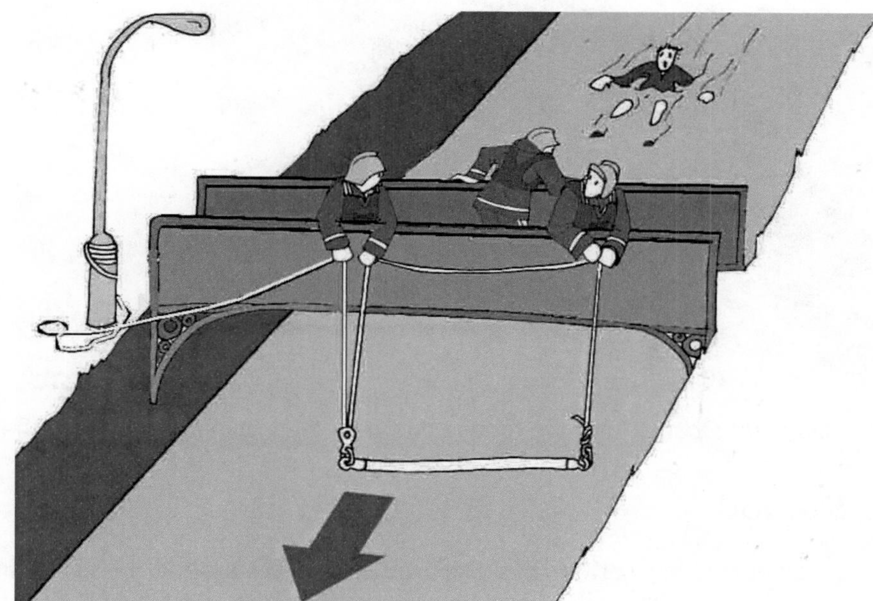

Diagram Ops28: Long Beach method.

Upstream spotters move as necessary so that they are always in line with the victim. The hose attendants move as needed to keep the upstream spotter in line with the middle of the inflated hose.

As the victim is about to go under the bridge, the upstream spotter shouts for him to raise his arms. To emphasize this, he raises his arms – this is the signal for the hose to be dropped onto the water. Once the victim is downstream of the bridge, the attendants drop the floating line upstream of the victim.

As the victim is carried downstream holding onto the hose, the rope system goes tight and wraps the hose around the victim. The whole system, secured to the bank or managed by a belayer, will pendulum toward the bank.

Notes

Diagram Ops29: After the rope is dropped, the victim is wrapped in the hose.

Charlotte Method

A similar method developed in Charlotte Fire Department, North Carolina. This uses three ropes to create the loop. There is no pulley in this system, so one rope goes to each end of the hose. The third rope goes from the far end of the hose to the bank. The advantage of this system, is that the length of rope required is a lot less. However, the forces experienced by the hose operators may be higher.

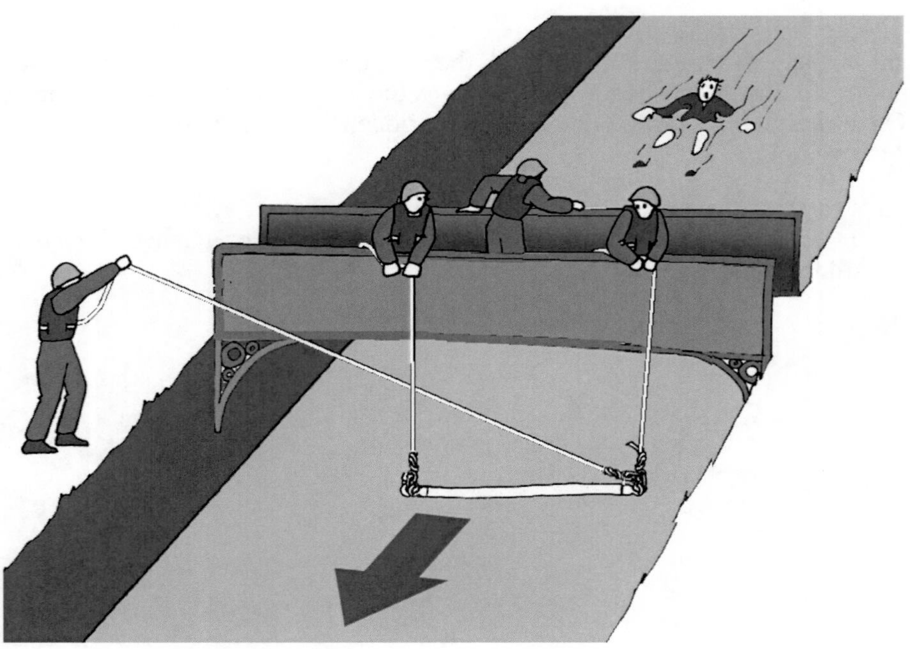

Diagram Ops30a: The setup for the Charlotte Method.

Notes

Diagram Ops30b: The catch. As the upstream spotter raises his arms, the rope handlers must retain hold of the rope to form the loop.

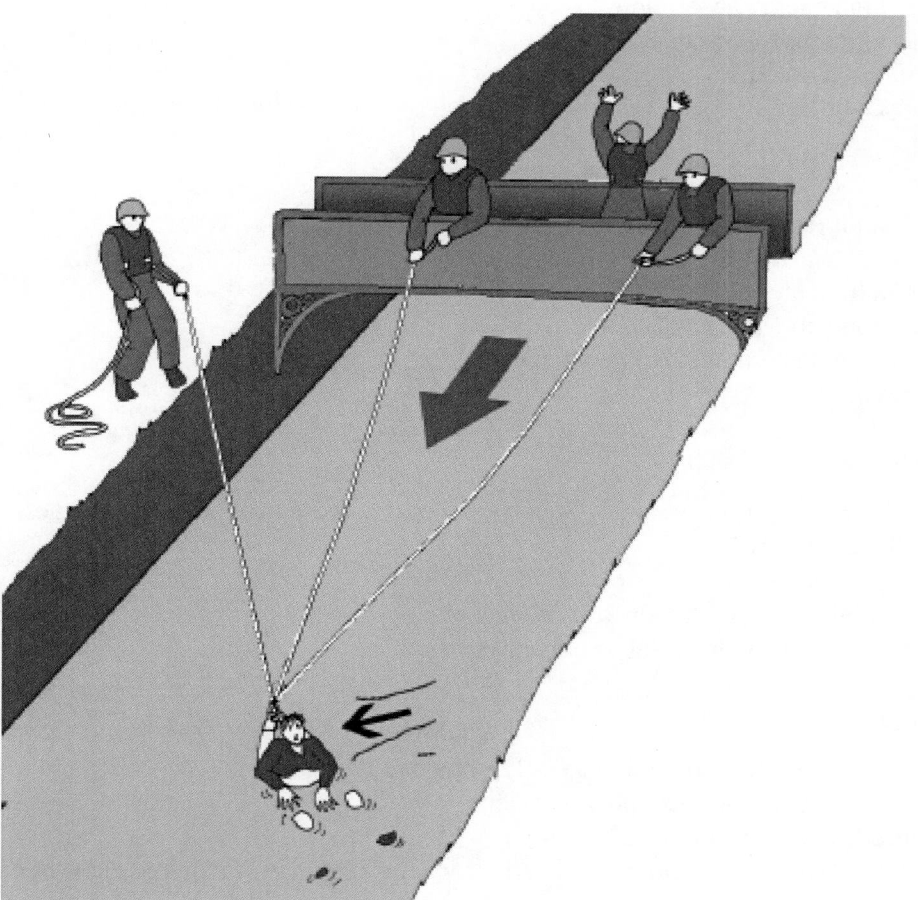

Diagram Ops30c: The recovery. The forces on the ropes will be at their highest as the victim swings in toward the bank.

Notes

Introduction to Technical Equipment

Proper use of the correct technical equipment is an integral part of many water rescue situations. By using a small amount of equipment and some basic techniques, a rescuer will be able to set up systems that may make a rescue much safer and more efficient.

Ropes

Ropes are used for a variety of applications in water rescue. It is essential to ensure that the correct type of rope is used for each application. The characteristics and properties of a rope will depend upon the method of construction and the materials from which it is made.

Rope Construction

Some common materials used in modern rope construction and their properties include:

Nylon

- Has high tensile strength
- Has high elasticity
- Has high energy absorption
- Has high impact resistance
- Softens at 446°F
- Does not float and can absorb water, which reduces its strength

Polyester

- Has high tensile strength
- Has low elasticity
- Has a high melting point (480°F)
- Has good abrasion resistance
- Has no reduction in strength when wet
- Does not float

Polypropylene

- Has strength is approximately 50% of nylon or polyester of the same thickness
- Will soften at 165°C
- Floats in water
- Has minimal strength reduction when wet
- Is not as abrasion resistant as polyethylene.

Polyethylene

- Has about 5% less strength than polypropylene
- Is about 5% heavier than polypropylene
- Has a low melting point (280°F)
- Is often used in non-critical applications where buoyancy is required e.g water skiing tow ropes

Notes

Aramids e.g. Kevlar

- Is resistant to high temperatures
- Has very high tensile strength
- Has very low stretch (1.5-3% stretch at failure)
- Has poor shock absorbing ability
- Does not float
- Is increasingly used in winching operations

HMPE (High Modulus Polyethylene) e.g Spectra, Dyneema

- Is very strong
- Has very low stretch (2.7-3.5% stretch at failure)
- Has poor shock absorbing properties
- Has a low melting point (275°F)
- Floats and has no reduction in strength when wet
- Is very slippery and does not hold knots well.

Kernmantle

Most modern ropes for water and rope rescue are "kernmantle" in construction. This German word means core (kern) and sheath (mantle). The central core of fibers provides the majority of the rope's strength, and these fibers are protected by a woven sheath.

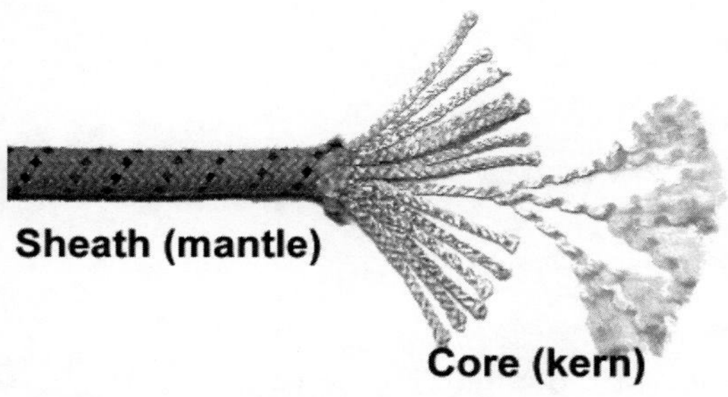

Diagram Ops31: Kernmantle rope construction.

The sheath provides a lesser portion of the strength, but also protects the core from abrasion, dirt and UV damage.

This construction method produces ropes that are strong, resistant to damage, and easy to handle. Some ropes found in throwbags can be of a braided construction as opposed to kernmantle construction.

Knots and Strength Loss

The fibers in ropes, in the kern and in the mantle, are oriented to line up with the length of the rope for maximum strength. The measure of this strength is commonly referred to as "tensile strength." The fibers have low flexural strength, meaning they are not strong along their horizontal axis, which is why ropes lose significant amounts of strength when tied in knots.

This loss of strength occurs when a rope is bent, as when tied in a knot or going through a carabiner or pulley. Four inches is the magic number for maintaining full strength in a rope. Any bend tighter than four inches reduces the rope's strength. Common knots used in rescue situations can reduce a rope's strength by 20-40%.[1]

1 NRS: *Know the Ropes* www.nrsweb.com

Notes

Floating Rope – Types and Usage

For water rescue, ropes that float are essential. They are easier to work with, and greatly reduce the possibility of entanglements with in-water objects.

Throwbag Rope

Most throwbag ropes are constructed from polypropylene in bright colors. This provides a high visibility rope that is soft to handle (packs well into the throwbag) and floats well. However, the NPFA also specifies that throwbag rope consist of low stretch or static line with a diameter of 7 mm (19/64") - 9.5 mm (3/8"). The NPFA also specifies a minimum breaking strength of not less than 13 kN (2923 lbf).

Throwbag ropes are not designed for use in hauling or high tension applications. Due to the low melting point, they should only be used in conjunction with rope grabs and prusik knots with extreme caution.

Combination Water Rescue Rope

A number of specialist water rescue ropes are now available that mix construction materials to create specialist properties for water rescue work. These water rescue ropes are designed for in-water use only and not for high angle work and rescue applications.

Nylon sheath / polypropylene core

Sheath provides abrasion resistance and core provides flotation.

Polypropylene sheath / HMPE core

Core material provides extra strength.

Water rescue ropes are now available that glow in the dark for low light rescue work.

Non-Floating Rope – Types and Usage

Water rescue also utilizes non-floating rope for tensioned systems and high line applications. These ropes will be almost exclusively made from nylon.

Notes

Static Rope

These are "low stretch" ropes commonly used for rope access and rope rescue applications. The definition of "static rope" is rope with a maximum elongation of 6% at 10% of its minimum breaking strength.

Their strength and relatively low stretch characteristics make these ropes ideal for high load applications such as tensioned diagonal and vector systems. Generally rescue rope is 11mm (7/16") - 12.5 mm (1/2") in diameter. While 11 mm rope is easier to work with and lighter to carry, any highline systems should be constructed with 12.5 mm rope in keeping with NFPA Standards on life safety rope.

Dynamic Rope

Dynamic line is also available, but it is designed for use by climbers and mountaineers and so stretches considerably in order to cope with the dynamic created by falling. It is not used in water rescue applications. It is not used in water rescue and could present a serious safety hazard.

It is not possible to tell from a visual inspection whether a rope is a dynamic, semi-static, or specialist water rescue rope because all 3 types can look and feel the same, and be the same color. Proper recording, marking, and logging of rope is required to avoid potentially lethal confusion.

Accessory Cord

Non-floating low stretch rope is available in a variety of smaller diameters for use as accessory cords and applications such as making prusik loops. The rule of thumb in choosing cord for prusik loops is that the cord should be approximately 60-80% of the diameter of the main line. Given that water rescuers primarily use 11mm - 12.5mm main line, prusik loops are generally made from 6 mm (1/4") - 8 mm (5/16") cord.

Webbing

Most webbing is made from nylon or polyester and due to its characteristics it may be preferential to rope in certain applications. It is cheaper than rope and due to its wide, flat surface it is less susceptible to abrasion[1]. There are fewer secure knots for use in webbing (normally a water knot is used) and as a result it is common to use pre-sewn webbing slings.

1 www.hse.gov.uk/research/crr_pdf/2001/crr01364.pdf

Notes

Use of Rope Protection

Ropes and webbing are highly susceptible to damage when rubbing on edges and rough objects, especially when under tension. Wherever ropes are at risk of damage, they should be protected. A variety of specially designed protectors are used, plus more general material such as canvas and salvage sheets. Testing undertaken has suggested that some of the best rope protection performance was achieved with canvas, which was also one of the cheapest materials.

Care of Ropes, Storage, and Recording

Ropes should be dried after use and then stored in a cool dry location away from light. If needed, ropes can be washed according to the manufacturer's recommendations. The life of a rope will be determined by how well it is cared for and the use it has had. Rope usage needs to be logged and each rope should have its own identification code, marking, and rope log.

The general rule is that ropes should be used for up to a maximum of five years once issued (unless condition or usage dictates an earlier retirement). Additionally, the rope can be stored for up to five years before being issued. This means that if a rope is purchased and stored but never issued and used, it should still be retired and destroyed after ten years.

Rope Log		
Rope ID:		
Diameter:		
Length:		
Make:		
Model:		
Color:		
Purchased From:		
Purchase Date:		
Date in Service:		
Batch Number:		
Serial Number:		
Date	**Use / Inspection**	**Name**

Table: Example of rope log sheet.

Technical Hardware

Carabiners

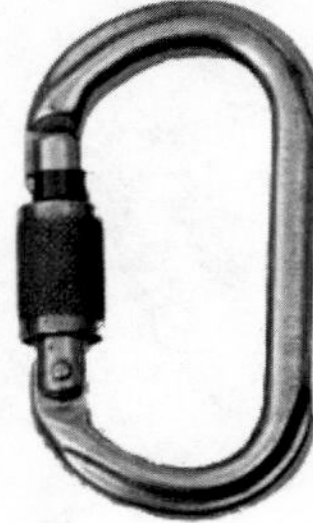

Diagram Ops32: Carabiners from left to right. Bent snap gate, Oval screwgate, D shaped screwgate, Pear-shaped screwgate

Carabiners are metal connectors that are used to clip together ropes, slings, webbing, etc. Carabiners come in many shapes and sizes. They are made from steel or aluminum alloy.

Steel has the advantages of being stronger and cheaper than aluminium alloy, but has the disadvantage of being prone to rust.

Aluminium alloy carabiners have an excellent strength-to-weight ratio and are generally used for water rescue applications. Although they do not rust, they are susceptible to corrosion, especially if exposed to salt water.

Carabiners are available as either snap gate or locking gate designs. As the name suggests, locking gate carabiners have a locking mechanism on the opening gate. This makes them safer for use in safety critical applications, such as clipping a rope to a quick release.

There are a number of designs for this locking mechanism, ranging from traditional screwgates to more modern twist lock designs. Screwgates require the user to manually lock the gate closed whereas 'twist lock' systems will automatically do so.

It is important that carabiners are used correctly to ensure they are used to their full strength. The load should be applied along the major axis with the gate locked. This ensures the carabiner maintains its full strength.

NFPA 1983 sets standards for carabiners and will have a stamp right on the hardware if the hardware is compliant. This means that approved carabiners will cost more than other, similar ones from the same manufacturer. It is up to the AHJ whether or not to purchase NFPA-approved hardware.

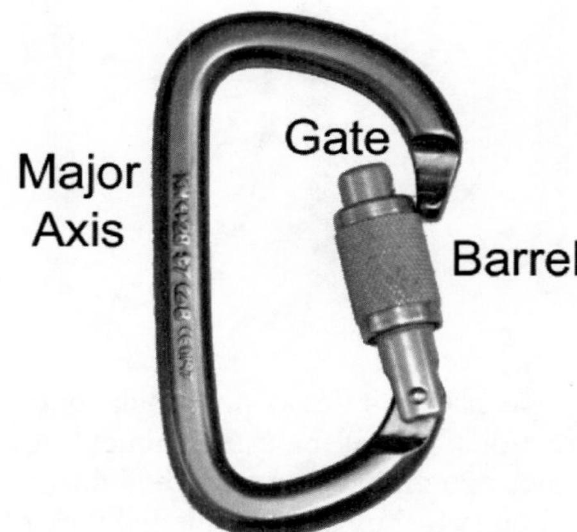

Diagram Ops 33: Locking carabiner

Notes

Belay Devices

Diagram Ops34: From left to right; Münter Hitch, Eight Plate, Belay Plate, Petzl GriGri, Petzl I'D

The above-pictured devices are used to control a rope under load, and are often referred to as belay devices or friction devices. In water rescue these devices can be used in a number of situations including tensioning lines and controlling the movement of boats. There are many variations available but whichever method is used to control a rope, it is essential the manufacturer's instructions are followed.

Rope Grabs

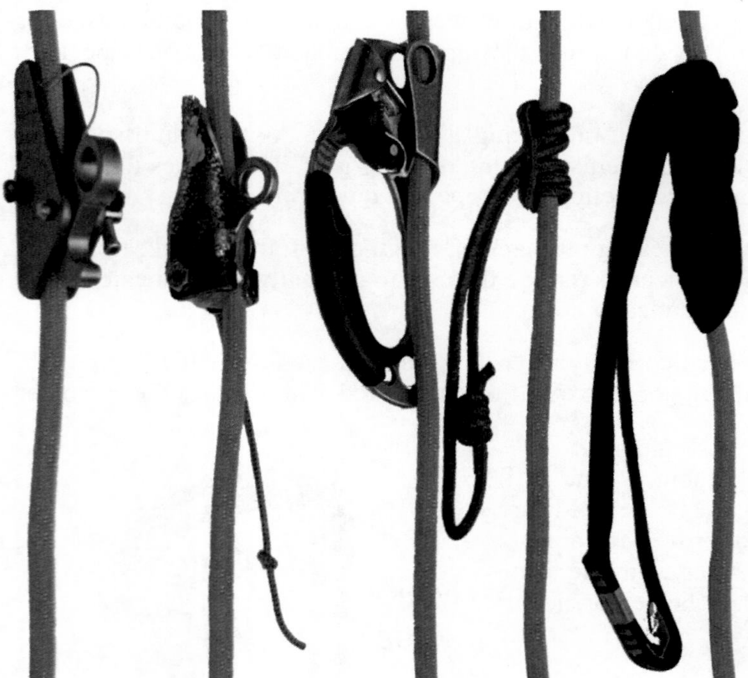

Diagram Ops35: (From left to right) Petzl Rescuecender, Petzl Shunt, Handled Ascender, Triple Wrap Prusik, Klemheist Prusik

A rope grab is a device that locks onto the rope to grip against a pulling force from one or both directions. It may be a mechanical device, or a non-mechanical device such as a prusik hitch. Some rope grabs have a toothed design. These are generally designed for use of a single person load only. If they are overloaded they can cause critical rope damage.

Notes

Pulleys

Diagram Ops36: Petzl Pulleys: (top row, from left to right) Mini, Fixe, Gemini; (bottom row, from left to right) Twin, Rescue, Tandem, Minder

A pulley is a wheeled device that is used to reduce friction when the rope changes direction. There are a wide variety of designs and shapes for use in particular applications such as prusik minding, knot passing and tandem pulleys.

Notes

Rope Systems

There are several rope systems that can be used for providing support during shallow water crossings, or perhaps more usefully to transport equipment. These are commonly known as the pendulum system and the continuous loop system and each has advantages and disadvantages. It should be emphasized that these are for use in shallow water only and that no one should be tied into these systems. If a rope is to be attached to a person in the water it must only be connected to a quick release chest harness on his PFD.

Continuous Loop

This system does not comply with the clean rope principle (see *page Ops-12*). It uses a length of floating rope tied to make a loop, or is often made from a number of throwbags tied together. It therefore needs to be operated with caution and nobody should be attached to the rope. This method should not be used if the ropes are required for support.

The loop means that once contact is established with the victim, it is difficult to lose, which is a significant advantage. By moving the rope in one direction equipment and people can be moved across channels, or to and from a stranded car, etc. This simplicity of operation is particularly useful at night. A general rule is that the length of rope used to make the loop should be twice the distance across which it is to operate.

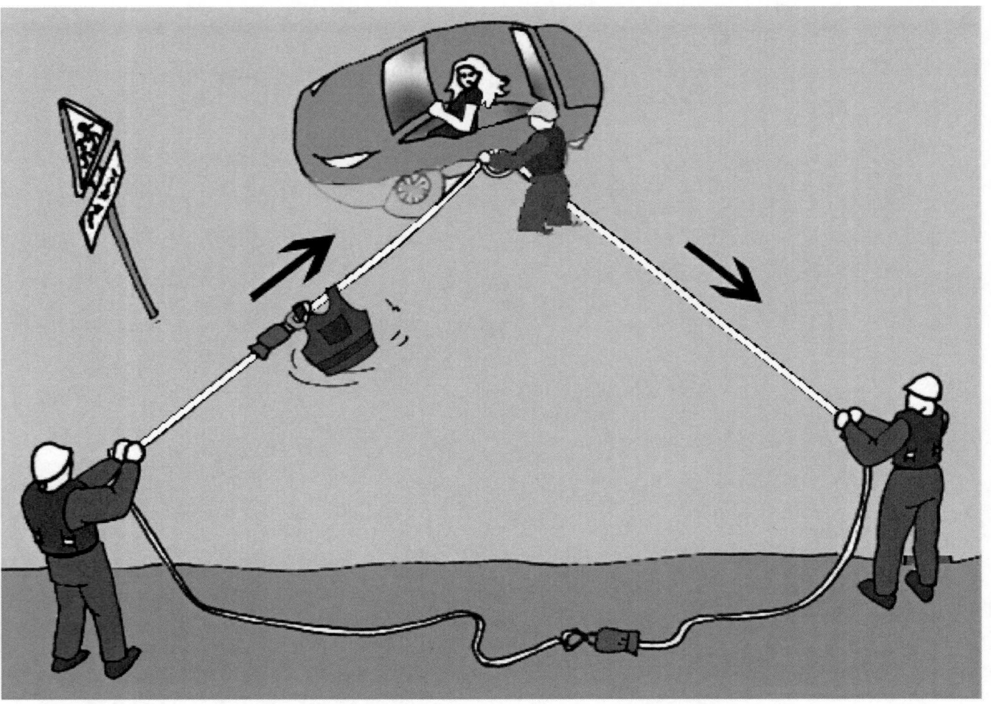

Diagram Ops37: Continuous loop system.

Pendulum System

Notes

This system uses two separate lengths of floating rope to help responders cross a channel or access a midstream object in shallow water. The advantage is that the system maintains clean rope but it can be a little more complex to operate and if the wrong rope is let go it can break down and must be rebuilt.

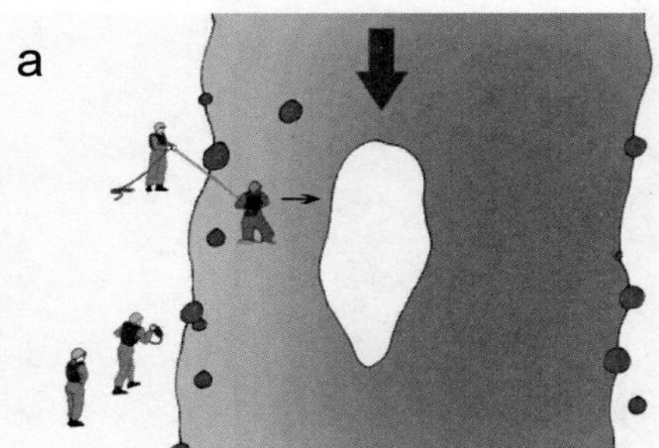

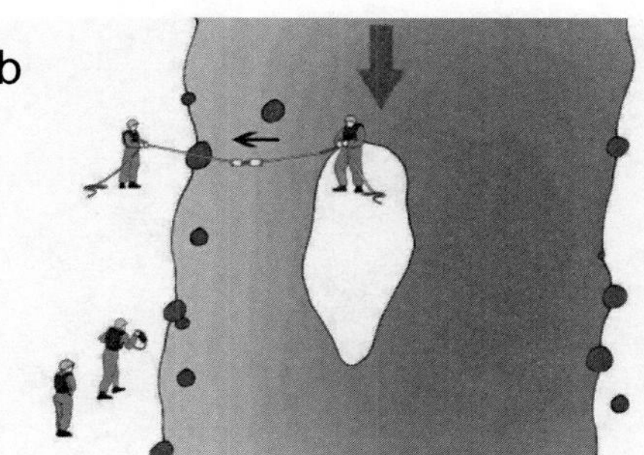

These initial two stages of setup are commonly used for setting up other rope systems, such as tensioned diagonals and boat tethers. The first rescuer will wade across, in order to get the first rope across the channel. Often this first stage is the most difficult part of the whole sequence.

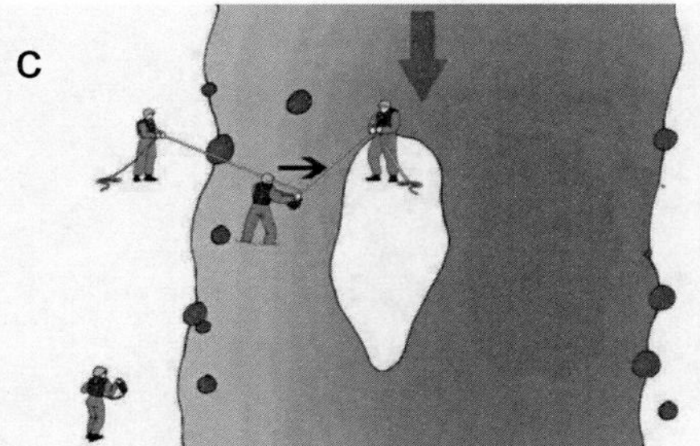

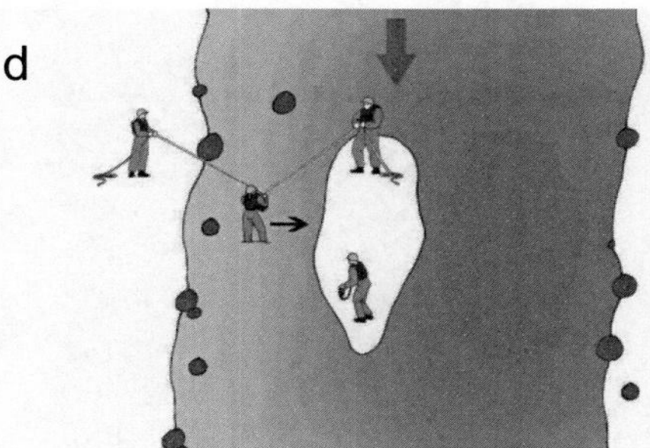

As with the setup, often the break-down of this system is used to get the final rescuer across a channel at the end of a tensioned diagonal and other rope systems.

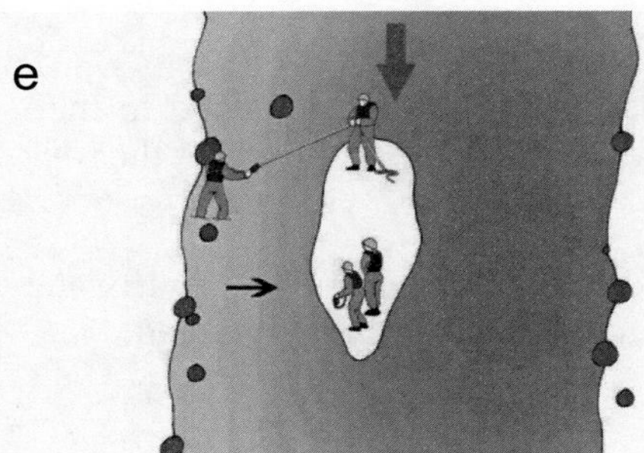

Diagrams Ops38 a-e: Moving personnel and equipment using a pendulum system.

Notes

Tensioned Diagonal Rope Systems

By using basic technical rope equipment, a rescue team can construct a tensioned diagonal rope system quickly and easily, which will be useful in many situations.

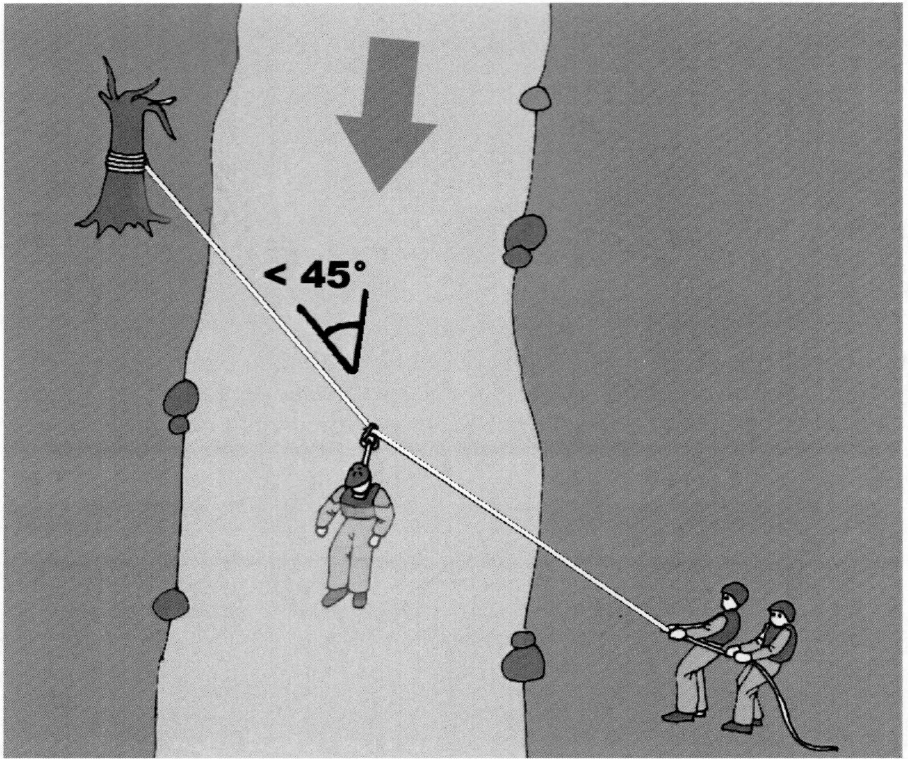

Diagram Ops39: Tensioned diagonal rope system.

Generally, the downstream end of the diagonal is either hand-held or secured using a no-knot. This ensures the system is releasable if required, such as if a rescuer becomes stuck on the rope, or slack develops, preventing the diagonal from working effectively. The upstream end is where the rope can be tensioned, using either hauling or mechanical advantage.

To traverse this system, rescuers may be clipped to the rope via a cows-tail attached to their quick release chest harness, or by holding on to a short length of webbing tape clipped to the rope using a carabiner.

The rigging of tensioned diagonal rope systems would need to be managed by a Swiftwater Rescue Technician®. However, first responders can be active members of the rigging team.

Notes

Low Angle Litter Management

Responders may find themselves carrying a stretcher or litter across flat or gently sloping ground. Low angle slopes are generally those where the ground is steep enough for a person still to be able to walk up with care and effort, but not end up tumbling down should he slip. Rescuers must be very careful when carrying victims over this ground, and treat it with respect.

Techniques for controlling a litter are:

Talus Belay

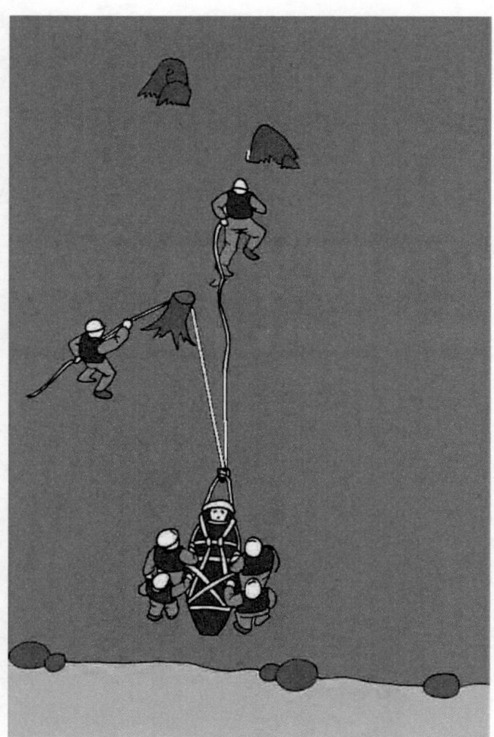

Diagram Ops40a and Ops40b: Talus belay moving up-hill

This system works well, as the litter is secured using a rope belay. The belayers have to work quickly to maintain progress. Obviously, this method requires conveniently placed anchors. Effective communications are essential to ensure that the stretcher always has at least one belay in place. At no point should the stretcher be without a belay.

Notes

Diagram: Ops41: Caterpillar.

Caterpillar

Here the rescuers move up or down the slope, or past obstacles, while not holding the litter. The litter is slid through their hands when they are in position, similar to a conveyor belt. This reduces the chance of the stretcher being dropped, and also reduces the risk of injury to a rescuer.

Change of Direction

Often it is more convenient to manage the rope on a path or road running along the watercourse at the top of the bank. By using a change of direction the hauler can move easily along the path at 90 degrees to the direction of travel of the load as it ascends the bank. A simple 2:1 mechanical advantage system *(see page Tech-37)* and a brake prusik *(see page Tech-29)* can also be incorporated if needed.

Diagram Ops42: Change of direction with 2:1 mechanical advantage.

Notes

Tethered Boat Systems

Systems can be rigged to enable a boat to be moved from one point to another without the need for continual paddling. These two or four point systems are useful in slower flowing water to gain access and to provide transportation for rescuers, equipment, or victims. They may also be used to "pick off" (rescue) a victim from a vehicle, mid stream rock, or low head dam.

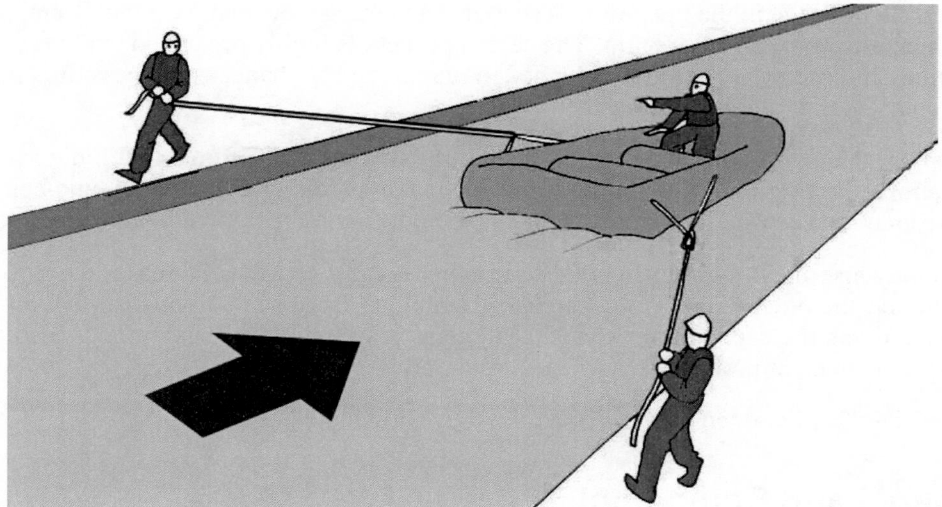

Diagram Ops43: Two point boat tether.

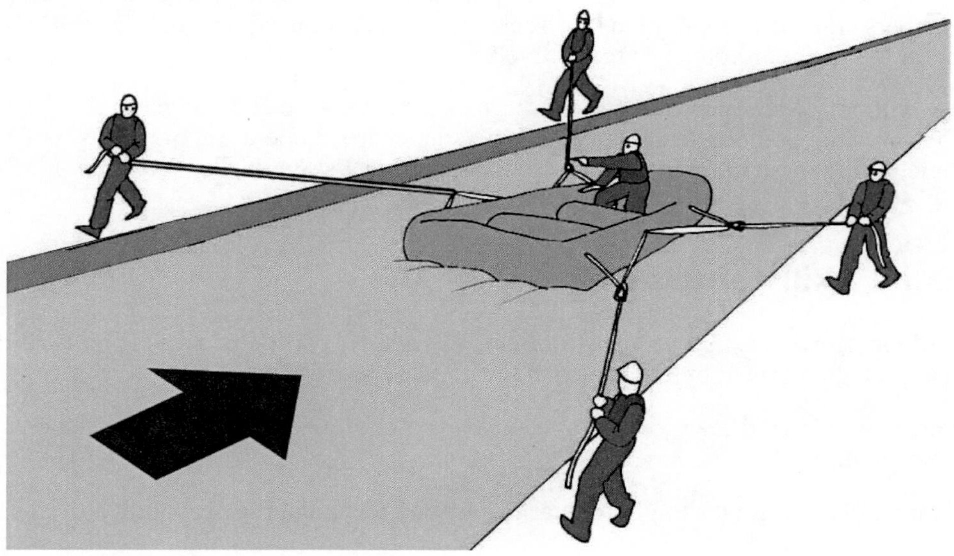

Diagram Ops44: Four point boat tether.

The four point system requires more rope, people and time to set up; however, it provides more control, particularly to the downstream end of the boat. Additionally, the boat can be held in a ferry angle position which assists with the crossing of the current.

The overall rigging and operation of a tethered boat system is the responsibility of Swiftwater Rescue Technicians®. However, the individual control ropes may be operated by first responders under supervision.

Notes

Searching Rivers and Floods

Foundation Knowledge

The first stage of a swiftwater or flood rescue is to locate the victim. In many cases this can be the most difficult stage in the operation. A search is an emergency—an individual is missing and could potentially come to more harm. The search process is highly organized, and very rational. Search areas and routes are carefully planned to maximize the chance of success. It is important that searchers stick to their assignment.

Natural river channels and flooded areas have a massive number of potential hiding places. In addition, limited access and fast moving water can make searching difficult and time-consuming. Many victims of swiftwater and flood accidents are not found for a considerable length of time.

Searches may also be at night or in adverse weather conditions. This increases the difficulty of the search and the potential risks to searchers. Searching large-scale floods can be a multi-day operation and has the capacity to exhaust searchers. Searching large-scale floods also presents particular management problems.

Searching rivers and flooded areas will require the following:

Personnel and Equipment

In-water and next-to-water searching will require specifically trained and equipped searchers. Only searchers trained to Operations or Technician level wearing appropriate PPE should be searching in the warm or hot zones respectively.

Searchers without swiftwater training can be used, but they need to be carefully managed to ensure they are not operating in a risk zone. If personnel are to operate at night they need to have had sufficient training in night operations, such as Rescue 3's *Swiftwater Technician - Advanced* course.

Specialist Skills and Capability

Specialist boat crews may be needed to effectively search particular areas. The type of boats required will be determined by the nature of the area to be searched.

Helicopters can be a vital search tool but can also present operational limitations and so should not be relied upon.

Steep terrain and river gorges might require teams with technical rope capability.

The use of search dog teams can be highly effective.

Communication

Effective communication systems are vital. If radio communication can be established, then it is generally the preferred option. Radios need to be protected from water, and specialist dry-bags are available for this purpose. Differences in radio systems between agencies can mean there

is difficulty in communication between teams from different agencies. Recent developments include small GPS trackers that can be given to individual teams, and their exact locations can then be relayed to the search control.

Notes

Lighting

Effective lighting is required to:

- Identify the location of searchers – chemical light sticks attached to the searchers' PFDs and helmets are highly effective and relatively cheap.
- Allow the searchers to see where they are going – waterproof head lamps are ideal for this purpose and most can be helmet-mounted.
- Allow the searchers to effectively search – this requires the use of handheld waterproof spotlights. These may be of limited battery life, thus limiting a teams' operational time.

Search Methods

Operations level rescue personnel may be called upon to search the warm zone in a swiftwater or flood incident. Searching is a lot more complicated than just walking along the water's edge looking for something. Active searching is mentally tiring and physically hard work. To enter the warm zone, proper PPE must be worn at all times and searchers should be provided with support.

The search area cannot be so challenging that searchers are just concentrating on staying out of trouble themselves. If searchers are being heavily taxed just to travel through the area, then they are not searching. The environment must be within the capabilities and experience of the search team.

Several methods of searching a river corridor have been developed by many different agencies, and local protocols will apply. However, the concepts are generally the same.

Searchers should imagine they are in the center of a cube. They must look ahead in the near distance, middle distance, and far distance. At each distance from themselves, they must look to the left, right, forward, backward, down and up. The size of the cube is going to vary depending on the terrain and environment. Ideally, a searcher's cube will overlap with the next searcher to ensure there is no chance of missing an area.

Searcher

This person is dressed in full water PPE but with minimal additional equipment. He is free to move wherever he needs to in order to search the river bank.

Backup

This person is also dressed in full water PPE with minimal additional equipment. His task is to ensure the safety of the searcher. He will be moving from safe location to safe location (eg. upstream of an eddy). Normally, he will be ready with a throwbag at all times, in case the searcher falls into the water.

Notes

Administration

This person does not have to be in PPE if he is able to remain in the cold zone. His task is to look after the searcher and the backup. He will navigate, use the radio, carry equipment, and so on. His job is to free up the searcher to search, and the backup to look after the searcher.

This system works well and can progress in an upstream direction relatively smoothly. However to move downstream, progress is slightly slower. The backup must first locate themselves in a downstream position, and only when they are in place, will the searcher begin to move downstream, searching as they go. The searcher stops when he meets the backup. Then the backup moves to a new location.

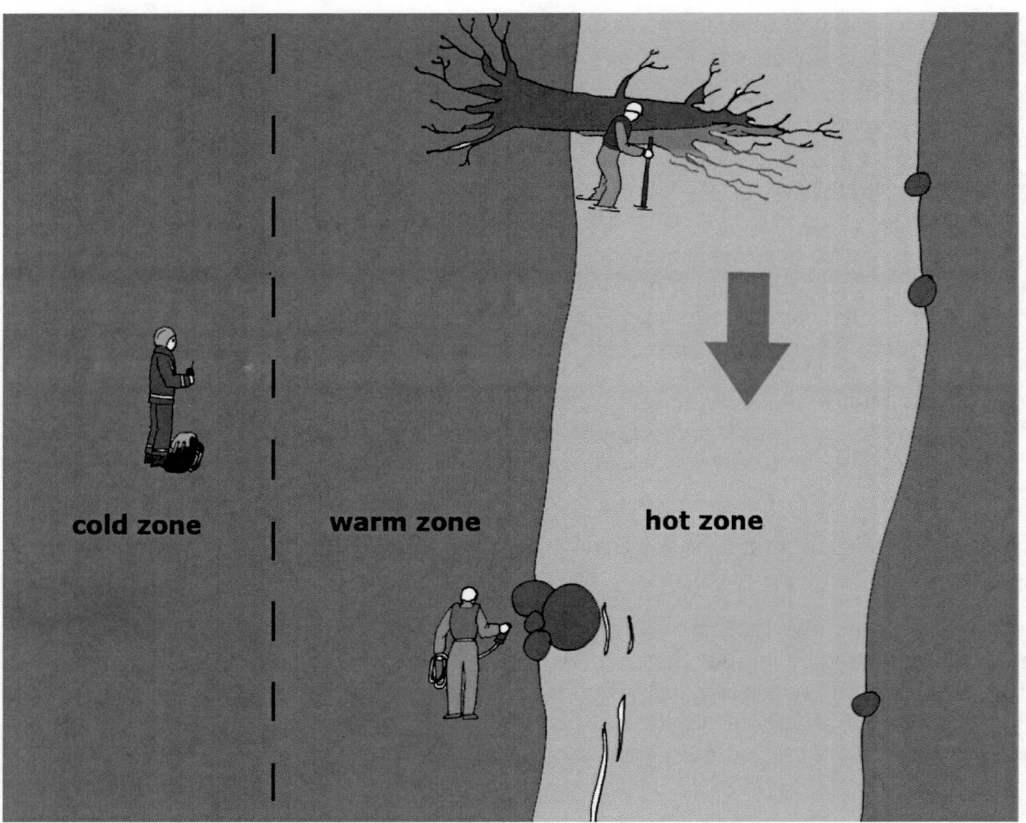

Diagram Ops45: Searching the hot zone with an administrator in the cold zone and downstream in place in the warm zone..

Operating in Poor Visibility

Notes

Working in swiftwater and floods at night and in poor visibility (e.g fog, very heavy rainfall) presents particular problems both in terms of risk to rescuers and effectiveness of rescue techniques.

Lighting

Provision of effective lighting is critical.

Personal Waterproof Lighting for Rescuers

This is generally achieved through the use of a helmet-mounted head lamp. Additionally, rescuers should be equipped with a helmet-mounted chemical lightstick (cyalume). These provide a constant marker light, some of which can last for up to 12 hours and are ideal for locating people and equipment. Reflective patches on drysuits, PFDs and helmets also help ensure rescuers are as visible as possible.

Lighting the Downstream & Operational Areas

Effective lighting must be provided for both the downstream area where the backup team(s) will operate and the operational area. This may be achieved through the use of floodlights attached to batteries or small generators, use of vehicle headlights, or hand-held search lights. Care must be taken in locating the lights to provide an overall illumination but not to blind any rescuers or victims through glare.

Lighting of Equipment

Throwbags, inflated fire hoses etc. can all be made more visible by attachment of chemical light sticks and reflective material patches. Small items such as carabiners and pulleys benefit from being marked with reflective tape. New developments, such as floating rope with a reflective tracer are now available. Boats must be well lit.

Training

If first responders are to operate at night, then they need to undertake familiarization training at night. Swiftwater rivers and floods are a much riskier environment in the dark and the chance of injury is increased. Rescue techniques should be practiced in the dark so that rescuers appreciate the difficulties of applying them in this environment. Effective downstream backup is critical for night operations. An in-water night exercise is included in the Rescue 3 Swiftwater Rescue Technician® Advanced course.

Communications

Reduced visibility can make it very difficult to communicate among team members and between teams on a rescue site. Hand signals may not be possible, and so an increased emphasis may need to be placed on whistle signals, radios, or the use of light signals (for example, flashing head lamps).

Notes

Notes

Swiftwater Rescue Technician®

Notes

Swiftwater Rescue Team Roles

In order for a Technician-level swiftwater or flood rescue team to operate efficiently, it should consist of the following team roles:

Team Leader

Responsible for determining the actions of the team. Responsible for incident size-up and team briefing. During the operation the team leader has a hands-off role to maintain an overall view of the situation as it develops and to plan for subsequent stages of the operation.

Rigger(s)

Responsible for setting up any technical systems that may be required. They will also be belaying ropes when the rescue is in operation.

Logistics

Responsible for managing team equipment and ensuring it is available where and when it is needed. They may also be tasked with maintaining lines of communication between team members.

Rescuer(s)

Team members who make contact with the victim(s). For example, they might be the swimmers in a swim rescue, or in a boat during a tethered boat rescue of people trapped on a car in moving water.

Medic

Will provide specialist medical support for both victims and other team members.

Smaller or Larger Variations

For teams with limited members, it is common for team members to take on multiple roles. For example a single person might provide logistics support as well as specialist medical support, or a rigger might set up a system and then take on another role once the system is operational.

At major incidents, teams must operate within a more formal Incident Command Structure (ICS) to ensure that such events are effectively managed. Large flood incidents will require responses from many different agencies. As such, a multi-agency incident command structure will need to be implemented.

See *page Aw-48* for more information on Incident Command.

Notes

Tactical Decision Making - The TEMPO Model

Tactical Decision Making During Swiftwater & Flood Emergencies

Adapted from an article by Battalion Chief Tim Rogers, Charlotte Fire Department, North Carolina, USA & Rescue 3 International Instructor Trainer

For many years, rescuers have used a traditional tactical model for water rescue events. This model was originally based on low risk to high risk methods of rescue. That tactical model is:

Talk — Reach — Throw — Row — Go/Tow — Helo

This model was often seen as a hierarchy of rescue - a mantra to be followed without question.

The Tactical Toolbox

However, the concept of a toolbox of rescue options introduced on *page Aw-11* recommends using the tactic that best suits the situation, rather than wasting time and resources by beginning with tactics destined to fail because of the particular circumstances of the incident (just because they come first in the "list"). For example, if victims are unconscious, attempting to rescue them using conditional rescue techniques such as "talk", "reach" or "throw" is not going to work no matter how skilled the rescuer.

Instead, the T.E.M.P.O. decision-making model puts the tools or tactics on an equal footing and allows the appropriate rescue strategy to be quickly identified and put into action.

A tactical decision-making model is of the most value to a new rescuer, because as experience is gained, the process will begin to occur subconsciously, through a natural flow of information and observation. The tactical decision-making model will also provide experienced rescuers with a framework against which to evaluate their decisions.

Goals of TEMPO

The TEMPO size-up model was developed ***specifically*** for swiftwater and flood rescue. Its goals are two-fold:

1. Provide rescuers with a checklist of those things that can influence the method used to rescue someone from the aquatic environment
2. Assist in the selection of the tactic that is most appropriate in the given circumstances.

Notes

Factors Affecting Decision Making

T	Time and Temperature
E	Energy and Equipment
M	Movement and Measurement
P	Plan and Personnel
O	Operations

Time and Temperature

Swiftwater and flood rescuers are almost always up against time and temperature. The time of day dictates how much daylight is available and the corresponding drop in temperature that arrives at dusk.

Time is never more critical than when air and water temperatures are low. Consider how much time it will take for the victim to succumb to fatigue and whether hypothermia (or heat related injury) could shorten this even further.

Remember that immersion in cold, still water cools the victim's body four times faster than exposure to air. Further, hypothermia based on immersion exposure undermines a victim's ability to use fine motor skills and/or think clearly.

Once victims are injured or hypothermic it may be impossible for them to assist in their own rescue. This single factor may limit tactical choices to true rescues, eliminating many of the rapid, low risk and low-tech tactics. It is hard enough to swim while shivering or injured and even more difficult to grab a rope and hold on in current. Making matters worse, the rescuers themselves are subject to the effects of time and temperature, as it will diminish their ability to function physically and mentally.

Response time is also to be considered as accessing remote locations adds precious minutes or hours to the movement of personnel and equipment.

Rescue as it relates to time has four stages:

- Activation/response time
- Set up time
- Rescue/completion time
- Recovery time

Notes

Energy and Equipment

Water flowing down a gradient is constant, relentless and fortunately, predictable. Even so it remains a truly dynamic environment where rescuers must be keen on matching the proper tactics and equipment with existing conditions. Rescuers must possess the necessary knowledge and practical understanding of hydrology and flow dynamics. Understanding current vector, laminar flow, helical flow, hydraulics, load, strainers, and eddies will enable rescuers to make better choices with regards to rescue tactics while keeping themselves safe. Furthermore, rescuers must have a full understanding of the capabilities and limitations of their water rescue equipment, as well as what assets are available through aid agreements.

Movement and Measurement

Water rescue sites are basically six-sided problems consisting of river left and right (as determined by facing downstream), upstream, downstream, and the river surface and riverbed. Part of the size-up process involves gaining as much information as possible concerning all six sides. At a minimum, attempt to place rescuers downstream, upstream, and on both banks. Situational reports from these personnel will provide the IC with a reasonable degree of situational awareness.

Situational reports from each team member should include current speed, channel width, a description of the channel (including hazards), and any other pertinent information. Where the water is going can also be critical during operations in flood control channels since the water may go below grade, go through a variety of culvert systems, or pass under fixed structures.

Each of the team members serves as part of the IC's reconnaissance system for gaining situational awareness. The upstream spotter advises the team of any hazards or load that may threaten the rescue effort. The downstream spotter acts as a lookout for the back-up safety system. This back-up team must create a system that ensures success should the initial rescue go bad. The site spotter advises the team leader on changes at the site with regard to velocity, depth, and temperature. With this in mind, it is imperative to establish a communications link between all three.

Plan and Personnel

Once the IC has gained situational awareness, it's time to determine what, if anything, can be accomplished based on the capability of existing personnel and equipment. When determining the appropriate rescue strategy, select the one that offers the highest degree of safety to the rescuers, and has a reasonable likelihood of success.

Be cautious with conditional rescue techniques (techniques that are dependent on victim assistance), or those that are too complex, requiring too much time. Be careful not to select a technique that exceeds the capability of on-scene and/or available personnel. In other words, and as harsh as this may sound, "You can't fake being prepared." This is the last limiting factor and also the most important with regard to rescuer safety. If rescuers have never been in current, the site of the real swiftwater rescue is a poor time to learn. Boat operations in current, for the first time, can end in disaster as well. Therefore, any plan with regard to tactical operations, no matter how simple, cannot exceed the capability of those who are expected to carry it out!

When possible the IC should delegate implementation of the plan so that he or she can remain focused on the development of a back-up plan (in case the first one fails), as well as ongoing size-up. Tunnel vision is the likely outcome if the IC becomes directly involved in plan implementation.

Operations

This is the tactical component that involves deployment and implementation of the plan.

All rescuers involved must use their individual judgement concerning each component of the plan. Given that swiftwater and floods are so dynamic, ie. they change so continually, this is no time for blind obedience. What made sense an hour ago, may make no sense now. Do not be afraid to move on to Plan B. There is little point in sticking with a technique that has proven unsuccessful.

Notes

Notes

Personal Equipment

All Swiftwater Rescue Technicians® need to be suitably equipped to be able to carry out their roles.

This equipment must be in good order, tested, and maintained and should conform to the relevant OSHA and NFPA Standards.

Basic equipment requirements are discussed on *page Aw-58 to Aw-64*.

In addition to that equipment, it is advisable that a Swiftwater Rescue Technician® also carries:

- Waterproof head lap that can be helmet-mounted
- Three locking carabiners (HMS shape)
- 10' length of webbing
- Cows-tail with locking carabiner (for use with quick release chest harness)
- A prusik-minding pulley
- Two prusik loops
- Waterproof notepad and pencil

If every Technician carries these few extra items, when the equipment is pooled, it will be a sufficient quantity to facilitate many uses.

Team Equipment

Notes

The amount of team equipment will vary depending upon team background, role and area of operation. Below is a list of suggested equipment. Using this equipment, Technicians will be able to undertake the rescue techniques they have been trained for.

An initial response team will tend to travel light, whereas a full emergency service team will have the capacity to carry a larger range of equipment.

Recommended SRT Team Equipment List

(Based on minimum of four team members)

- 4x floating ropes (min. 50m but may need to be longer according to sites worked)
- 1x low stretch or static 11mm -12.5 mm kernmantle ropes (min. 50m but may need to be longer according to sites worked)
- 25x locking carabiners
- 3x pulleys (prusik-minding if using prusiks)
- 3x rope grabs or prusik loops
- 2x belay devices
- Lengths of webbing and/or selection of sewn tapes
- 2x rope protectors
- Bags for ropes and technical hardware.
- Boat for tethering, paddling and wading (must be suitable design for operational area)
- 6 x paddles
- 2 pairs of fins
- Poles (non-metal) for shallow water techniques
- Litter basket
- Spine board
- Victim PFDs (adult and child)
- Medical kit
- De-contamination equipment
- Scene lighting
- Search lighting
- Handheld waterproof radio communications
- Basic Life Support equipment
- Oxygen administration equipment

Fire rescue teams will generally also have access to:

- Hose inflation equipment
- 2x inflatable rescue platforms
- Compressed air cylinders

Notes

In-Water Rescue Techniques

Use of a Quick Release Chest Harness

It is important that all Rescue Technicians' PFDs are fitted with an integral quick release chest harness, and that all technicians are familiar with its use.

Quick release chest harnesses are specially designed to allow ropes to be attached to them that can then be released under load by the rescuer in the water if required.

The threading of the chest harness must be done in accordance with the manufacturer's instructions. It should be ensured that there are no twists in the webbing, and that the webbing has passed through all of the loops on the buoyancy aid. Different manufacturers use different webbing and cam buckles, and all vary in their instructions for use. Some recommend just using the plastic buckle for in-water use while others recommend threading both the metal and plastic buckles for in-water use.

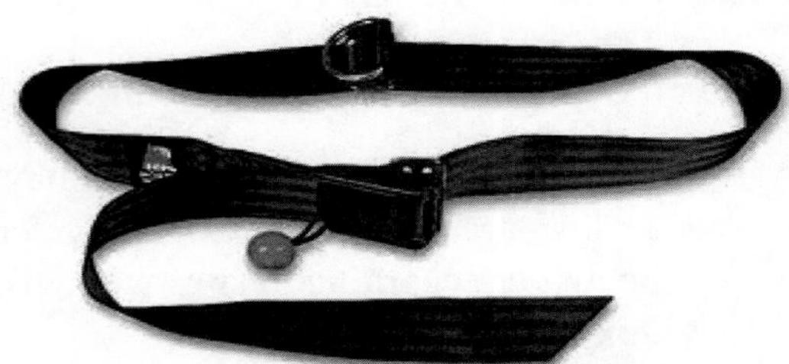

Diagram T1: Chest harnesses are usually integral parts of rescue PFDs but may be purchased separately.

Ensure that the cam buckle is fully closed, and that the end of the webbing is left to dangle free. It should not be tucked in anywhere, as this creates a risk that the harness may not release correctly.

Diagram T2: Direct attachment to the harness.

The attachment of a rope to the harness must only be done a) directly to the harness using a locking carabiner, or b) using a "cows-tail" (a piece of flexible webbing attached to the chest harness with a metal ring or locking carabiner). This is to ensure the attachment stays in place and does not clip accidentally onto other parts of the PFD, creating an entrapment hazard.

There have been a number of near miss reports arising from the use of non-locking carabiners for attachment. In operation, the gates of non-locking carabiners have opened and snagged on non-releasable webbing on the PFD. Be sure carabiners are the locking type, and that they are properly fastened.

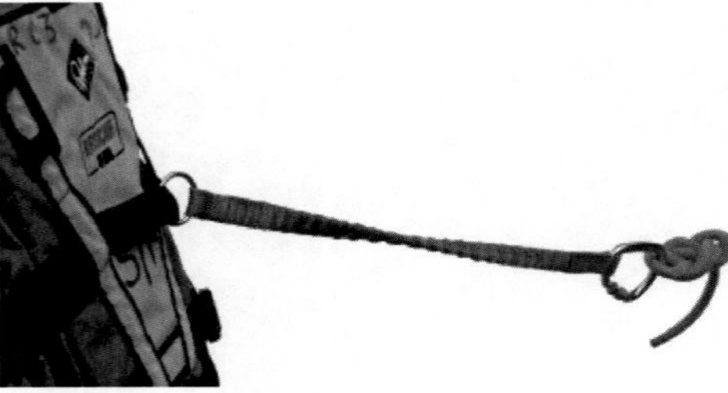

Diagram T3: Using a cows-tail to connect to the harness.

Notes

Swimming Rescues

Swimming in swiftwater and flood water to rescue victims can be very risky. Rescuers run the risk of being swept away. Once contact is made with the victim, it can be very difficult for the rescuer to swim to safety while maintaining contact. To reduce the risk to rescuers and greatly increase the chance of a successful rescue, the rescuers can be attached to a floating ropes via quick release chest harnesses.

Tethered Swims

Tethered swim rescues have a major advantage in that they are true rescues. They do not rely upon victims taking an active role in their own rescue. Victims who would be unable to hold onto a reached object or thrown line due to cold, injury or fear can be rescued with this "hands on" or "go" rescue technique.

A swimming rescue is high risk because the swimmer is exposed to numerous hazards in the water. However, it may the only option available. When the rescue is within a rescuer's capability and all safety systems are in place, it is a highly effective rescue technique.

As well as the swimmer's task, the bank team has a vital role to play including belaying the rope, upstream spotting, and downstream safety.

If a throwbag is to be attached to the rescuer's chest harness, the bag end should be clipped to the harness, leaving a "clean rope" at the other end.

The floating rope is attached to the rescuer's quick release chest harness with a locking carabiner. This should be checked to ensure it is correctly attached by another team member.

It is important that the belayer pays close attention to the rescuer. Belayers must manage the line carefully to stop excess rope forming a loop in the water, but they must not restrict the rescuer's ability to swim.

Where possible the rescuer should approach the victim from slightly upstream. This often means that the victim will have almost passed the rescuer's position. Ensuring it is safe to approach, the rescuer should take a secure grip with both hands and allow the rope to become taut which will pendulum the rescuer and victim into the bank.

Belayers on the bank need to anticipate the increased load they will experience once the victim is being recovered, and choose a suitable belay technique.

Diagram T4a & b: Tethered swims are true rescues.

Notes

"V" and "Y" Lowers

As well as swimming rescues, a quick release chest harness and rope can be used to move a rescuer to a particular position in the water flow to perform a rescue. This can be particularly useful when dealing with entrapped victims.

There are two basic systems.

In a V-lower, a rope from each bank is attached to the rescuer's quick release chest harness.

Diagram T5: V-lower set up.

In a Y-lower only one rope is attached to the rescuer's harness. Another rope from the opposite bank is clipped to this rope, which allows for the rescuer to be moved around the river channel.

Diagram T6: Y-lower set up.

Current Must be Considered

The rescuer is held in a defensive swimming position against the water flow by means of ropes and the quick release chest harness. This position allows for an air pocket to be formed if the water flows over the head and shoulders of the rescuer.

Even with the formation of this air pocket, both “V” and “Y” lowers are most effective in slower currents. In high speed flows and difficult water conditions, a highly trained and experienced team is required to manoeuvre the in-water rescuer.

Notes

In-Water Victim Management

Notes

For information on medical conditions in a swiftwater and flood environment see section beginning *page Aw-72*.

For effective victim management in the water, the victim must be brought to a bank or an eddy. From that stable position, the victim can be packaged onto a spine board or into a litter.

Complications arise when a spinal injury is suspected. If the victim is face down in the water, it is imperative he are immediately rolled over onto his back. Airway always takes priority over spinal injuries and there are several techniques to roll a victim and maintain spinal alignment.

Studies[1] suggest that spinal injuries are not emergencies that occurs very often in a water environment. However, there are no significant clinical studies on spinal cord injury management techniques in this setting. There are only anecdotal reports and opinions. Therefore, it is not possible to recommend one technique over any other. Treatment of spinal cord injury is primarily focused on doing no more harm.

PFD Technique

If the victim is wearing a PFD, the rescuer should carefully approach him and cross his arms. Both thumbs should be pointing down. The victim's head should be squeezed between the rescuer's forearms. Gripping the PFD shoulder straps, the rescuer untwists his arms, turning the victim face-up.

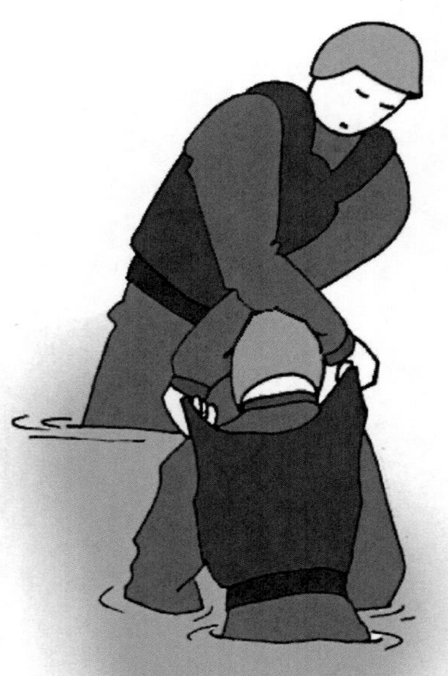

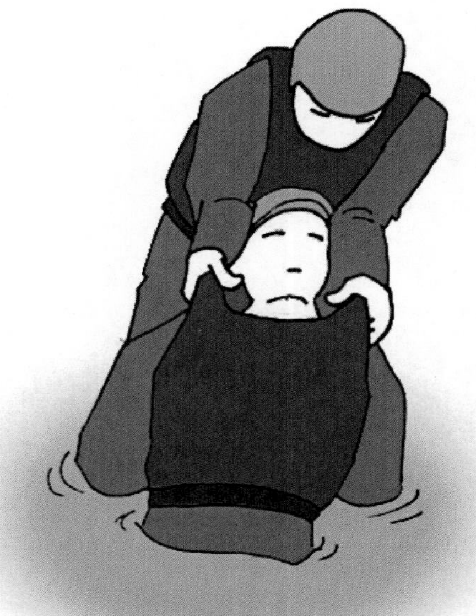

Diagram T7 a & b: PFD roll technique.

1 Watson RS, Cummings P, Quan L, et al. (2001) Cervical spine injuries among submersion victims. J Trauma 51:658–662

Extended Arm Grip

This technique is favored by the International Lifesaving Federation (ILSF) and is also sometimes known as the 'Head Splint'.

The rescuer approaches the victim and gently raises the victim's arms up to either side of the victim's head. The victim's arms are then squeezed against the victim's head to provide cervical spine stabilization. The rescuer places his thumbs on the back of the victim's head to prevent it from slipping backward. If necessary, the victim can be rolled face-up.

Diagram T8a: Place hands on victim's arms, squeezing the victim's arms against his head.

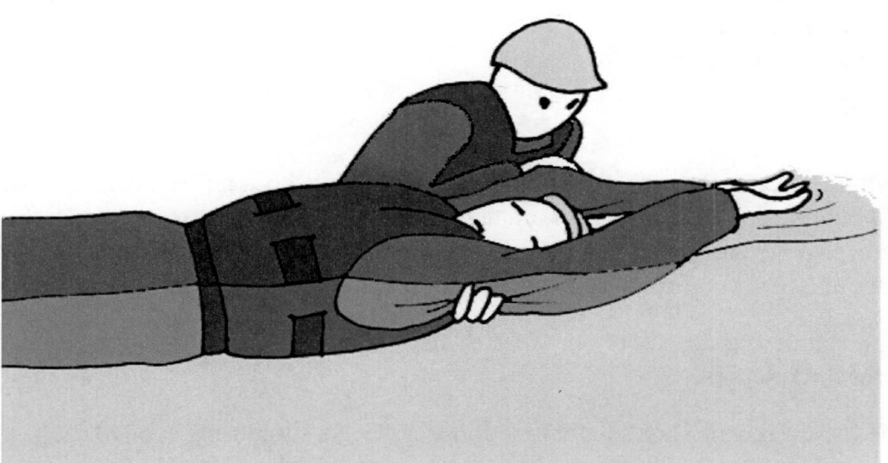

Diagram T8b: Gently roll the victim onto his back, while squeezing him into your chest and maintaining a secure grip on his arms. Stay low in the water to aid stabilization.

Once the victim is rolled onto his back using the appropriate technique, the head and neck should be continually supported and the victim then fitted with a neck collar and transferred to a spine board with head blocks -- all in a safe area of water.

Victims are to be transported across an area of water must ***never*** be secured to the board as this could result in victims being held upside down underwater should the board be lost downstream.

Notes

Foot and Body Entrapments

Victims trapped by part of or their entire body, held in place by the force of water and unable to release themselves, presents a very difficult rescue situation.

Time is a critical factor in these rescues. Victims of foot entrapments in swiftwater often have little time in which they are able to keep their heads above water. Even if the victim is trapped with their head above water they will quickly succumb to the effects of cold water immersion – more dramatically so if they are not wearing equipment such as a drysuit or wetsuit.

There are various forms of entrapment:

- Foot entrapment
- Body entrapment
- Boat wrap
- Kayak and canoe pin

The rescue priorities, as always, are:

- Self
- Team
- Victim

The stages, as always, are:

- Locate the victim
- Access the victim
- Stabilize the situation
- Transport to safety

Due to the time-critical nature of entrapment, rescuers may be tempted to put themselves in danger to resolve the situation. However, an assessment of hazards ***must*** be done before rescue attempts begin. Due to the urgency of the situation and the numerous methods of resolving it, the team leader must gain control quickly and communicate the action plan to all team members.

The priority is stabilizing the situation—that is, maintaining the victim's airway and in effect buying time for the rescuers.

Generally, the lowest risk method of stabilization is getting a supporting rope to the victim. This will probably only be effective in relatively narrow channels. It is difficult (if not impossible) to do this if victims are unable to help in getting the rope under their bodies or are unable to hold onto it. Once a support rope is established it may be possible to use this to send out a floating object or a pole to the entrapment victim. The victim may be able to use them to stay above the water, but again, the force of the water may make this difficult or impossible.

Notes

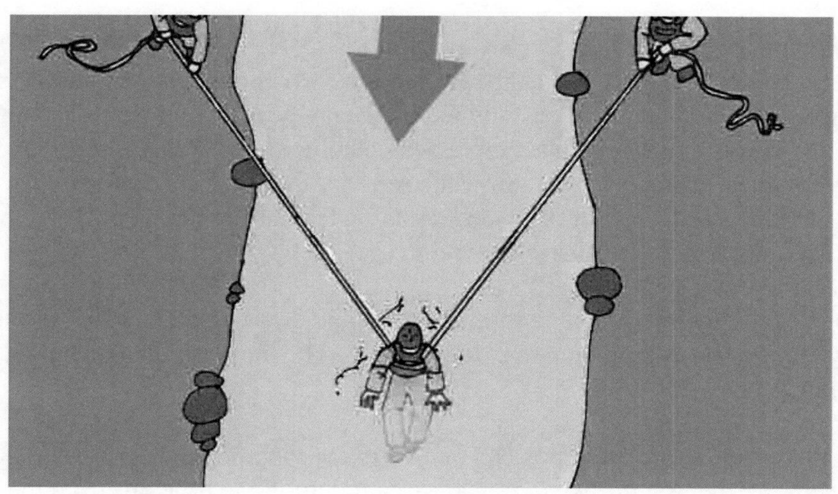

Diagram T9: Moving upstream allows the maximum pulling force to be applied.

Anecdotal evidence suggests that most successful foot and body entrapment rescues are as a result of a "go" rescue. In other words, the rescuer enters the water, makes contact with the victim, and supports the victim while the rescuer attempts to release the victim from the entrapment. This can be a very high risk solution, especially as the rescuer(s) may be exposed to the same entrapment hazard. The level of risk can potentially be reduced by:

- Tethering the rescuer using a quick release chest harness
- Team shallow water techniques (such as the wedge)
- Poles and/or paddles to provide support to rescuers

Approaching the victim from upstream has the risk of the rescuer getting entrapped as well. However, there is the benefit that the rescuer will create an eddy, thus reducing the force of water on the victim directly downstream. Approaching from downstream is generally a safer option for the rescuer, but it can be difficult to make progress upstream to the victim.

If a "go" rescue is not an option, then there are a number of rope options available. These require a lot of practice by rescue teams in order to be able to apply them quickly enough to be useful, and even then they may be of limited success. It is often difficult to get access to both sides of the river to set up an initial stabilization rope.

Single Bank Methods

Notes

There are also a number of single bank methods that can be attempted:

- A throwbag or floating rope is thrown into the current upstream and beyond the victim. Once this has floated down past the victim it may be retrieved from the bank. Options here include hooking it with a simple device known as a "Snag Plate" that can be left permanently attached to a throwbag rope for this very purpose, or a swimmer on a tether. Once both ends of the rope are on the bank, they can be pulled to provide support and potentially release the victim.

- Two packed throwbags can be joined with a tape or a sling. They are both thrown over the victim, one upstream and one downstream. The loop can then be pulled to provide support.

- The clean end of one throwbag can be tied to the loop on the bag of another. The rescuer with the first throwbag runs upstream, letting the rope fall from the bag. The rescuer with the packed bag is positioned downstream of the victim and throws his packed bag high over the victim.

All the above options will be most successful if they are applied as soon as possible, and if the victim is still head up and able to assist in his own rescue. Once the victim's head is forced underwater very little time remains to implement any system.

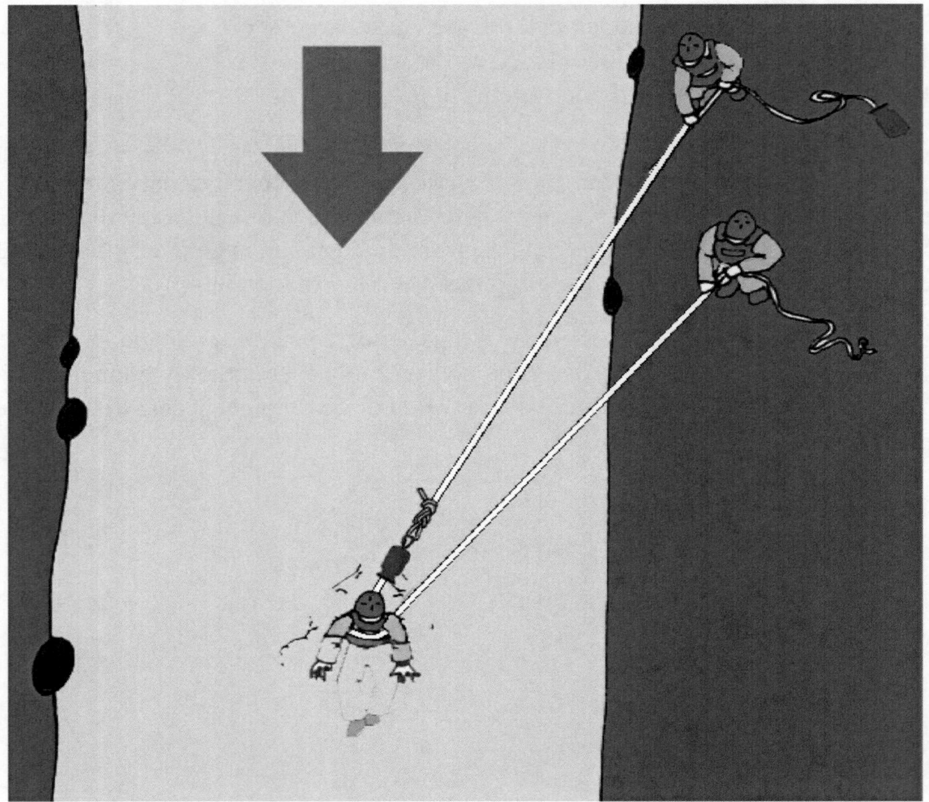

Diagram T10: Recovering an entrapment victim using a single-bank method.

Notes

All of the above methods just put a loop around the victim. There are no cinches. With an uncontrolled cinch it is possible to apply a huge amount of force through the line and further injure the victim. Controllable cinches do not have the same issue, but they are complicated to set up and require a lot of personnel and equipment, which is not practical in most entrapment situations because of limited time. Cinches can be very useful when attempting to recover equipment, and there are no time pressures or risk of physical injury.

A quick release chest harness can be a vital tool in dealing with entrapments for both the victim and rescuer. If the victim is wearing a PFD fitted with a quick release chest harness and cows-tail (as many whitewater kayakers do) then it may be possible for him to clip a throwbag that has been thrown from the bank into his harness to provide support and potentially release him.

Rescuers can also use a quick release chest harness to set up a "V" or "Y" lower (see *page Tech-10*) in order to lower the rescuer to the victim under control from both banks. As mentioned above, once the rescuer is in place behind the victim an eddy is formed which can be used to assist with the release.

Notes

Ropework for Water Rescue

In order to carry out many of the tasks associated with rescue from water it is essential a Swiftwater Rescue Technician® is suitably skilled in and experienced in the following areas:

- Tying knots and hitches
- Building anchors and anchor systems
- Belaying
- Creating mechanical advantage systems

Rope Terminology

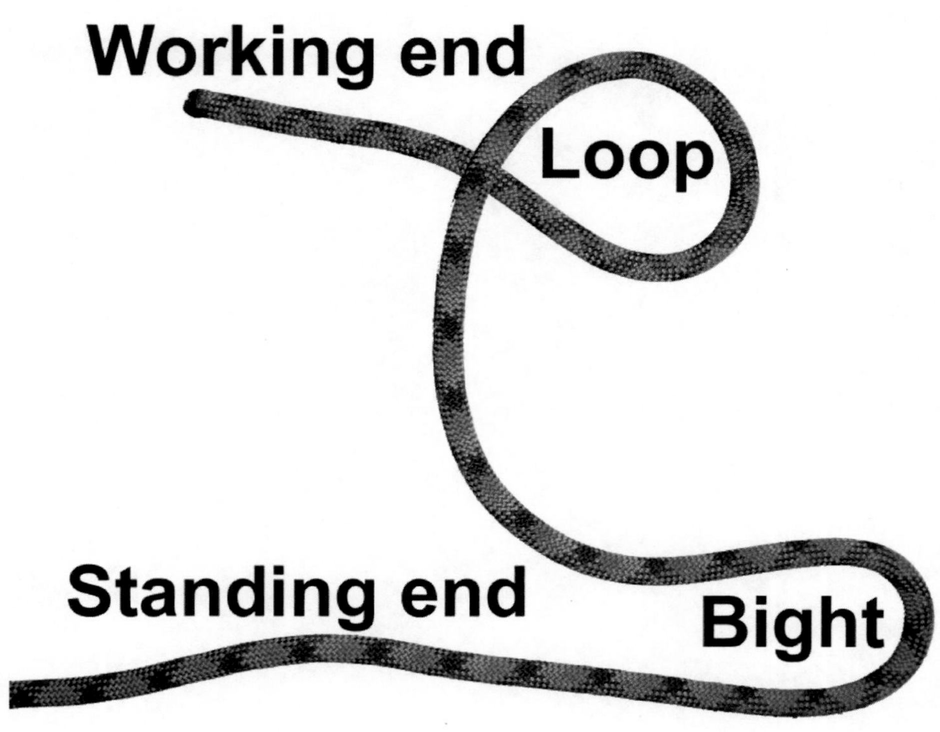

Diagram T11: Parts of a rope

Knots & Hitches

There are a multitude of knots and hitches. However, only a small number of them are needed by a Swiftwater Rescue Technician®. These knots and hitches must become second nature, so that they can be tied reliably and quickly when needed, including at night and underwater.

If sufficient length of tail is left, then knots should not require the tying of additional stopper knots. A general rule of thumb is to leave 6" of tail.

Once a knot is tied in a rope it will reduce the strength of the rope. This is due to the rope going through a sharp turn. The fibers on the outside of the turn will end up taking the majority of the load,

Notes

while the fibers on the inside of the turn may take very little. The exact amount of strength loss will depend on how tight the turns are in the knot and will vary from knot to knot. Knots should be dressed so that they look neat, well tied and load evenly. This will help maximize the strength of the knot.

As a general rule of thumb, deduct one third of the tensile strength of a rope once it has a knot tied in it.

An investigation into the relative strengths of basic rescue knots tied into 12.5 mm and 7 mm accessory cord was undertaken in the US by The Cordage Institute. A copy of the full report is available:

www.ropecord.com

After use, knots should be removed from the rope before the rope is returned to storage. Knots left in the rope for extended periods tend to set and become difficult to untie. If a knot is untied after having been in place for a long time, the rope will be weaker where the knot was than before the knot was in place.

The website www.animatedknots.com (also known as Grog's Knots)is an excellent resource with step-by-step photos of how to tie most common rescue knots.

Overhand Knot

This simple-to-tie knot is commonly used as a stopper knot on the end of a rope.

Diagram T12: Overhand Knot.

Overhand on a Bight

By first doubling over the end of the rope to form a bight, an overhand knot is tied to create a loop. This is easy to tie but can be difficult to untie once loaded.

Diagram T13: Overhand on a Bight.

Figure Eight Knot

Similar to an overhand knot but with one extra turn. The figure eight shape is easily recognizable.This is commonly used as a stopper knot on the end of a rope.

Diagram T14: Figure Eight Knot

Notes

Figure Eight on a Bight

By doubling over the end of the rope to form a bight, a figure eight knot is tied to create a loop in the end of rope. It is important that this knot is only loaded in one direction.

Diagram T15: Figure Eight on a Bight.

Figure Eight Follow Through (Re-threaded Figure Eight)

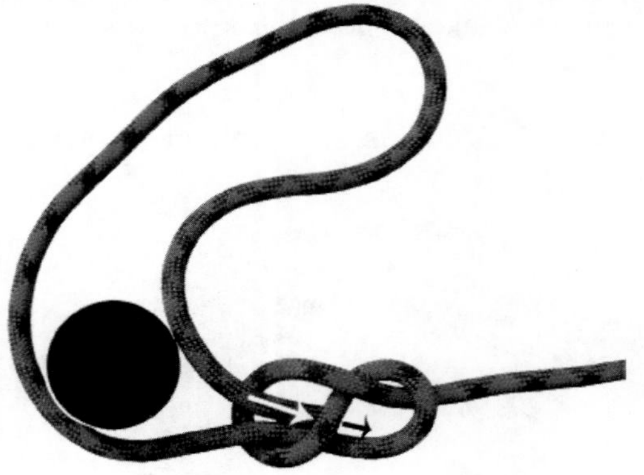

Diagram T16 (a-d): Re-threaded Figure Eight

This knot allows a loop to be made at the end of a rope around an object such as a tree or post, when a figure eight on a bight cannot be tied. It is commonly used in anchor applications. Begin by tying a figure eight (see above). Then take the end of the rope around the object before re-threading it through the initial figure eight knot.

Alpine Butterfly

Notes

This knot creates a loop in the middle of a rope that can be loaded in multiple directions. It can also be used to isolate a damaged section of rope.

Diagram T17a: Begin by wrapping the rope around the hand, so that there are three strands in the palm.

Diagram T17b: Take the strand nearest the thumb, and move it to the finger tips, lifting it over the top of the other two strands.

Diagram T17c: Take the new strand that is nearest the thumb, and move it to the finger tips, lifting it over the top of the other two strands.

Notes

Diagram T17d: Slide the thumb underneath the strands and take hold of the furthest strand (the one that has just been placed there). Pull the hand out.

Diagram T17e: Remove the hand completely. To dress the knot correctly, pull the ends of the rope apart.

Diagram T17f: The Alpine Butterfly correctly dressed. This is the reverse side of the knot shown in the above picture.

Water Knot (Tape Knot, Overhand Bend, Ring Bend)

Notes

This is used for tying together two pieces of similar webbing or joining two ends of the same piece to make a loop. It is important that this knot is dressed properly to maximize its strength.

Diagram T18a: The Water Knot starts with a simple overhand knot (see above). Ensure that the webbing sits flat and is not twisted or wrinkled.

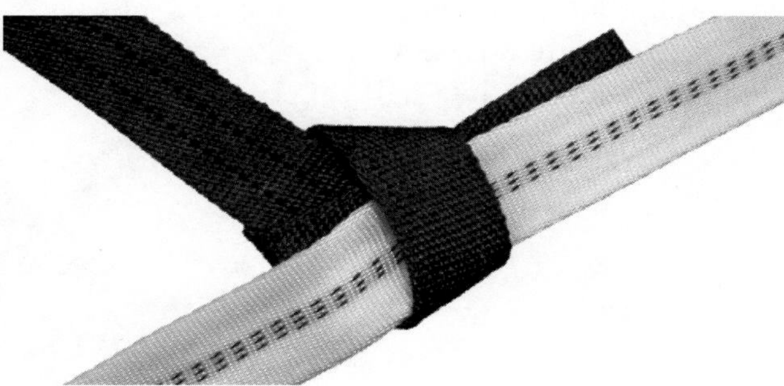

Diagram T18b: Starting from the working end of the first piece of webbing (dark), feed the end of the second webbing (light) into the overhand knot.

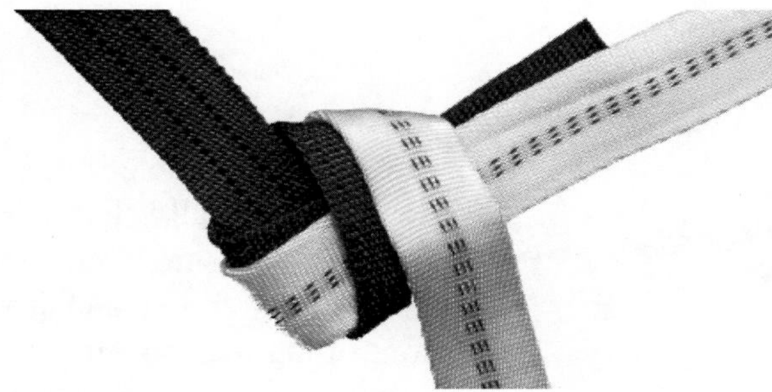

Diagram T18c: Feed the light webbing all the way through the overhand knot.

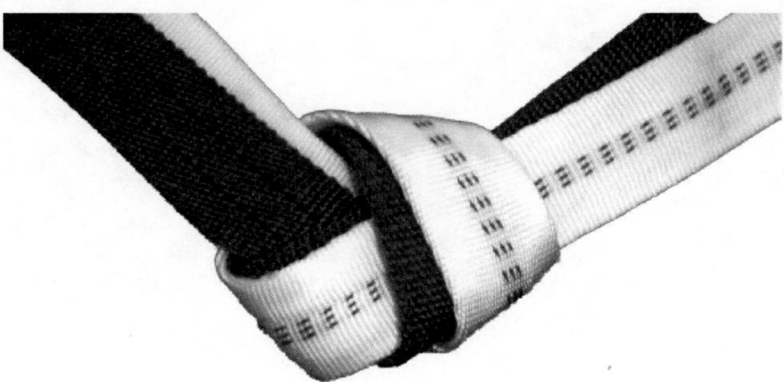

Diagram T18d: The completed knot, tied loosely to show the construction.

Notes

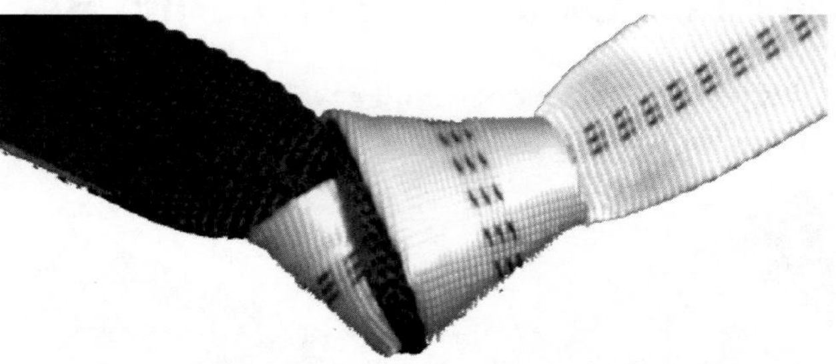

Diagram T19: The Water Knot - loaded. Note: Once the water knot has been fully loaded it can be impossible to untie.

Clove Hitch

This can be used to secure the middle of a rope around objects such as carabiners or fire hoses. As they are prone to slippage they should not be used on the end of a rope.

Diagram T20: Clove Hitch.

Münter Hitch

This is a movable hitch that is normally tied around a specially shaped carabiner (HMS or pear shaped). The hitch creates friction as it moves over the carabiner and itself. It can be used for controlling the movement of loads. It will reverse automatically so rope can be let out or taken in.

Diagram T21: Münter Hitch.

Tying off a Münter Hitch

Notes

Diagram T22a: Form a loop in the rope.

Diagram T22b: Push a bight of rope through the loop.

Diagram T22c: Pull enough of the bight of rope through to tie an overhand knot around the tensioned part of the rope.

Notes

Diagram T22d: The tied off Münter Hitch.

Double Fisherman's Bend

This is used for joining the ends of two similarly-sized ropes. It can be very difficult to untie once loaded. This is commonly used with accessory cord (6-8mm) to make prusik loops (see Prusik Knots below).

Diagram T23a: For clarity, ropes of two different colors have been used. Start with the two ends of the rope overlapping.

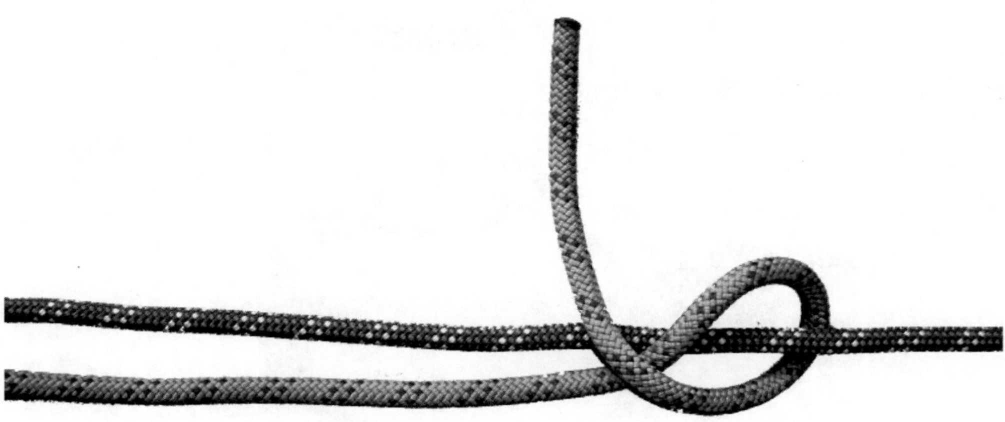

Diagram T23b: Loop one of the ropes around the other.

Notes

Diagram T23c: Continue to loop the rope around – travelling back on itself. A cross should have formed.

Diagram T23d: Feed the working end of the rope underneath the cross to form the first double fisherman's knot.

Diagram T23e: When correctly tied and dressed, the knot should form a neat cross shape on one side.

Diagram T23f: Repeat the process with the other rope. Note the difference between *Diagram T23 b (previous page)* and this one - the working rope is wrapping around in the opposite direction.

Notes

Diagram T23g: Continue to wrap the rope around until another cross is formed.

Diagram T23h: Feed the working end of the rope underneath the cross. At this stage, ensure that the two crosses formed by the two knots are on the same side. This is a common error. If the crosses are not next to each other, it is necessary to untie one of the knots and re-tie it in the opposite direction.

Diagram T23i: Both Double Fisherman's Knots tied correctly.

Diagram T23j: The Double Fisherman's Bend, tightened and dressed. Note the compact and neat appearance of the knot.

Notes

Prusik Hitches

Originally developed by mountaineers for ascending fixed ropes, these hitches are very useful in water rescue situations – particularly in constructing mechanical advantage systems. They are created by making a loop of cord or webbing and wrapping this around a larger diameter main rope. For example a 12.5 mm (1/2”) rope would require an 8mm (5/16) prusik loop. The narrower cord will tighten when loaded to grip the main rope, but when unloaded, can be slid along the main rope and repositioned. There are a large number of prusik hitches with different properties and applications. Two of the most common for water rescue applications are:

Triple Wrap Prusik

This is tied using cord that is approximately half the diameter of the main rope. It cannot be released under normal working loads. However, iIt will slip if excessive loads are applied.

Diagram T24a: When starting the Prusik hitch, ensure that the Double Fisherman’s Bend is slightly to one side. Otherwise the knot can end up inside the Prusik hitch.

Diagram T24b: Wrap the prusik loop around the main rope and feed it back through itself - to form a loose “Larks Foot”.

Diagram T24c: Wrap the prusik loop around the main rope again, and feed it back through the loop again.

Notes

Diagram T24d: Wrap the prusik loop around the main rope for a third time to complete the Triple Wrap Prusik.

Diagram T24e: The Triple Wrap Prusik in action. Notice that the pull is from the center of the knot.

Notes

Kleimheist

If a loop of webbing is being used, then the kleimheist is the best prusik knot to use. As with a triple wrap prusik, it cannot be released under normal working loads but will slip if excessive loads are applied.

Diagram T25a: Start with the end of the webbing loop a few inches clear of the main rope.

Diagram T25b: Wrap the webbing around the rope at least four times.

Diagram T25c: Feed the remainder of the webbing loop up through the end of the loop. The direction of pull is from left to right.

Anchoring

Notes

The ability to select reliable anchor points and construct anchor systems are key skills for the Swiftwater Rescue Technician®.

Good anchor selection is a result of experience and judgement gained over time. "Bombproof" anchor points such as large boulders and trees may be sufficient as single anchor points, even for some of the largest forces found in water rescue situations (e.g. anchoring submerged vehicles). However, these are often not available, or more than one anchor point may be needed so that the load is shared – multiple point anchors.

Single Point Anchors

No-Knot (Full Strength Tie-Off)

This is one of the simplest anchor systems to construct but also one of the most versatile. The rope is wrapped around a suitable object (tree, post, etc.) and surface friction secures the rope in place. The surface friction of the object will determine how many times the rope needs to be wrapped around the object.

Wrap in a upward direction – this stops the rope unwrapping

Keep your wraps tight and tidy.

As there is no actual knot tied in the rope, the rope's strength is not reduced. It is also a clean line.

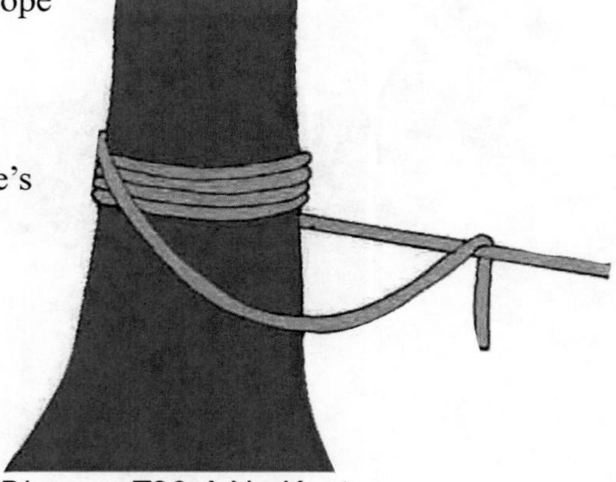

Diagram T26: A No-Knot.

The unloaded end of the rope can be clipped onto the loaded line with a carabiner for added security. However, the line will no longer be clean.

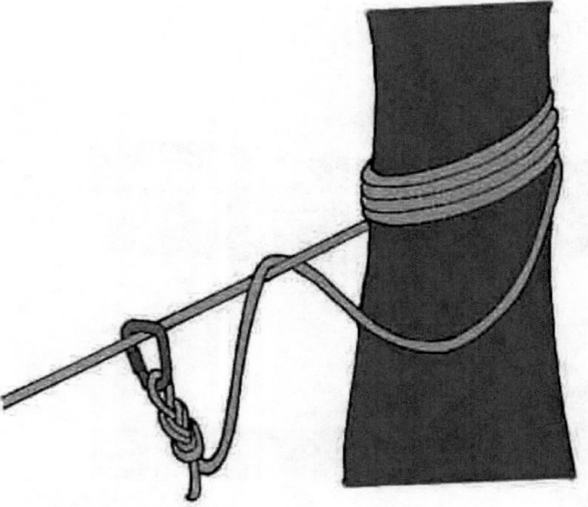

Diagram T27: Full Strength Tie-Off.

Notes

Basket Hitch

This is a sewn sling or knotted sling for wrapping around an object or for threading between two objects. Both ends of the webbing are then clipped together to complete the anchor. Sewn slings work best here as any knot tied in webbing will have the full load applied to it and consequently can be difficult to untie.

Diagram T28: Basket Hitch.

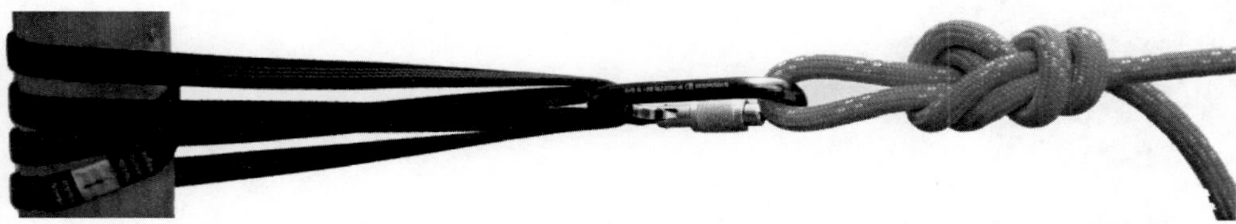

Diagram T29: A wrapped basket hitch. The extra wrap means that the hitch grips the post better, and is less likely to slide down it.

Single Point with Re-Threaded Knot

A similar anchor can be constructed by tying a figure eight follow-through knot around the anchor point. This can be used in place where a full strength tie-off would not be suitable. It does not need a webbing sling and carabiner but can result in the figure eight knot being difficult to untie.

Diagram T30: Single Point with Figure Eight Follow-Through Knot

Wrap Three - Pull Two

This is a very versatile and useful anchor (see photo next page). It is constructed by wrapping a length of webbing around the anchor three times and joining the ends with a water knot. Two of the wraps are then pulled to isolate the knot on the third wrap, which cinches onto the anchor object. The two other wraps are connected to the rope system with a carabiner.

Notes

The advantages of this system are

- The knot is isolated from the full load and thus remains easy to untie after use
- The anchor point is made of multiple wraps of webbing and thus has increased strength – this assumes the object they are wrapped around is of sufficient size and strength.

Diagram T31: Wrap Three - Pull Two

Multi-Point Anchor Systems

The forces involved in swiftwater rescue can be applied in many directions, due to the constantly moving water. Conversely, in rope rescue, the forces are created by gravity in one fixed direction.

Depending upon how multi-point anchor systems are constructed, they can be made so that they will work in a range of directions should the loading direction move (load-distributing anchor) or only work in one set direction (load-sharing anchor).

Anchors

Load

Load-Distributing Anchor

As its name implies, it distributes the load to multiple anchors as the load direction changes. Advantages include:

- Should one anchor fail in the system, the other will take the load
- Ideal for use in water-based applications where the direction of loading may change e.g. while recovering a pinned boat.

Boatman's Anchor

When anchoring to the D rings on an inflatable craft, it is essential that a multi-point anchor is utilized because the D rings are only glued onto the raft. By using a multi-point anchor this will spread the load across several D rings and also ensure that if one fails, there is a back up. One of the easiest ways to set this up is with a boatman's knot.

Notes

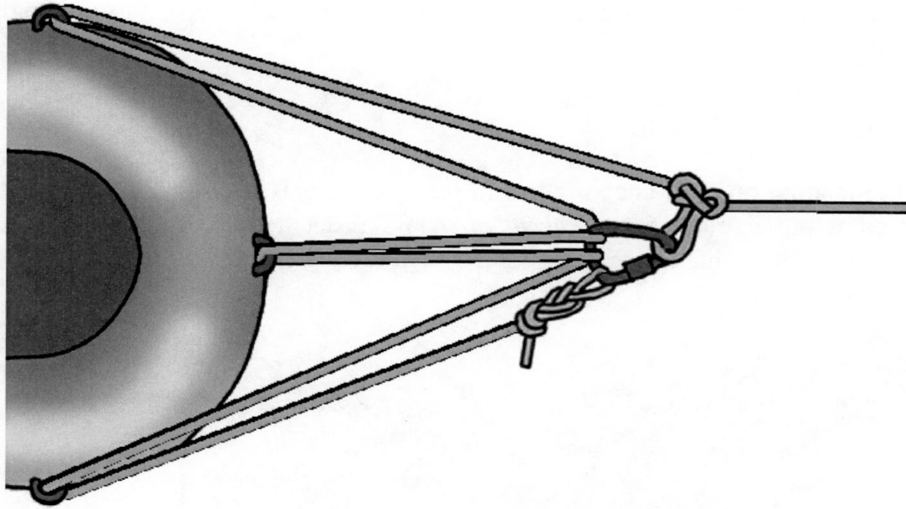

Diagram T33: Three Point Boatman's

Load Sharing Anchors

These anchors are set up to work in one direction only, so should one anchor fail, the others will not be shock-loaded. The force will be taken up by only one anchor point. For this reason, load sharing anchors are generally only used for applications where the direction of the load is set by the action of gravity, e.g. vertical/high angle rescue solutions.

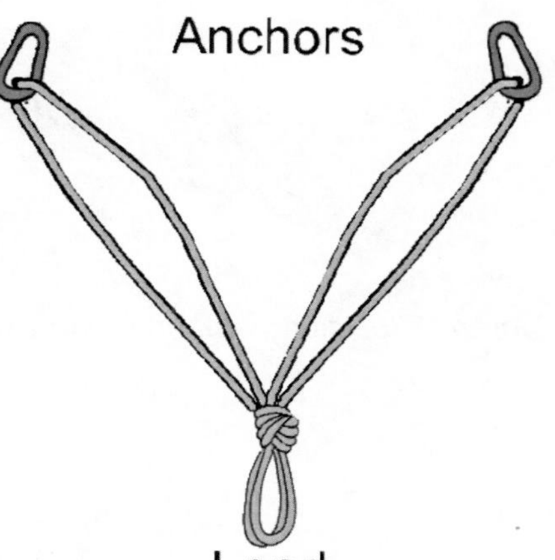

Diagram T34: Two point load sharing anchor with sling.

Internal Angles

Whenever a load is shared between two or more anchor points, the actual amount of loading each anchor receives is dependent upon the internal angle created at the focus point.

If the load is shared between two anchor points next to each other, so that both legs of the anchor system are essentially parallel, then each anchor point will receive half the force of the load. As the anchor points move apart, the internal angle will be increased, and each anchor point will see increased loading.

Notes

Increased Angle = Increased Load

At an internal angle of 90°, each anchor will see a force of approximately 70% of the load.

At an internal angle of 120°, each anchor point will see a force equal to the full load.

As the internal angle increases above 120°, the loading on each anchor point will be increasingly larger than the load being supported. For example at 160°, each anchor will receive a force equal to three times the load.

Estimating an Internal Angle

In order to reduce the loading on each anchor point in the system, it is necessary to keep the internal angle as small as possible and ideally at ***90° or less***. An outstretched hand creates an angle that is approximately 90°so that internal angles can be quickly estimated.

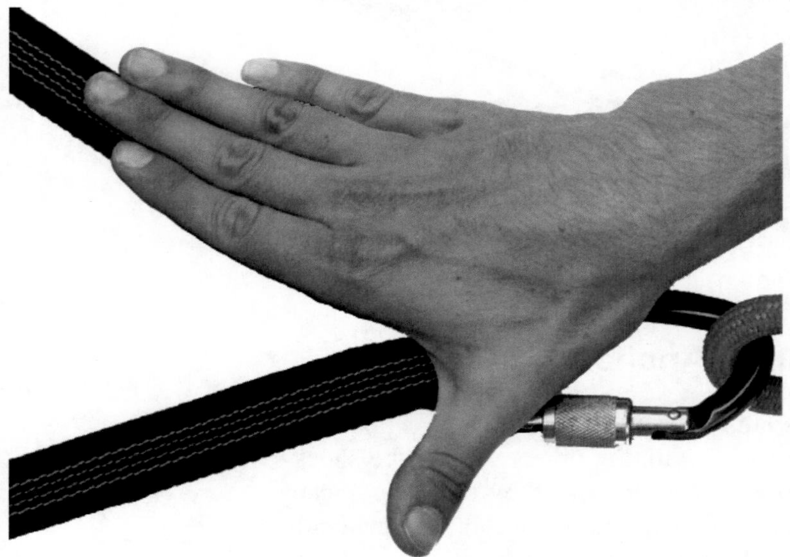

Diagram T35: Using a hand to measure the internal angle of an anchor system.

Notes

Mechanical Advantage Systems

Mechanical Advantage (MA) can assist the rescuer in moving a heavy load or opposing a large force. Commonly, rescuers will use mechanical advantage to either tension ropes, stabilize objects, or haul loads.

Energy cannot be created, so mechanical advantage works on the principle that a large load can be moved over a short distance by a smaller load moving over a longer distance.

In order to lift a 3kN (1 kiloNewton=225 lbs/force) load up one meter, a 3:1 MA system can be built. The load will then move by applying a 1kN force to it. However, the cost is that three meters of rope will need to be pulled through the MA system to move the load one meter.

Mechanical advantage can be achieved through a number of methods. In water and rope rescue, mechanical advantage is usually created by the use of pulleys and rope.

Depending upon the arrangement of pulleys, a vast range of mechanical advantage systems can be created. These can be divided into three categories:

- Simple mechanical advantage systems
- Compound mechanical advantage systems
- Complex mechanical advantage systems

Swiftwater Rescue Technicians® need to know a few, easy-to-remember methods of creating mechanical advantage. If these do not work it is often because the pull is being applied in the wrong direction, as opposed to not using enough MA.

In swiftwater applications, rescuers should read the water and, whenever possible, use it to help rather than hinder operations. Therefore the direction of the current must be considered when calculating the "ideal angle of pull" for systems.

Basic MA Systems

"Boy Scout" ("Strong Arm") Method

Not a true MA system since the force is increased by adding more people into the system to haul. It can however often be the simplest, quickest and most efficient solution – assuming the manpower is available.

Diagram T36: Boy Scout Method

Notes

Vector Pull

Once a line is tensioned and secured, a force can be applied at right angles to the line to create a mechanical advantage. Once the vector force is applied it will reduce the angle on the main line which is operating as a force multiplier. Consequently the effectiveness of the vector pull in creating mechanical advantage is quickly diminished.

Diagram T37: Vector Pull

3:1 Simple MA System

This easy-to-rig system is the most common basic mechanical advantage system.

This system can be rigged either on the rope itself (internal MA) or using a separate rope attached onto the haul rope (external MA).

Notes

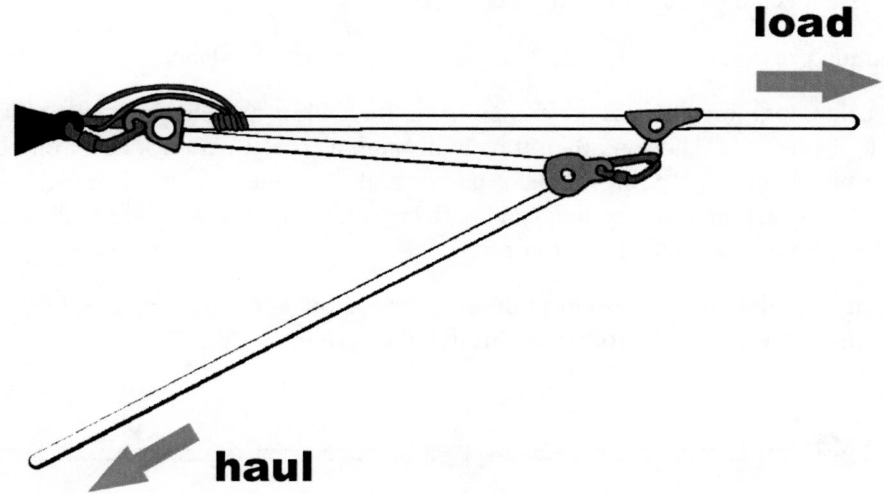

Diagram T38: Simple 3:1 Mechanical advantage (internal).

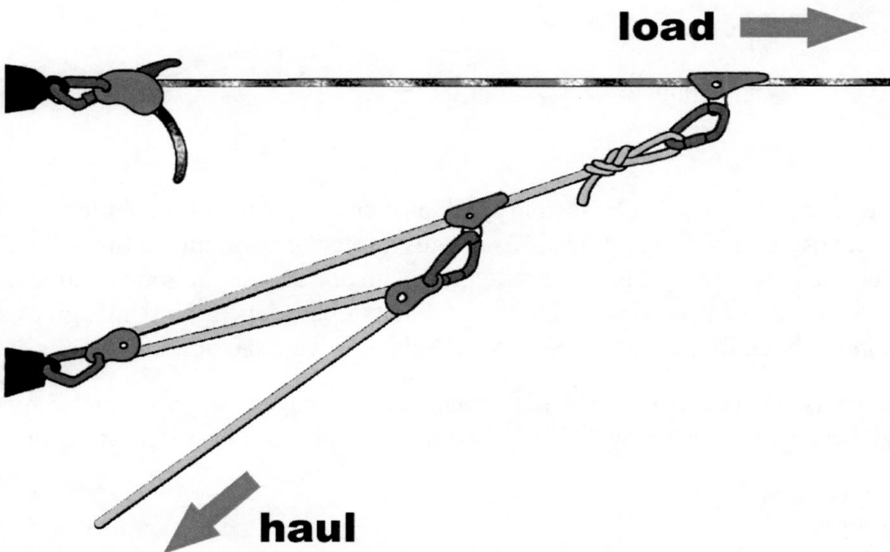

Diagram T39: Simple 3:1 Mechanical advantage (external or piggy back). Note: these diagrams are expanded for clarity. Ideally the haul rope will be as close to the load ropes as possible.

Notes

T-Method - Calculating Mechanical Advantage

Working out how much mechanical advantage a system creates can be difficult to learn. The T-Method is one of the easiest and most practical ways of doing this, which works regardless of whether the system is simple, compound, or complex.

The underpinning principal of this method is that everything must balance.

Always start calculating mechanical advantage from the haul team. The haul team always pulls with the force of one unit. The rope then travels through a pulley with a load of one unit. The result is one unit in the rope going into the pulley and also one unit in the rope leaving the pulley. These units must therefore be balanced with two units on the other side of the pulley, and anything else attached to it, such as a carabiner.

If this principal is applied to the system in the diagram below and assuming a nominal force of one unit from the hauler, it can be followed through the system.

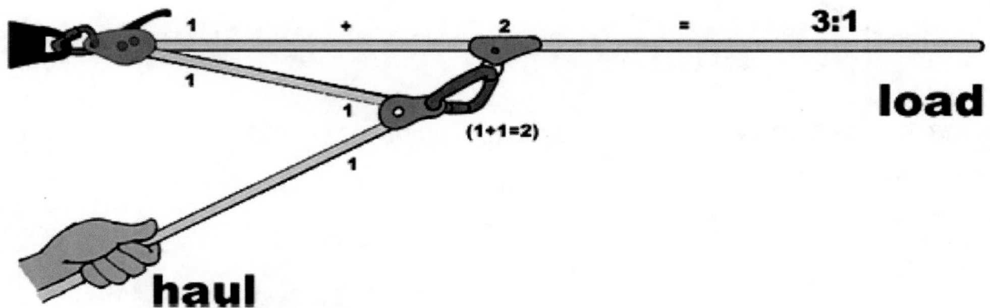

Diagram T40: 3:1 system explained using "T"-Method.

This force of one unit from the hauler is in the rope as it enters the travelling pulley. It remains in the rope as it leaves the travelling pulley. This creates a force of two units in the pulley, which is carried through the carabiner and into the rope grab. The one unit in the rope continues through the ID. The one unit in the rope is added to the two units in the rope grab which gives a total of three units being applied to the load. Thus the mechanical advantage of the system is 3:1.

T-Method can be used to calculate the **ideal** mechanical advantage of any system. No mechanical advantage system ever works that well. T-Method does not account for external factors such as:

- Frictional loss
- Heat loss
- Rope stretch
- Slippage, and many other things.

Rope-Based Rescue Techniques

Rope Crossing Techniques

It is often necessary to get a rope from one side of a channel to the other in order to carry out some forms of rope-based rescue, and to enable teams to cross a channel. Often this can be the most difficult part of the whole rescue. For efficient time management, this needs to be tasked early as it will take a lot of time. Also, once a rope is across the channel, it should be among the last things to come down. Lots of time will be wasted if a rope has to be crossed again.

There are many ways this may be done:

- Use of a bridge
- Throwing
- Wading
- By boat
- Swimming
- Rope launcher
- Catapults, bows and guns

It may be necessary to first send over a small diameter rope as a messenger line, to facilitate getting a larger rope over.

It should also be remembered that while getting a rope across a large expanse of water may be achievable, it may still be impractical to work over such a distance, as tensioning it or building it into a rope-based system will be very difficult.

While relatively straightforward in theory, all the above line crossing techniques (yes, even the bridge crossing) require practice by all team members.

If a rope is to be crossed by swimming or by boat, then the initial rope transported must be a floating rope. Once this is across the channel it can be used to pull over any non-floating ropes that need to span the channel.

Tensioned Diagonal

For basic information on this technique see *page OPS-32.*

This is a technique using a rope tensioned at an angle to the current vector. People and equipment attached to the rope will move down the rope and across the channel, simply due to the force of water.

Tensioned diagonal rope systems can be used for:

- Crossing rivers, channels and flooded streets
- Accessing mid-channel features including cars in the water
- Evacuating from trapped boats to the bank
- Accessing entrapped victims

Notes

The key safety consideration is that the downstream end of the rope is releasable under load and is a clean rope. If anyone gets into difficulty on the rope, the downstream end can be released easily. The person will then move downstream, away from the rope, to be rescued by downstream back-up.

Securing a downstream end in a manner that is both releasable and clean can be achieved by a number of methods, including:

- Body Belay
- No-Knot

As a general guideline, the angle of the rope should be as close to the current vector as possible. This minimizes the force on the rope when people are sliding down it. A maximum of 45° to the current vector is advised. At this angle, the system still functions, but any greater than this and there is a risk of people getting stuck in a downstream V part way across.

In slower current it can be possible to hold the rope with one or several team members on the downstream end. This is useful for quick set up and ensures the angle and placement of the diagonal is ideal. The key to this hand-held method is setting the angle correctly to ensure the loading on the downstream personnel is relatively low.

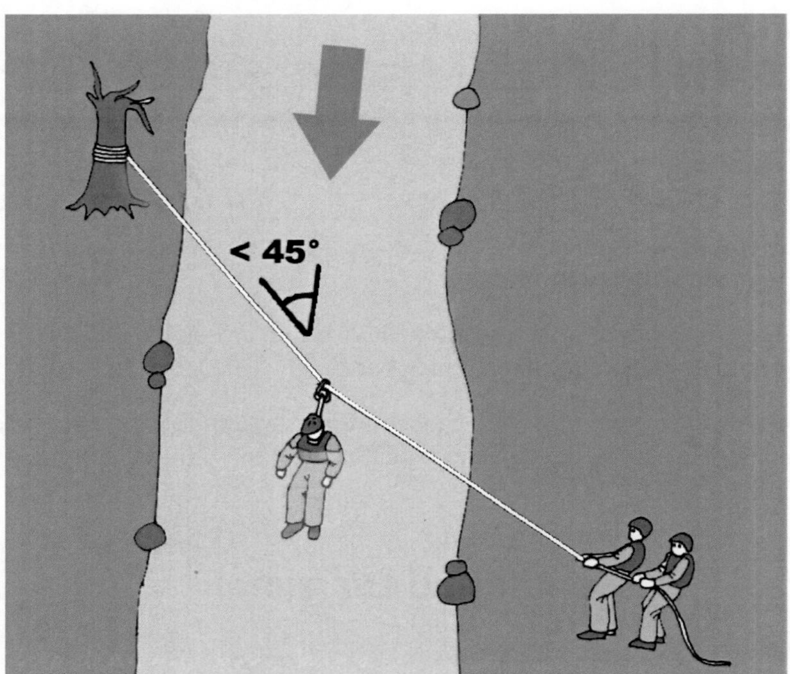

Diagram T41: Hand-held diagonal.

If the system will experience large forces, it may be necessary to tension the rope using a mechanical advantage system. Placing the mechanical advantage system at the upstream end of the rope is the easiest way of applying tension to the system and ensuring the downstream end is still clean and releasable.

Notes

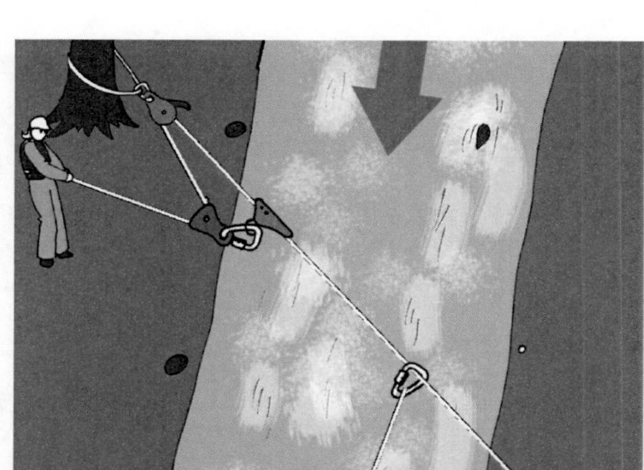

Diagram T42: Tensioned diagonal, showing no-knot on downstream end and tension system on upstream end.

When using the system, rescuers can either clip onto the tensioned line with a cows-tail attached to their quick release chest harness, or use a short length of webbing attached to the tensioned rope with a carabiner. To avoid entrapment, this webbing should not be a loop or contain any loops big enough to trap a hand. Small stopper knots tied in the webbing provide grip for the user.

The addition of a tag-line to the system allows rescuers to be held in place to effect a rescue or to recover equipment back upstream.

Diagram T43: Tensioned diagonal, using a recoverable tag-line to transport people instead of a cows-tail.

Tethered Boat Operations

Notes

For basic information on this technique see *page Ops-35.*

The initial setup of this system requires the team to get a rescuer and a rope over to the far bank. While this is taking place, the boat should be prepared for the task. For example, the anchor points should be rigged with a suitable load distributing anchor system (see *page Tech-34*).

The principle of the two-point boat tether is fundamentally the same as the pendulum method (see *page Ops-31*) except there is a boat on the rope system rather than a person. The two-point setup can be used for transferring the necessary personnel and equipment across the channel.

The key to operational success is that the belay points remain mobile, so that effective control of the boat can be maintained. In order to remain mobile, the terrain around the operational area must be quite open so that belayers are not restricted.

If additional control is required, then additional ropes can be attached on the downstream corners of the boat – making a four-point tether.

Once the task is complete, the empty boat can be sent over to the far side, loaded with personnel and equipment (depending on the boat's capacity), and then swung back to the bank on a single rope.

Notes

Paddle Boat Handling Skills

Introduction

In water rescue, a boat can be one of the most useful tools at the swiftwater rescuer's disposal. However, the wrong boat used in the wrong environment, or even the right boat used by an inexperienced crew, can put the rescue team in danger, or in need of rescue itself.

It is important that a rescue team chooses craft that are transportable, dependable, and appropriate for the type of environment in which they are to be used. Teams should receive Swiftwater Rescue Boat Operator training after their Swiftwater Rescue Technician® training if they are to use powered rescue boats. It is then essential for the crew members to ensure that they get adequate practice with their chosen craft to develop experience and judgement. Only with all of the above in place will any boat be a valuable asset to the team. Without the above, any boat will be at best a hindrance, and at worst a potentially life-threatening device.

For more information on boat types, see *page Aw-66.*

Paddling a Boat

The traditional method of paddling a whitewater raft is with one experienced guide and a crew made up of at least four less experienced people. The guide issues commands and his decision is final. Simple commands such as "all forward", "all back", "left turn" and "right turn" are used to maneuver the boat downstream.

With rescue teams, it is much more common for a boat to be "R2'd" or "R4'd" which means there is no guide and either two or four paddlers. If one member of the crew is more experienced than the others he may still make some of the route-finding decisions, and call out commands, but if all paddlers know the objective and are experienced, they will be able to paddle together as a unit to achieve their goal.

Swiftwater Handling

Understanding hydrology is essential if rescuers wish to control a boat in moving water. Learning to "read" a river is the key to effective boat handling. Whether water is running over a natural river bed or down a flooded urban street, the river features that form, such as waves, hydraulics, and eddies are universal. The boat handling skills that are needed to effect a successful rescue are the same no matter the environment.

The hydrology dictates the direction of the boat. It is essential to consider the features immediately ahead when planning the next move.

Speed, angle and trim (tilt of the boat) are particularly important in swiftwater paddle boat handling. When all three elements are used effectively, whitewater can be run safely and efficiently.

Notes

Speed

This can relate to both the speed of the water and the speed of the boat, and more importantly the difference between the two. It is important to distinguish between speed over water and speed over ground, or headway. For example, when ferrying, the boat has very little (if any) speed over ground (it makes little headway), but may have considerable speed over water.

Another consideration is the speed required to travel through a hydraulic. If the boat is too slow, it will stall and possibly flip. Speed is required in order to punch through the powerful recirculation of a hydraulic feature. In addition, in order for the crew to retain control of the boat, it must be travelling either faster or slower than the water to retain directional control. Otherwise the boat will simply float down the channel under the control of the water.

Angle

The angle of the boat in relation to the current vector determines which direction the boat will head. To use ferrying as an example again, the closer the angle of the boat to the direction of flow, the slower or more controlled the lateral movement will be.

Trim

In swiftwater, correct application of trim (tilting the boat to either side or from front to back) can make the difference between a successful ferry and a complete capsize. By placing the crew's weight on the downstream side of the boat, which tilts it, more of the bottom of the boat is presented to the flow. This has the added benefits of increasing the speed of the ferry and preventing the water from swamping over the upstream side of the boat, potentially capsizing it. Conversely, if the boat is tilted toward the upstream side, the force of the current will build up against the upstream side of the boat and could easily flip it.

If the boat is incorrectly trimmed fore and aft (front and back), it will be difficult to achieve the speed necessary for successful maneuvering. With too much weight in the bow, there is a greater possibility of the boat ploughing into a large wave and water swamping the boat. It also makes steering difficult due to the effect of the water on the bow. If too much weight is in the stern (back), the boat will not be able to power through the recirculation in a hydraulic, and may get flipped over backward.

As can be seen from the examples above, it is necessary to continually adjust the three elements of speed, angle and trim to successfully negotiate moving water.

Notes

Ferrying

This is without doubt one of the most important skills to master in moving water. At its simplest, ferrying is a method of moving across the current without moving downstream.

The boat can be pointing either up or downstream, although more power can be applied while paddling forward and there is less chance of water coming over the bow than over a transom (depending on type of boat used). As already mentioned, the speed of the water dictates how much power must be applied to maintain the ferry, and the angle and trim must constantly be adjusted to ensure that the boat moves in a controlled manner across the flow and does not swamp.

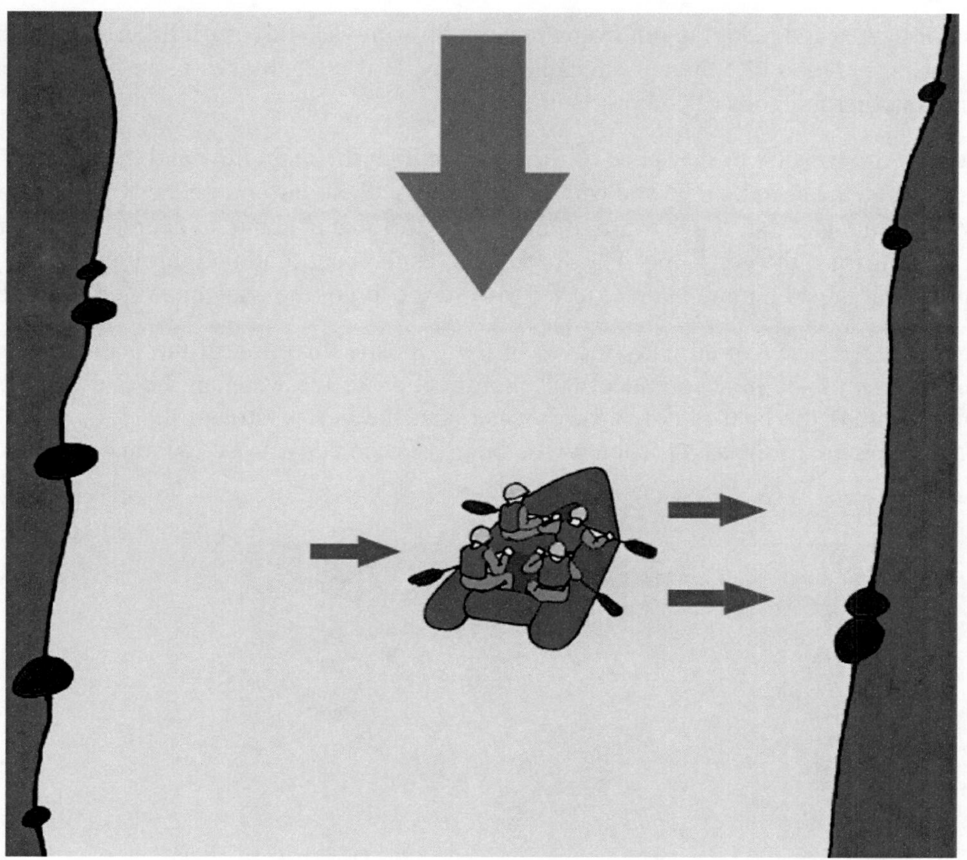

Diagram T44: Forward ferrying across the flow.

Imagine a victim has tried to cross a flooded road in his car. The car has become swamped and the victim is now sitting on the roof of the car awaiting rescue.

One of the simplest and quickest methods of rescue is for a boat to ferry across the current from an eddy close to the car. The crew must apply the correct amount of power or speed. The crew must constantly adjust the angle of approach and the trim of the boat. The boat moves across to the car by ferrying up to it, and the victim enters the boat. The crew then assumes the opposite ferry angle and paddles the boat back to the eddy that it started from.

Notes

Eddy In and Eddy Out

These are the terms used for entering the main flow (eddying in) and exiting the flow (eddying out). By varying the amount of speed, angle and trim, these maneuvers can be applied to a wide range of conditions.

It is vitally important that a crew is able to eddy in and eddy out. In fact, if the crew cannot attain the relative safety of an eddy at will, it presents a real risk to rescuer safety, and the crew should not be on the water.

Dynamic Eddy Out

Dynamic (or high speed) eddying out from the main flow into an eddy is useful in strong currents or when it is imperative that the crew makes the eddy. However it takes more skill to perform correctly than other methods of eddying out.

It is important to be aware of the speed of the water in both the main flow and the eddy, in order to properly gauge the speed, angle and trim of the boat. As the crew approaches the chosen eddy, facing downstream and moving forward, it must angle the boat at about 45 degrees to the current and accelerate toward the eddy line. The speed enables the boat to punch through the eddy line and then the boat must be immediately turned toward the top of the eddy and tilted downstream.

Remember that the water in an eddy moves in the opposite direction to the main flow, so the downstream tilt must be in accordance with the direction of the water in the eddy, not of that in the main flow. If the boat is not tilted downstream, the new upstream tube could be easily swamped and the boat flipped. As soon as the boat is in the eddy, the crew must rebalance the boat.

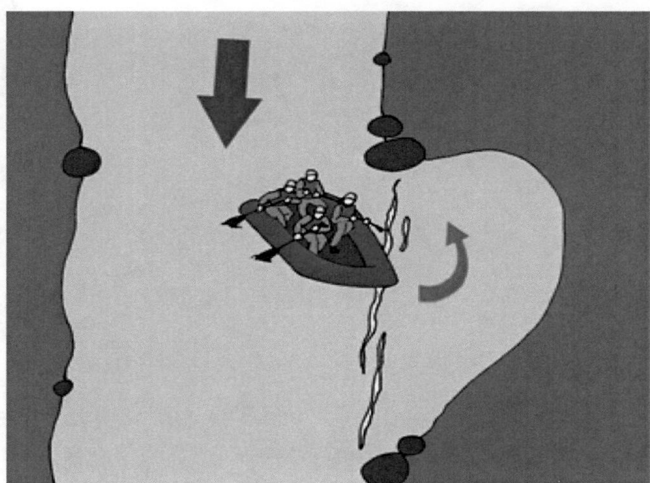

Diagram T45: Dynamic eddy out.

This maneuver can be very dynamic given the fact that the boat is moving quickly when it suddenly encounters the water in the eddy moving in the opposite direction. This can spin the boat quickly towards the top of the eddy, and throw an unprepared crew overboard, or instantly swamp the boat. Therefore it requires a lot of crew co-operation and awareness. With practice, this maneuver can become a high speed carving turn with the boat coming to rest in the eddy.

Notes

Ferrying Out

A more controlled method of eddying out of the current can be accomplished by turning the boat to face upstream (in a paddle boat) and maintaining an upstream ferry angle. The crew controls speed, power and angle to ferry in a controlled manner across the river or downstream to the chosen eddy and across the eddy line.

This method does not involve dynamic movements of the boat or crew and so may have a lower chance of dipping a tube and flipping the boat as it crosses the eddy line. However, some strong eddy lines can be very difficult or impossible to cross in this manner, and will require a dynamic move in order to punch through into the eddy. Strong eddy lines are usually the result of a strong main flow.

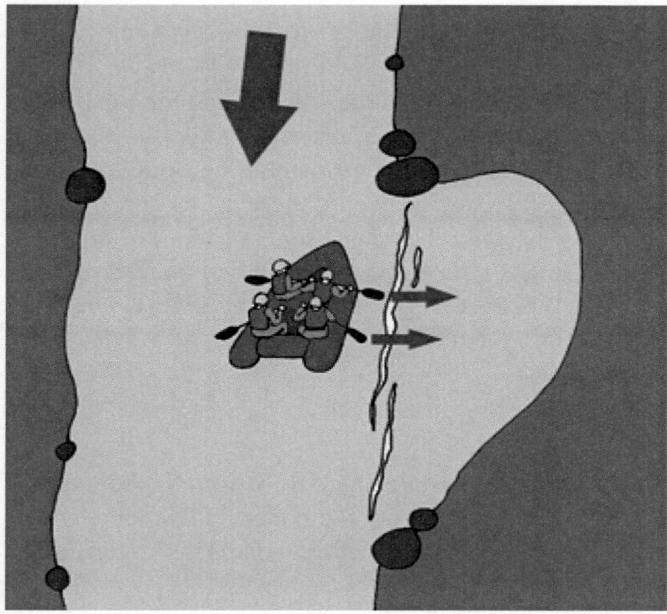

Diagram T46: Ferrying out of the current.

Hitting the Top

Once the boat enters the eddy it is necessary to stay alert and continue to control the position of the boat. Many eddies are powerful and the current will quickly sweep a boat toward the top where it can easily collide with the bank or be swept back into the main flow. Some eddies are calm and quiet and take very little maneuvering, allowing a crew to sit and rest. With practice it becomes easy to judge the character of an eddy while still in the main flow.

Notes

Dynamic Eddy In

A dynamic method of leaving an eddy or ferrying back into the main flow is to start from the bottom of the eddy and accelerate towards the top and punch through the eddy line at around a 45 degree angle. As the boat passes into the main flow, it will have to quickly reposition on the downstream side (relative to the main flow) to ensure the correct trim. With the correct application of speed, angle and trim as the bow enters the main flow and starts to turn downstream, the boat will carve a dynamic yet controlled turn. In this way, the crew can continue downstream without sinking the upstream tube, swamping or flipping the boat.

Ferry In

As with ferrying out of the current, this technique of re-entering the current utilizes lower speed and does not require the rapid alteration of angle or trim when leaving the eddy. However, it will only work if the eddy line is not strong. Begin near the bottom of the eddy, facing the top of the eddy, and set the backward ferry angle toward the main flow. Once across the eddy line and into the main flow, speed can be reduced until the boat is moving downstream at the same speed as the flow and then a turn downstream can be initiated. This works well if there is lots of room and time, or if it is not possible to initiate the turn from the eddy. There is also less chance of dipping the upstream tube or edge. However, if the eddy line is strong, the boat will be bounced off the eddy line and back into the eddy when the attempt is made to ferry across. In this case, a dynamic move is necessary to punch through the eddy line into the main flow.

Fade In

A third method of eddying into the main flow is to "fade" into the main flow from the bottom of the eddy (commonly called "fading out of an eddy" or "falling out the bottom"). Here the eddy line is less powerful and therefore less likely to affect the balance of the boat. This is generally not possible in eddies with powerful lines.

Understanding Hydrology

Notes

Scouting

Learning to read any section of moving water either from the boat or the bank is an essential skill to develop so that crews may plan a safe route through any obstructions. More experienced crews will read and react as they go, taking only a few moments to scan the stretch ahead as they approach. The next step would be to observe a stretch of river from the vantage point of an upstream eddy, but this could limit the range of vision. If conditions begin to border on the upper range of the crew's ability, if the water is completely unknown, or if the local river is unrecognizable due to flood conditions, it is recommended to observe from the bank. This is called "scouting".

Eddy Hopping

A technique of scouting from the boat is called "eddy hopping". This can be extremely effective, and involves moving slowly downstream from eddy to eddy, but only if the next eddy is in line of sight. It is good practice to ensure that two clear eddies can be seen before leaving an eddy. Using this method, the water in between the eddies can be seen and the route planned. Standing up in the boat allows a better view but should be done with care. Once in the next eddy, look for the one after that, and only move on if it can be seen. If a section disappears around a bend or over a drop, the route must be scouted from the bank.

Scout from Water Level

It is a good idea to get an overall view of the section of water at hand and decide whether or not it is possible to run given the crew's ability and equipment. It is important to scout as close to water level as possible, as features observed from a high vantage point like a bridge may be easily underestimated.

Five minutes spent scouting a section of water can save hours trying to extricate a wrapped boat later. If a decision is made that the section is unrunnable, consider whether it is possible to carry the boat around.

If the decision is made to run the section, it is worth building up a picture of where the boat needs to be at certain points in the section. One method is to walk downstream getting an overall picture and then walk back to the boat inspecting in more detail and identifying landmarks. This way the water can be broken down into small sections and a plan developed for where the boat needs to be at any one time to avoid hazards en route. There is no "one correct way" to run a section of water. There are usually several viable routes. The judgement needed to make the call of whether any section of water can be run safely can only be built up over time.

Notes

Momentum and Drift

Momentum and drift can be used as advantages on all moving water. This is using the flow of the water and river features to assist in maneuvering. In a paddle boat, this is essential. No matter how strong the crew is, the river never tires.

With power boats it is easy to neglect momentum and drift because there is a motor to get you out of trouble. However, to develop as competent and safe boat handlers, and especially paddle boat handlers, rescuers must learn to “feel” what is happening to the boat.

Waves can be used to accelerate across the water or to correct the position of the boat in the middle of a rapid. Even rocks can be utilized to speed up or slow down a turn if contact is made at the right time and in the right part of the boat.

For paddle boats, reacting in plenty of time and planning ahead are essential. Knowledge of how powerful the water is, where the current is going, and how to utilize this power to assist, must become second nature.

Boat Flips

Notes

Boat flips need not be disasters if they are managed correctly. However, a lot depends on the section of water, how deep it is, what is immediately downstream, and how many crew are in the boat.

The severity of a flip is dictated by the nature of the section of water. A flip on a shallow, continuous stretch of rapids can be very difficult and dangerous. A flip on a pool-drop river, where hard rapids are followed by long sections of calmer water, gives the crew time to right the boat and recover personnel and equipment.

The correct handling of a flipped boat depends on crew members staying calm and working as a team. The first priority is a head-count to ensure that everyone is safe. The crew members should swim to the boat as quickly as possible so that they can assist with righting it. A designated team member (usually the helm) needs to climb on to the hull of the flipped boat. How this is achieved depends on the type of boat.

Whitewater rafts are often equipped with flip-lines or carry lines that make it fairly easy to climb aboard. If not, it is possible to use the drain holes in the floor as hand holds to assist in boarding. In an IRB without a motor, it is usually easier to climb aboard at the transom, as this is the lowest point.

Alternatively, a carabiner may be used to clip one end of a line to the side of the boat, either through the safety line, a carrying handle, or a D-ring. The other end of the flip-line can be attached to another carabiner, a paddle or something heavy, and can be thrown over the bottom of the upturned boat. Once the line is over the boat, it can be used to scramble up.

Once on top, if the flip-line is already attached, it can be used to pull the boat right-side up. Have a crewmember, usually lighter than the one actually righting the craft, move to the same tubethat the flip-line is attached to. This crewmember's task is to hold onto the lifeline or handles and ride the tubeas the boat rotates right side up. Riding the tube will deposit the rider in the boat, leaving that crewmember in position to assist the rest of the crew into the boat.

Diagram T47: Righting a flipped raft.

This takes a little practice. The easiest method involves standing on the edge of the boat while grasping the flip-line. Keeping the legs and arms straight, lean backwards over the water using your weight to start the flip. It might be necessary to pump your legs to start the motion. Keep in mind the weights of both the person flipping the boat and the person riding the tube as the righting member will need to compensate for the other's weight.

Notes

Do not rush this stage, as the boat may not come all the way over. Once you are sure the boat is past the "point of no return", jump clear but stay as close as possible as you will need to reboard the righted boat as quickly as possible. If one person is unable to right the boat, add personnel to more flip-lines as needed.

Once the boat is the right way up, and the crew back aboard, it is good practice to get to shore or a safe eddy to regroup and sort out crew and equipment.

Righting flipped powerboats is covered in the Rescue 3 *Swiftwater Rescue Boat Operator* course.

Boat Wraps

A wrap occurs when a boat gets held against an obstacle by the force of the water. Such an obstacle may be a rock, log, or bridge pillar. Picking routes that avoid these obstacles, as well as keeping the raft fully inflated and topped off, are the best method of avoiding a wrap.

If contact with an object is imminent, all attempts should be made to turn the boat so that the front or back of the boat hits first. This dramatically reduces the chance of the boat becoming wrapped but it is necessary to immediately turn the boat downstream and free of the obstacle.

If the boat hits the object side-on, the side may rise up the face of the object which in turn, will drop the upstream side into the water, where the current will force the side further under. This exposes the internal compartments of the boat to the full force of the river, which will gradually push the boat against the obstacle until it literally wraps around the object. The upstream tube of the boat is likely to be held deep under the water.

High Siding

Wraps can often be avoided if the crew works quickly upon impact. As the side against the obstacle begins to rise, the helm should give the command "High side!" Without hesitation, the crew members should move to the side that is rising and hope that their weight is sufficient to re-balance the boat against the force of the water. It may be difficult for the crew to move out of position without danger of wrapping and may require outside assistance to get the boat off the obstacle.

If there is no high-side attempt, chances are that the tube furthest away from the object (usually the upstream tube) will be forced under the water, which in turn will swamp the boat and flip it. Crew may be thrown from the boat or pinned between the boat and the obstacle, Alternatively, they may be able to scramble up onto the upper tube or on to the obstacle that caused the wrap.

It is important that heads are counted continually to keep track of the crew. If there is the possibility that a person may be trapped between the boat and the obstacle, it may be possible to cut the floor (if made of hypalon) of the boat to free trapped people.

Notes

The Basics of Unwrapping

If high siding fails, and the boat wraps around an obstacle, the general procedure for removing boats from a wrap situation is:

- Attempt to dislodge the boat immediately by moving crew to the front or the back of the boat. This can change the balance of the boat and allow the water to push the boat off the obstacle.
- If this does not work, then crew should be transferred from the boat to the bank by making use of techniques such as tensioned diagonal, individual throwbag rescues, or the use of a second boat to evacuate people. If using a tensioned diagonal remember to attach the tensioned diagonal to the boat in such a way as to pull the boat toward the rock, in order to prevent the boat from accidentally unwrapping while evacuating people. No attempt should be made to dislodge the wrapped boat before people are safely on the bank.
- The upstream spotter should be positioned so he can warn other river users of a wrapped boat. Spotters should direct river users to move in order to avoid the hazard.
- The 15 Absolutes still apply. Remember that you may need to respond quickly in order to provide downstream safety for the crew members, in the event that they fall in and get washed downstream.
- To unwrap the boat, start with the simplest methods. Take the time to read the water, and taking the current into consideration, work out the ideal angle of pull. Working with the water is always going to be more effective and efficient than fighting against it.

Tensioned Diagonal

Using a tensioned diagonal is a fast and effective way of evacuating crew from a boat.

Note that the crew member is being transported into a safe eddy and there is also a Technician in the eddy to receive the person and act as downstream back up with a throwbag if required.

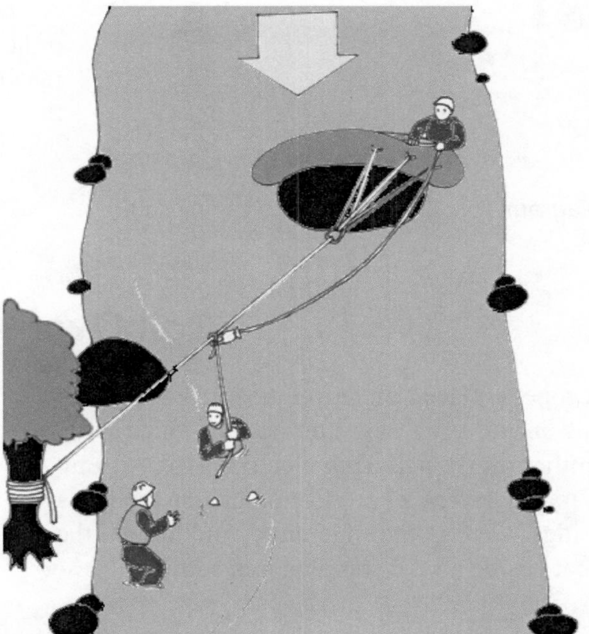

Diagram T48: Using a tensioned diagonal to remove crew from a wrapped boat.

Notes

"Boy Scout" (Strong Arm) Method

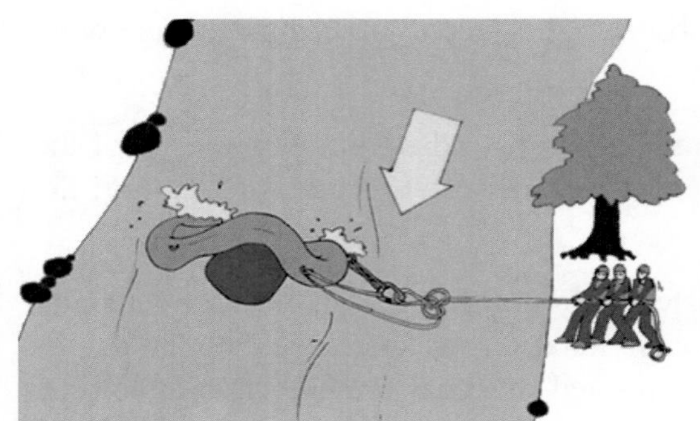

DiagramT49 (right) Using the Boy Scout method to haul a wrapped boat off a rock.

The Boy Scout method is the simplest method of unwrapping a boat using a rope. It is simply a case of getting as many people on the rope as possible, and pulling as hard as possible. If this method doesn't work at first, try altering the angle of pull. Again, it is important to consider the angle of the current when determining the haul angle.

"Boy Scout" Method (with a Vector Pull)

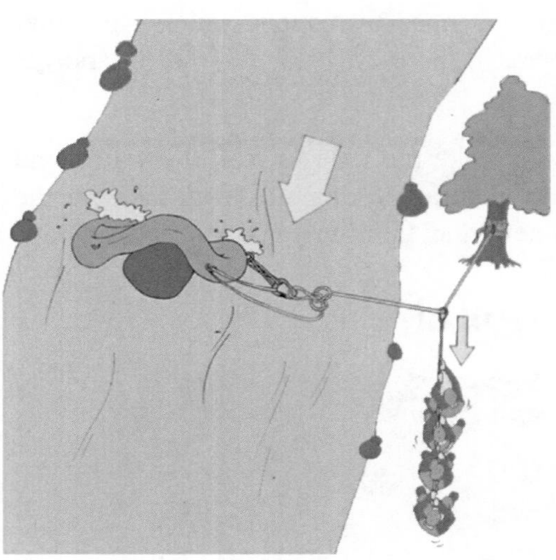

Diagram T50: Boy Scout with vector pull.

Initially the rope is tensioned by using a "Boy Scout" pull. The rope is then tied off with a releasable hitch, in this case a no-knot. A second rope is then clipped to the tied-off rope and a vector pull is applied at 90 degrees to the tied off rope. The force on the anchors and on the tensioned rope can be huge. It is important that a load-distributing anchor system is used to attach the rope to the boat.

A vector pull only works if the ropes are very tight. Once the angle created by the vector pull reaches 120° there is no additional benefit to using the vector pull method. The forces are only high when the internal angle is very wide.

Roll Over Method

A rope is placed under the boat. As tension is put on the haul rope, the boat is rolled over, spilling the water. This method is very useful if trying to free a boat from a height such as a bridge. Getting the rope under and around the boat can be a very complex procedure.

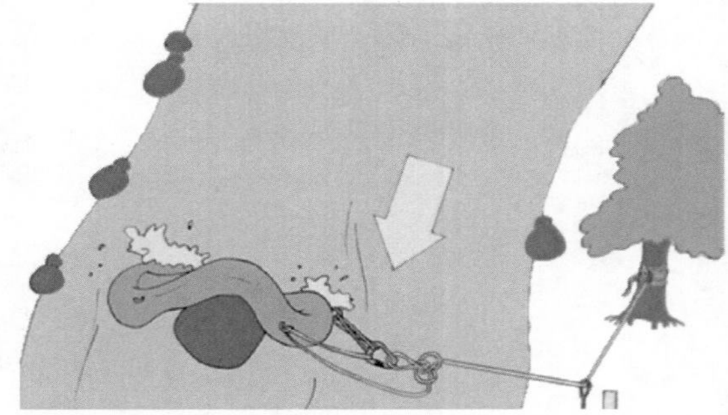

Diagram T51: Rollover method.

Notes

The "Peel"

The peel is a term used for "peeling" the wrapped boat off an obstacle. This is unlikely to work on its own for boats that are severely pinned, as the pull is directly against the force of the water. But it is intended to upset the forces on the front and back of the boat enough to dislodge it from the obstacle. The boy scout/strong arm method can be used and if more force is needed, it can be converted into a mechanical advantage system.

The "Pull"

When pulling a boat from an obstacle it is worth taking the time to evaluate the best angle. Too far upstream and the pull is against the flow of the water. Too far downstream and the pull is against the obstacle that the boat is wrapped against. If needed, mechanical advantage can be added to this system to increase the force of the pull.

Peel and Pull

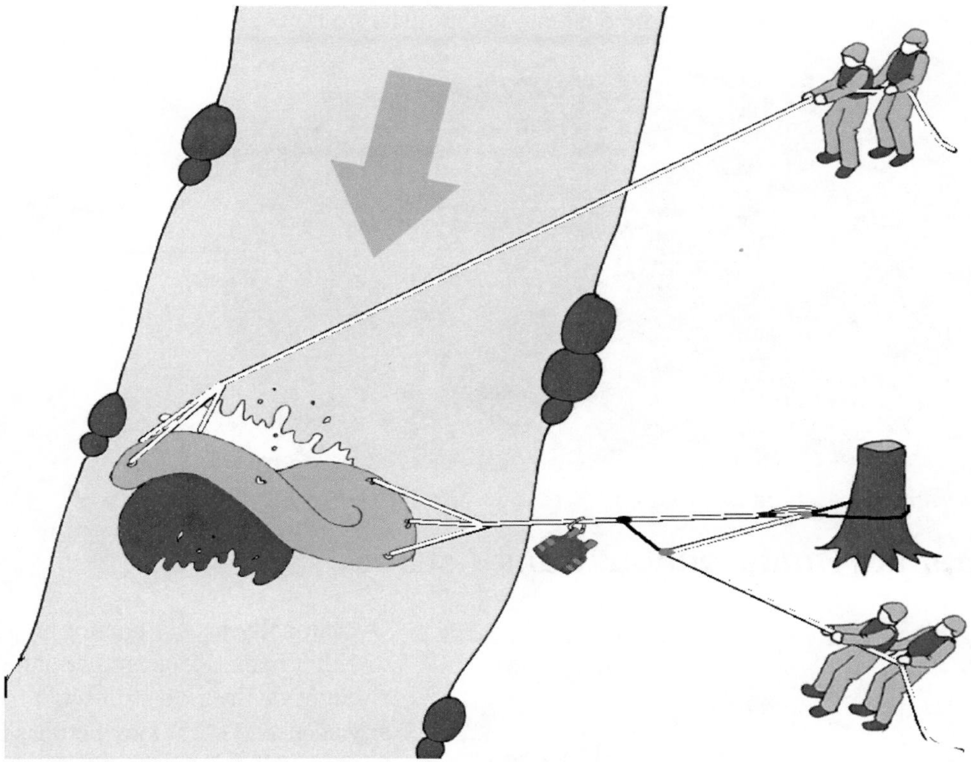

Diagram T52: Attempting to free a wrapped boat using the peel and pull method with dampener in place.

It is often beneficial to combine the peel and pull methods to free a wrapped boat. This is simply one end of the boat being peeled off the rock while the other end is pulled off. This method requires more equipment, as two ropes are being tensioned at the same time. Each rope should be attached to the boat with a load distributing anchor system.

In the diagram, the Technicians have set up a 3:1 mechanical advantage system to pull the boat off the obstacle, and a second rope is used to peel the other side of the boat from the obstacle by

Notes

using the boy scout method. The Technicians are using a spare PFD attached to the rope to act as a dampener. If the anchors on the boat fail, this dampener prevents the hardware (which is under tension on the boat) from flying back and hitting the haulers.

On busy commercial rivers, the dampener hanging down clearly shows where the rope is crossing the river, in case any river users move past the upstream spotters.

Be very alert when applying mechanical advantage to a wrapped boat from the shore. When the boat begins to come off the obstacle, the initial movement is likely to be small, but when the boat comes loose it will do so very suddenly. All personnel should be prepared for this eventuality. No one should be standing on the downstream side of the ropes or he may be injured as the boat dislodges and swings toward the bank. Crew on shore should be prepared to release tension from the system if needed. Crew, if left on the rock, could be stranded.

In-boat Mechanical Advantage System

Another method of unwrapping a boat is to use a throwbag or a long bowline to form an in-boat mechanical advantage system. By hauling on this either from in the boat or from the bank it may be possible to upset the balance of the boat enough to dislodge it.

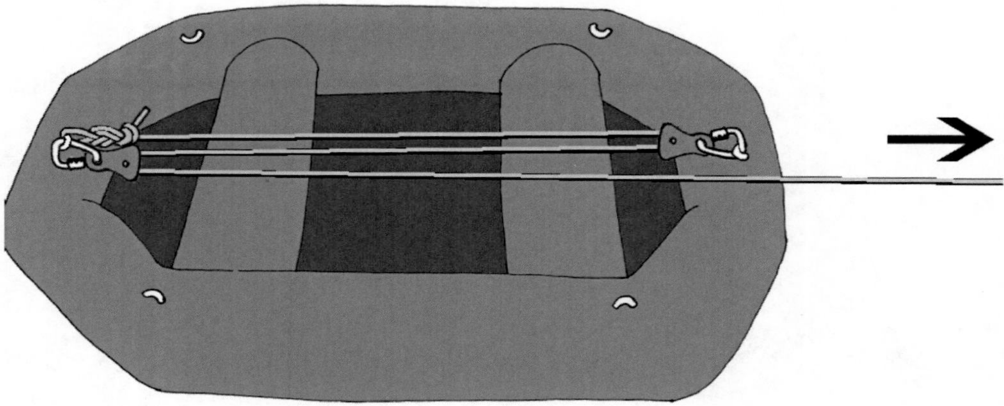

Diagram T53: In boat MA system.

Unwrapping Boats without Bank Access

Occasionally access cannot be gained to either bank. Ropes may not be long enough, or the river too wide to gain any access. If so, it may be possible to lever the boat from the wrap.

A load distributing anchor is set on the upstream side of the boat. The rope is then taken and wrapped around a paddle, oar or cut branch.

Using body weight, Technicians may be able to lever the boat just enough to start spilling water which may allow the boat to slide free.

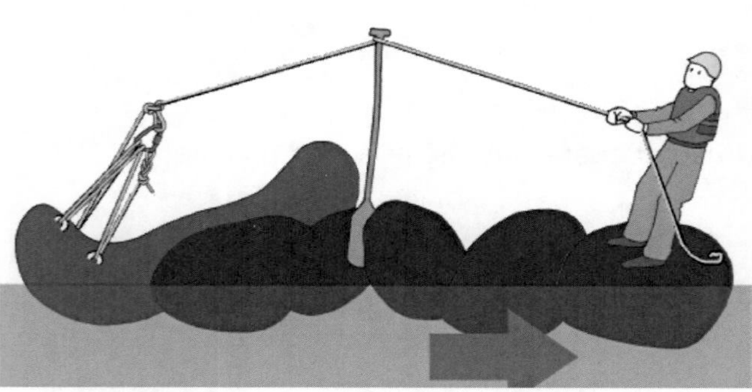

Diagram T54: Levering a boat off an obstacle.

Summary

There is no doubt that boats are exciting and dynamic, and in the right hands a valuable rescue tool. However, there is considerable potential for things to go wrong.

All boat crews must know their boats and equipment inside out. They need time to practice and become familiar with them in as many different scenarios and grades of water as possible. With the correct training and time to practice, experience and judgement will be gained – the essential tools to perform any boat-based rescue.

Notes

Notes

Searching Rivers and Floods

Refer to *page Aw-37* for basic information on search.

There are three main situations that require a Swiftwater Rescue Team to be involved in the search component of a swiftwater callout.

- The team is on a rescue site and learns from the victims that another person has been swept away
- The team is called in as a special resource by another agency
- There is large scale flooding

Determine Who You Are Looking For

This is generally the job of the police and the search manager, who will interview reporting parties, family members, bystanders, etc. They will then brief the search team(s) with as much relevant information as possible on the missing person. Minimum information would be a physical description and name. Useful information would include the person's activities prior to becoming a missing person, his clothing, his state of mind, and any other relevant details.

Establish a Point Last Seen (PLS)

Determining the point last seen is a vital step for the search manager as this allows the initial search areas to be determined.

The PLS is the last place that witnesses report seeing the missing person. For example, this could be the place where witnesses saw a boat capsize or where the victim was seen being washed away by flood waters.

For moving water events establishing the PLS will generally set the upstream boundary for the search area, unless particular circumstances or witness reports dictate otherwise. For example, if the search area is in a tidal estuary, and the tide has turned between the time the person went missing and the arrival on scene of the search teams, the search may include the area upstream of the PLS.

A vital piece of information connected to the PLS is the time that the person was last seen. For a water search, this is of particular importance because it may allow a team to establish a downstream limit to the initial search and to estimate the victim's condition *(see Tempo Model page Tech-2)*

Establish Downstream Containment

Once a PLS and time last seen are determined, the elapsed time and knowledge of water conditions can be used to determine the maximum downstream extent of the search area.

For example, if the person was last seen falling into a river half an hour ago and the average flow speed is three miles per hour, he might have travelled 1.5 miles in that time. If team members can get in place at a bridge two miles downstream within this thirty minute time frame, they will be able to secure this position.

Notes

This serves to limit the downstream extent of the search area, but also puts a team in place to rescue the victim should he reach that point. Once this team is in place, the search manager can concentrate resources in the area upstream of the containment. The sooner that a downstream point can be secured, the smaller the defined search area will be. For large area floods, it may be impracticable to secure a downstream point, but flow information can be used to determine, prioritize and increase search areas as time develops.

In-water features may limit the maximum downstream extent of the search area regardless of elapsed time. For example a retentive low head dam that holds swimmers and debris, or a cross channel strainer, will not let in-water victims continue downstream.

Diagram T55: Search area plan showing PLS and downstream containment.

Hasty Searches

Sending out initial or hasty search teams is going to be one of the first actions of a search manager. These are small, lightweight teams of two or three searchers. Their aim is to move quickly along their determined route, either ground-based (warm zone) or water-based (hot-zone) doing only cursory searching. They may not find the missing person, but they will discover a wealth of information that can be provided to the search manager to enhance the search plan.

A hasty team will normally be deployed to each bank so that time is not wasted crossing from side to side. Water-based hasty teams may only be deployed if water conditions and team capability are appropriate.

Area of Probability (AoP)

Notes

The information received from the hasty teams will allow the search manager to determine areas where there is a high probability that someone will be found. These are referred to as areas of probability (AoP).

For example, a fallen tree on the outside of a bend with the main current flowing through it would be an area with a high probability of trapping a person who was being carried downstream in the river. Therefore it would be an identified as an AoP.

Searchers and search managers will need to have a good understanding of river and flood hydrology to allow them to correctly identify an AoP. Alternatively, local experts may be available who will already know the AoPs in the search areas – local fishermen, canoeists and park wardens may all be of use in determining AoPs.

Some of the AoPs identified by the hasty team will also represent significant hazards to searchers working near them and upstream of them. These may require special management or safety cover. Search teams may need to be removed until it is possible to work in the area at less risk, e.g. after daylight increases, or when water levels have dropped.

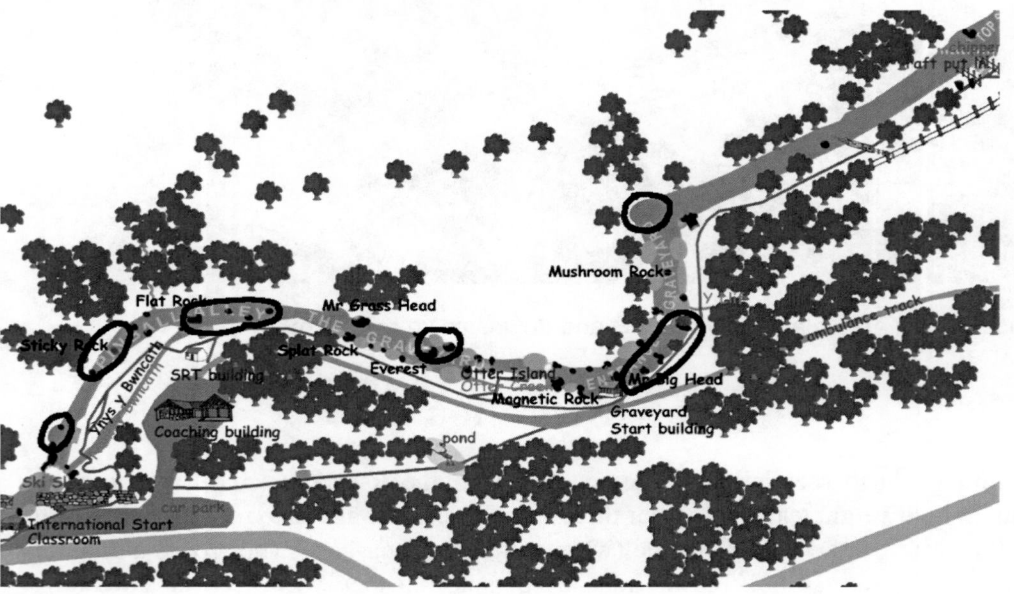

Diagram T56: Search area plan as above, updated with information from the first hasty search, and with AoPs identified

Hasty Searches (again)

Notes

After hasty teams have searched an area, it is common for that area to be searched again by a different hasty team or by the same team moving in a different direction. In a river scenario, the river-right team and river-left team might swap banks and work their way back in the opposite direction.

By having a number of different people look through the area, there is a greater chance of spotting something. It is more efficient to quickly search an area many times than it is to slowly and thoroughly search an area once. This is particularly important if the missing person is still assumed to be alive.

Detailed Searches

If the hasty teams have not found the missing person, than detailed searches may need to be undertaken. These are very time consuming and very resource intensive. It will generally require assistance from other teams or agencies.

Good information about AoPs from the hasty searches will allow search areas to be prioritized for a detailed search. Generally, if a detailed search is required in a water environment, it means that searchers are now looking for a body to recover, rather than a missing person.

Notes

Rescues from Vehicles

Rescues from vehicles are possibly one of the most common water-related incidents faced by rescue personnel.

Sixty percent of flood deaths in the USA are attributed to people driving their vehicles into moving water. In the UK, during the summer floods of 2007, over 70% of the rescues carried out involved vehicles in water. The pressures on the rescuers to act are often great. Changeable conditions and problems such as access, stability, extrication, communication, crew safety, time constraints and entrapment all have to be overcome.

The stages of a rescue involving a vehicle in water are the same as in any other water rescue.

- Locate
- Access
- Stabilize
- Transport

The common problems are:

- Access
- Stabilization
- Extrication
- Hazardous Materials
- Vehicle-Specific Hazards

Access

It is common to have to access the vehicle or its immediate area in order to stabilize the vehicle. At any moment, the vehicle could move and so rescuers are at great risk during this period. In order to access suitable anchor points on the vehicle, windows may need to opened, removed or broken. This involves glass management training and skills.

Stabilization

Stabilization is a key requirement in order to provide operational time, ensure the safety of rescuers, and increase the potential success of any rescue.

Extrication

It may be necessary to extricate passengers from the vehicle. This could involve skills similar to those needed to deal with road traffic collisions but in a very different environment.

Notes

Hazardous Materials

For vehicle rescues, extra PPE should be considered to protect against the extra hazards posed by the vehicle. Safety glasses and gloves that are designed to protect the hands from cuts and sharp objects are necessary.

Consideration should also be given to the presence of hazardous materials such as gasoline, diesel, and battery acid which may have leaked into the water. These substances may also contaminate and damage ropes, technical equipment, and PPE (eg. deteriorating seals on dry suits) as well irritate the skin. All equipment should be de-contaminated and checked after use.

Vehicle-Specific Hazards

The electrical system of a vehicle is an unknown entity when immersed. Generally, it will cease functioning soon after immersion and render all the lights, safety systems and other electrical functions inoperable. However, there are cases reported where the lights, wipers, radios and horns of an immersed vehicle operate sporadically for a considerable time. Also keep in mind that the average American sedan carries approximately 70 amps of electricity on board, while it only takes about half an amp to cause ventricular fibrillation.

On land, it is usual operational procedure to disable electrical systems prior to extrication, in order to reduce fire risk and to disarm safety systems such as airbags. However, in the water, it is not usually possible to disconnect the power. With this in mind, rescuers should treat all safety systems as active, and due care should be taken not to encroach into the deployment zones of airbags.

Rescuers need knowledge of the water and associated features to enable them to assess the scene and develop an action plan. By having a practical understanding of hydrology, they can assess the forces at work upon the vehicle, and therefore determine the best way to gain access to the vehicle, extricate occupants, and evacuate them.

Notes

Vehicle Anatomy

It is essential that rescuers have a basic understanding of the terminology associated with vehicles so that they can use common terms when working along with other rescue services.

The columns supporting the vehicle roof are named alphabetically from front (the A-columns) to back. These columns are designed to be strong points and support the integrity of the passenger cell. The front and rear cant rails run between the two A-columns and rear columns. They also support the roof panel. Body panels are designed to add strength to the vehicle and resist buckling.

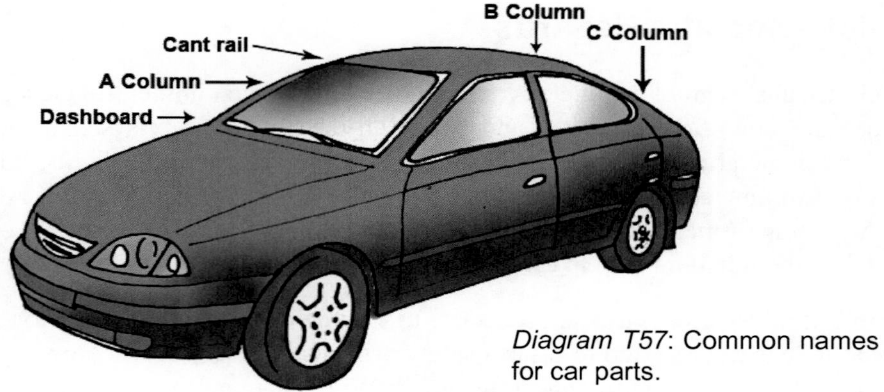

Diagram T57: Common names for car parts.

Glass Management

Rescuers should try to leave as many windows in place as possible to avoid flooding the car and altering its stability. However, it is likely that in order to secure the vehicle, windows will have to be broken to allow an anchor point to be made. Additionally, glass may have to be removed to extricate the victims. Normally, the preferred windows to remove are on the downstream side of the vehicle, where the pressure is less and the chance of the vehicle flooding is less. Where possible, the victims should assist by opening windows themselves from the inside. Opening windows rather than breaking them saves victims and rescuers from possible injury due to sharp edges from the remaining window glass as well as chips and slivers.

There are different types of glass found in vehicles:

Toughened glass

Safety glass is usually fitted to the side and rear windows. Safety glass will shatter into small cubes when hit with a hammer or a window punch. The broken glass can then be easily cleared away.

Laminated glass

Laminated glass has a thin layer of plastic sandwiched between two layers of glass. Laminated glass is designed not to shatter, but to either chip or crack. If the windshield is hit by a stone chip when driving, the driver can carry on in relative safety. On high-end cars, laminated glass is sometimes fitted to the rear and side windows for increased security.

Dealing with laminated glass can be time consuming and awkward. This is why many teams leave windshield in place. It is easier to remove the safety glass side windows.

Vehicle Hydrology

Notes

A vehicle in moving water will create much the same water features that an obstacle like a rock creates in moving water. All the same principles apply.

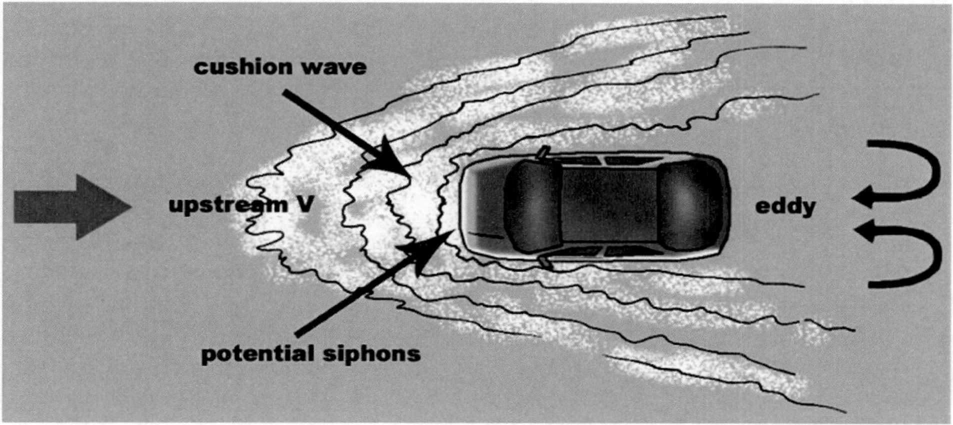

Diagram T58: Vehicle Hydrology.

The high pressure area on the upstream side of the vehicle is a dangerous place in which to work. Hazards such as siphons may exist *(see page Aw-39)*. These occur when there is a space between the vehicle and the ground that allows moving water to flow through it, creating a siphon effect. Clearly, if water is flowing through this gap then it is likely that debris and possibly a person could get pushed into it and become trapped.

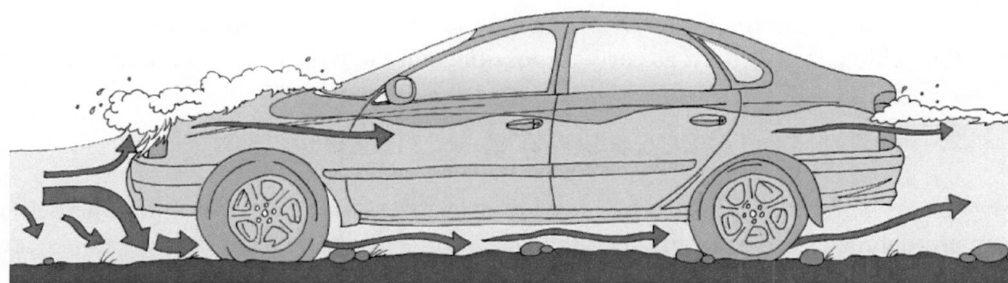

Diagram T59: The siphon hazard of a car is clearly shown from the side.

The low pressure, downstream side poses a considerably lower risk for rescuers. However, should the vehicle dislodge, it will move downstream into this low pressure area and onto rescuers. Therefore, before any rescuer enters this area it is essential that the vehicle be stabilized to reduce any movement.

Notes

Vehicle Behavior in Water

The behavior of a vehicle in water is not an exact science. However, by studying past incidents and looking at research done in the US we can start to predict a trend as to how a vehicle could be expected to behave.

As a general rule, a vehicle that has moved with the water will come to rest with the engine pointing upstream. This is because the engine compartment is the heaviest part of the vehicle and begins to drag first.

The stability of the vehicle in moving water is largely dependent on the type of surface underneath it.

On soft ground, the wheels are likely to sink in. The water pressure will push down on the body and anchor the car. As a result, the siphon effect may be reduced, but the cushion wave will increase. When embedded in soft ground, the vehicle is less likely to roll but still requires anchoring.

When on hard ground such as the road, the wheels cannot bed down. Given sufficient water volume and force, the vehicle is more likely to slide or roll downstream and therefore, in this situation, it is paramount to secure the car as quickly as possible.

Wherever possible, the occupants should be encouraged to remain still, to prevent altering the stability of the vehicle once it has come to rest. A stable vehicle is much easier to deal with than a moving one. Imagine dealing with a rescue from a vehicle that is that is moving unpredictably along the road.

If a vehicle moves or rolls, it is likely to sustain further damage which can create problems of water ingress, access to doors and panels, and injuries to occupants.

Because there are many unseen forces at work, and the unpredictable can happen at any time, it is essential the vehicle is stabilized as early as possible and the risks assessed continually.

Accessing a Vehicle

Once a plan has been formed, rescuers will need to gain access to the vehicle in the water. Access techniques are detailed earlier in this section. The priority at the vehicle is to establish secure anchors. Rescuers should avoid entering the vehicle until it has been securely anchored.

It is likely that rescuers will only have access from one bank initially. The decision will have to be made whether to use both banks or to remain operating from one side.

The presence of antennas, door mirrors, wipers, and damaged body panels all add to the difficulty and risk when working with ropes around a vehicle in the water. Ropes may snag on these protrusions, or become abraded or cut by sharp edges.

Anchor Points

Notes

During the initial assessment, rescuers should try to decide how to secure the vehicle to limit any further movement. Strong points on vehicles are the upright posts, wheels, axles, and towing points. Depending on the situation, it will usually be difficult to secure anywhere apart from the upright columns, as all of the other points will be underwater.

To secure to the columns, either glass must be removed, windows opened, or a door opened. Where possible, steel straps or protected webbing loops should be used, as there may be sharp edges, hot metal, and contaminants present.

Diagram T60 Anchor running through door frame and sun roof

Diagram T61 Anchor running around B Column

Diagram T62 Anchor running around C Column

Notes

Vehicle Stabilization

How to stabilize a vehicle can only be decided at the time of an incident, taking into account a number of factors. These include:

- Is there access to both banks?
- Can the vehicle be secured to both banks?
- Where are suitable anchor points located on the banks?
- If the vehicle can only be secured to one bank, what direction could it move in?

In order to answer these and other questions, rescuers need to be able to read the water conditions. Rescuers will also need the necessary rope skills to create safe and effective anchor and belay systems.

It must be remembered that the potential loads created by vehicles in swiftwater are very large as a result of a combination of the following:

- Vehicle size, shape and mass
- Water velocity
- Water depth
- Nature of the surface the vehicle is on
- Whether the vehicle is pinned against another object
- Number of people in/on the vehicle

Some of these factors are relative constants, e.g. vehicle size, while others are variable. The load on stabilization ropes will be affected by changes in water levels or by changing the number of people on the vehicle.

With the potential for large loads, careful consideration must be given to the methods of anchoring and the equipment used.

Anchor Systems

- Back up anchor points
- Combine several anchors into one “bombproof” anchor
- Use load sharing anchors if the vehicle can be stabilized from both banks
- Use load distributing anchors if potential movement of an anchored vehicle still exists.
- Use multiple ropes and independent anchors to create redundancy
- Use appropriate mechanical advantage and belay systems

Belay Systems

- Ensure a controlled release is possible

Equipment

- Choose type of rope carefully
- Protect rope and equipment from edges and glass hazards
- Use dampening gear to protect personnel should equipment failure occur

Notes

Extrication of Victims

Rescuers must decide, during their scene size-up, which is the best way to extricate the occupants of the vehicle. Depending on the orientation of the car in the current, it may be that the downstream doors or a window are the only options. However, a sunroof (if present) could also be considered.

Gaining Access

It is likely that to secure the vehicle at least two windows will have to be opened or broken to allow the strap to be fixed. These windows can then be used to extricate the victims. If the vehicle is sideways to the flow, then it may be possible to open the downstream doors to extricate the victims. Care must be taken not to make openings on the upstream side which will alter the stability and possibly wash the victims out of the vehicle. If an upstream door must be opened, tethered rescuers can form a shallow water wedge *(see page Ops-10)* directly upstream and create an eddy to facilitate the opening of the door.

When deciding on openings, rescuers should attempt to choose the largest available such as the rear window or tailgate, as this will ease the extrication of victims. Hopefully the extrication can occur without the use of hydraulic tools to cut away or ram body panels to create space, as this will make the job much more complex. It is often best to avoid the laminated front windshield due to the difficulty of removal. It is also likely that the front is facing upstream; therefore the integrity of the windshield is useful in preventing water from entering the car and adding strength to the front of the vehicle.

Victim Care

Care must taken to check the number of occupants in the vehicle. Not all may be visible; for instance, a child secured in a safety seat will be below the window line and possibly below the water level.

Rescuers should use PFDs for the victims. A PFD will assist the rescuers in handling the victim and provide additional buoyancy.

Where possible, the victims must be encouraged to remain still inside the vehicle. Often when rescuers approach, victims will move toward them in the belief they are helping. In fact, they may seriously affect the stabilization of the vehicle, making the incident worse.

If the victims are to be moved to a boat, it should be positioned as close as possible to facilitate the transfer. Rescuers will have to be positive and take control of the situation, often taking a firm grip on victims as they are assisted from the vehicle. If victims are unable to assist with their own extrication due to injury, then the rescuers may have to use extra equipment, such as spine boards.

Notes

Additional Problems

Too Far

To extend their reach across wide channels, rescuers should consider the use of a hydraulic platform positioned on the bank. Consider also mobilizing a tow truck to assist with stabilization or the possible removal of the vehicle from the water.

Submerged Vehicle

There is no hard and fast rule that states a passenger compartment will maintain an air pocket for a given amount time. History shows all scenarios are different. Sometimes a vehicle floods immediately and sometimes it takes a while.

However, even if the car is becoming submerged, it is never an acceptable risk for swiftwater rescuers to attempt improvised, sub-surface rescues in any form. Even to duck under the water momentarily carries enormous risk. The danger of entrapment is massive. Sub-surface rescue is the responsibility of dive rescue technicians only.

Animal Rescue

Notes

The problem of what rescuers should do about animals during a swiftwater or flood incident has come increasingly to the fore thanks to widespread media coverage. Whether the incident involves a family pet left behind when a home is evacuated, or the plight of hundreds of cattle stranded on slowly diminishing islands in a flood, emergency services are finding themselves tasked with responding.

The difficulties involved in keeping victims and rescuers safe is hard enough without adding victims that have large teeth, hooves, and claws …not to mention survival instincts that cannot be moderated no matter how well we attempt to communicate with them. For these reasons the rescue of animals is beyond the scope of the Swiftwater Rescue Technician® training course.

However, responding to an animal in peril is not only the humane thing to do, it may also stop untrained persons (bystanders, owners, etc.) from endangering themselves in order to save an animal.

To be able to effectively undertake such rescues at low risk, you need to be trained and knowledgeable in:

- Swiftwater rescue techniques
- Animal behavior, rescue, and transportation techniques

Rescue 3 offers a *Technical Animal Rescue (TAR)* course that provides the skills needed to help rescuers deal with animal rescue situations, whether they are the result of a major incident or due to smaller scale circumstances such as a single trapped animal. Rescue 3's *TAR* class will help meet the hands-on education requirements for FEMA's *Animal Emergency Response* positions.

Notes

Working with Helicopters

There is no doubt that helicopters can be vital assets in swiftwater and flood rescue. Time and time again, major swiftwater and flood incidents have demonstrated how the well-coordinated use of rescue helicopters can save lives.

Helicopters have the capability to reduce time taken, both in the deployment of rescuers and in the transportation of victims. Those helicopters equipped with winches have the potential to undertake mid-channel and over-water pick ups. They can greatly increase search capability with the use of specialist tools such as Forward Looking Infrared (FLIR) cameras.

However, helicopters also create their own set of problems in a rescue situation. They create noise and downwash from the rotors that can make ground-based communication and logistics much more difficult. There can also be communication difficulties between rescue teams on the ground and rescue helicopters overhead, due to incompatible radio equipment.

Most helicopters are limited to operating only in daylight, and require fairly stable weather conditions in which to fly. They have an inability to access the narrow canyons through which rivers often run. In addition, only certain helicopter pilots are certified to hoist human cargo. Finally, helicopters are very expensive to maintain and operate.

Sometimes, such as was the case in the 2007 flooding in the UK, a helicopter solution is the only option. At other times, while the use of a helicopter might be of benefit, rescuers should not be reliant on their use. If possible, rescuers should begin to undertake traditional rescue methods rather than waiting for a helicopter to arrive.

Rescuers should also differentiate between helicopter-supported rescue and helicopter-based rescues.

Helicopter-Supported Rescues

Here the helicopter may transport personnel and equipment to the rescue site where a landing zone is established. Once the rescue is completed through other means, the helicopter may be used for transporting casualties to further medical assistance.

Helicopter-Based Rescues

Here the helicopter deploys rescuers to or evacuates casualties directly from the rescue site. This includes techniques such hoist operations, short hauls, single skid landings, etc.

Notes

Unstable Surface Rescue

In some jurisdictions, Swiftwater Rescue Technicians® can be called out to a rescue from mud and ice – often collectively treated as unstable surfaces.

Ideally a pre-plan should exist for areas that are prone to incidents involving mud or ice and specialized equipment should be available.

While there are some similarities with swiftwater rescue in terms of skills, equipment and PPE, specialized training is recommended.

Rescue 3 provides an *Ice Rescue Technician* course that is a mix of ice strength theory, practical rescue skills and medical issues associated with prolonged exposure to cold. Mud rescue training is primarily available in the UK; however, many ice rescue techniques can be successfully applied in mud. The following is a brief summary of rescue considerations in both environments.

Ice Rescue

People who fall through the ice into the water are often unable to climb back out onto the ice surface.

As long as the victim remains at the surface, then surface ice rescue techniques may be applied. Rescue 3 offers an *Ice Rescue Technician* course.

However, due to the rapid effect of cold water, conditional techniques are soon ineffective. If a "go" rescue is necessary, full PPE must be worn which ideally includes a specialized ice rescue suit with inherent buoyancy. Rescuers are tethered and approach the victim from different directions, leaving the short route to safety untravelled as they will return along this with the victim.

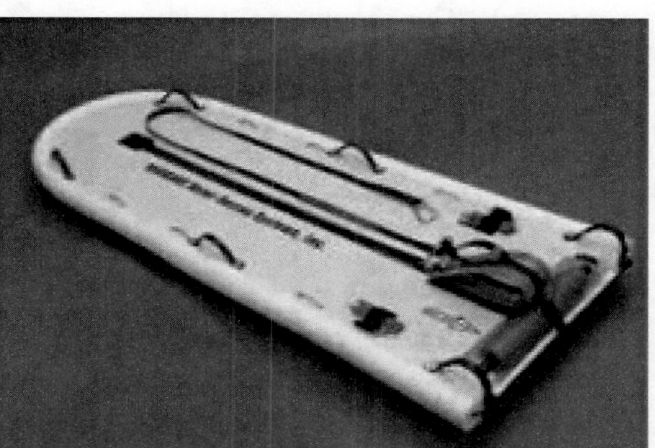

Photo T63: An ice rescue sled.

Rescuers can move in a splayed position on their bellies, using ice picks for purchase in the ice, or use a buoyant rescue board or sled to aid them if the ice fails.

Great care must be taken in handling a victim of an ice incident as rough handling could put him into defibrillation. Hypothermia is always a complicating factor.

If a victim is under the ice then dive rescue teams are required.

Notes

Mud Rescue

The use of inflatable pathways or sleds is also a key factor in mud rescue. Alternatively, for large areas of mud, the use of hovercraft have proven very successful.

Depending upon the consistency of the mud, it will have very different properties and require different rescue approaches. The common techniques and equipment for releasing people trapped in mud are:

Air Injection

This is achieved through the use of a specialist Mud Lance connected to a breathing apparatus cylinder. This allows compressed air to be forced into the mud which will hopefully help release a trapped person. In certain types of mud, this can be very successful.

Water Injection

An alternative approach is to force water into the mud and again, depending upon mud type, this could also be successful. This could possibly be achieved through use of a fire hose. Alternatively, fire extinguishers have also been used successfully and have the added benefit of being able to operate remotely.

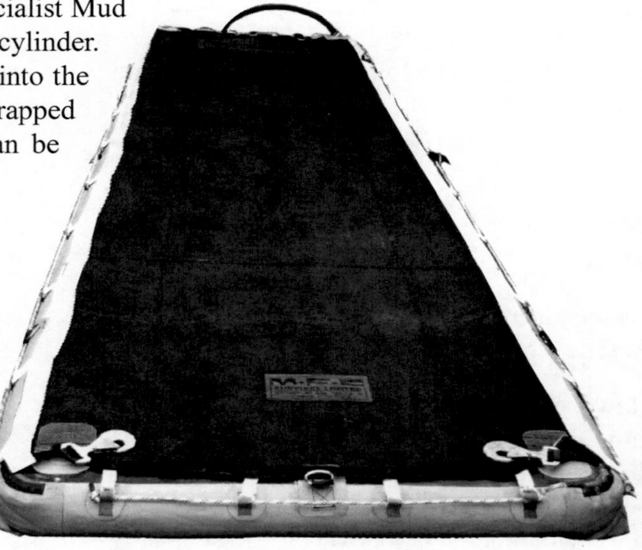

Photo T64: A mud rescue pathway.

Digging

This is probably the highest risk approach for the victim of a mud entrapment. As victims struggle in an attempt to avoid entrapment, their limbs can end up being spread out or twisted in odd positions. Additionally, the effects of compression from the mud and cold can result in the victims losing feeling in their limbs. As a result, it is difficult for rescuers to dig around the victim without hitting a limb. Should they do so, it may not initially be felt by the victim, and severe damage may be the result of continued efforts.

Hazardous Issues

Mud rescues include significant hazmat and decontamination issues. The mud may contain significant physical, chemical and biological hazards in addition to the entrapment hazard. Effective PPE is needed for rescuers. Although this will be very similar to their existing water PPE it will ideally be a separate set of equipment dedicated for mud rescue due to the difficulty of cleaning residual mud.

Canals and Locks

Notes

Although not common in the US, locks can be found on canals and rivers and are used to make the waterways navigable up and down inclines.

Rescuers should be aware of the additional hazards present around a lock:

- Sudden turbulence when the lock is opened
- Very deep water
- Sluice gates
- Potential for falls from a height
- Mud and debris at the base of locks and canals
- Mechanical controls that operate the lock.

When the sluice gate is released, a rush of water creates a large amount of turbulence downstream. A victim submerged in the lock may be drawn through the sluice with this rush of water and entrapped.

When attending an incident in a lock, ensure the controls are secured to eliminate the risk of any unexpected flows.

Notes

Notes